# FROM A SPARROW TO A STORM

The untold story of the Watts Baby; arrested and imprisoned 48 hours before the revolt known as the 1965 Watts Riots. Endorsed by Congress Women Maxine Waters, and Yvonne Brathwaite Burke.

Told by Mother and Author;
Reverend Elizabeth Bissett

Published by Anita Bissett

*Elizabeth Bissett*

outskirtspress

DENVER, COLORADO

From a Sparrow to a Storm
All Rights Reserved.
Copyright © 2012 Anita Bissett
v3.0

Anita Bissett: Publisher
Elizabeth Bissett: Author
Patricia Farmer: Chief Editor

Outskirts Press, Inc.
http://www.outskirtspress.com

ISBN: 978-1-4327-5750-2

Outskirts Press and the "OP" logo are trademarks belonging to Outskirts Press, Inc.

PRINTED IN THE UNITED STATES OF AMERICA

# Dedication

I humbly dedicate this book to the memory of my beloved departed Mother, the Sparrow who bravely endured the Storm.

Respectfully, I acknowledge the individuals who lost their lives in the revolt known as the 1965 Watts Riots. I fondly embrace the community of Watts in South Central Los Angeles, and all who were involved in defending me in a pivotal place and time in American history. Their proud heritage of unwavering faith and self determination has not been forgotten.

Warmest heartfelt gratitude is extended to Maxine Waters, and Yvonne Brathwaite Burke. They are exemplarily defenders of human rights, with a depth of concern, seeking justice in both word and deed. I thank them for acts of kindness and ultimate professionalism.

As a young attorney Yvonne B. Burke, represented my Mother pro-bono in court. After I was arrested, Maxine Waters was a friend to her, a confidant, co-worker, and teacher at the head start pre-school. My Mother was blessed to have crossed both their paths.

My greatest hope is for legislation to be adopted to better protect abused and neglected foster children, and to eliminate existing statutes of limitations for crimes committed against them.

I am compelled to bring to light my Mothers story, in hopes of bringing awareness to, and help better the fragile lives of these silent victims ....the foster children.

# Table of Contents

CHAPTER ONE . . . . . . . . Warrior Chieftain . . . . . . . . . . . . 1

CHAPTER TWO . . . . . . . . Spiritual Faith . . . . . . . . . . . . . .17

CHAPTER THREE . . . . . . . Forgotten Tradition. . . . . . . . . . . .25

CHAPTER FOUR . . . . . . . . Ideology Of Love. . . . . . . . . . . . .37

CHAPTER FIVE. . . . . . . . . Flickering Light . . . . . . . . . . . . .45

CHAPTER SIX . . . . . . . . . Critical Thinking. . . . . . . . . . . . .53

CHAPTER SEVEN . . . . . . . Alone In A Marriage . . . . . . . . . .69

CHAPTER EIGHT . . . . . . . The Strength Of A Woman . . . . . . .79

CHAPTER NINE . . . . . . . . Adrift. . . . . . . . . . . . . . . . . .91

CHAPTER TEN. . . . . . . . . Betrayed . . . . . . . . . . . . . . . 111

CHAPTER ELEVEN . . . . . . The Subpoena . . . . . . . . . . . . . 123

CHAPTER TWELVE . . . . . . A Stable Home. . . . . . . . . . . . . 143

CHAPTER THIRTEEN. . . . . Just Another File . . . . . . . . . . . 159

CHAPTER FOURTEEN . . . . In My Heart . . . . . . . . . . . . . 173

CHAPTER FIFTEEN . . . . . . Spiritual Heritage . . . . . . . . . . 189

CHAPTER SIXTEEN . . . . . . Go And Live . . . . . . . . . . . . . 203

CHAPTER SEVENTEEN . . . . No Mercy . . . . . . . . . . . . . . . 221

CHAPTER EIGHTEEN. . . . . Back To Court Again. . . . . . . . . 237

CHAPTER NINETEEN. . . . . Fate Of A Child . . . . . . . . . . . 255

CHAPTER TWENTY. . . . . . Self Determination. . . . . . . . . . 265

CHAPTER TWENTY-ONE. . . . My Children On Gurneys . . . . . . . 279

CHAPTER TWENTY-TWO . . . Disrespect Your Father, Disrespect Me . . 299

CHAPTER TWENTY-THREE . . The Man Who Loved . . . . . . . . . 311

CHAPTER TWENTY-FOUR . . . The Miracle Of My Family. . . . . . . 333

# CHAPTER ONE

# *Warrior Chieftain*

Father was the son of an Achee Chieftain and the village witch doctor. One of the numerous Indonesian jungle tribes, the Achee were not a people to be taken lightly. It took the Dutch colonialists some forty years to conquer them. Had my forefathers kept their mouths shut, they might never have been conquered at all. Legend had it that no Achee warrior could be killed except by a weapon passing through an opening in his body such as the mouth, nostril, or ears. A new Dutch commander took stock of the situation and came up with a plan that he hoped would bring the hostilities to an end. He realized that much of the Indonesian culture revolved around feasting and festivals. One evening he invited the chiefs to a feast to be held in their honor. Armed only with their sense of invulnerability and mindless of the perilous possibilities that attending such a feast could pose, the chiefs accepted the invitation. As the chiefs opened their mouths to eat, the Dutch soldiers rammed the barrel of their rifles down their throats. Surrender agreements were signed. The chiefs were released. The conflict was over.

I cannot vouch for the veracity of this legend. But, through my brother-in-law, I met Devi Jah, the world renowned Balinese temple dancer who appeared in the movie "The Portrait of Dorian Grey".

During an appearance at the Pasadena Civic Auditorium, she invited me and my husband to her performance and then backstage afterwards. It was there that she introduced me to three Malayan men. When she informed them that my Father was Rodrick Beden of the Achee tribe their jaws dropped open. Their brown skins turned a pallid yellow. Their eyes gaped as though they had seen an apparition from hell. When I offered a hand of greeting, they backed away in fear. At least to some meaningful extent, the legend was true.

What brought my father to New York was an act as ill advised as that of his forefathers accepting the invitation to dine with the Dutch. He fell in love with a girl who had been betrothed to the son of another chief. Word of their nocturnal rendezvous spread from village to village. To prevent a tribal war, my grandparents had no choice but to banish their son from the tribe forever. Their line of succession ended with my dad. They took him to Djakarta and secured a job for him on a Dutch freighter. On one of his trips to New York, he jumped ship and situated himself as yet another denizen of the Big Apple struggling to scratch out an existence during the Great Depression.

Mother eventually met and married Father. He was once her ex-husbands' closest friend. Their meeting took place not long after my Father settled in New York. Mother's husband was from a proud and wealthy Hindu family who worked as a motion picture projectionist until his job became a casualty of the Depression. The humiliation of losing his job and not being able to support his family was, for him, unbearable. He walked out on Mom and my half sister Gracie and was never seen again. My Mother concluded that his inordinate pride either drove him to die of starvation of commit suicide. Dad felt sorry for her and did all he could to help her through very rough times. Mother was thirty eight years old when I was born in July, 1936. Being an unwed mother, to her, was a disgrace in the eyes of God that she found intolerable. She persuaded dad to marry her in order to legitimize a husband and family. But as she once told me "There are people who are light in the streets and darkness at home." Such was my father. For him there were far more compelling necessities in life than home and hearth.

Somehow Dad acquired a three story building in Brooklyn to lodge the Indonesian crewman on leave from the Dutch freighters. Because of their respect for my father, the seamen always showed up bearing gifts. We were presented with necklaces, earrings, and bracelets of gold and silver from all over the world. There were also trinkets and statues carved of ivory including an elephant so heavy that we could only keep it on the floor. The nickels and dimes they gave me kept me well stocked with coloring books, crayons, and tracing paper.

One of the crewmen took a special liking to me. I figured him to be Javanese because he looked more Chinese than Malayan. He was old and skinny. I called him Grandpa. Whenever he came to New York, he would sit in the rocking chair and silently watch me play for hours. When I got tired, I crawled into his lap and he would rock me to sleep. I spoke no Malayan and he spoke no Spanish. But this man exuded a love and tenderness towards me that transcended any language. There was a comforting strength about him that encouraged me to explore the full range of my imagination. Once I got up the courage to walk over to him and say: "Grandpa, ven." I took him by the hand and led him to the trolley that went to downtown Brooklyn and the department store where my mother frequented. I was about five years old and knew nothing about the cost of things beyond pennies and nickels. But everything I pointed to he bought. How we managed to get the typewriter, train sets, dolls and a huge perambulator on the trolley and back to my remains a mystery. But he did. I never saw Grandpa again. Much later I learned that his freighter had been sunk by a German U-boat. Through an insurance policy, Grandpa left me ten thousand dollars in the care of my father. I never saw a penny of it. To my misfortune, Dad saw his agenda as far more important than that of providing for his child.

Dad began attending night school to learn to read and write. Undoubtedly, it was there that his interest in politics was piqued. He soon plunged himself full force into his new found passion. He equated his own experience of growing up in Indonesia under the yoke of Dutch colonialism with the human devastation and desperation spawned by the Depression. He concluded that capitalist exploitation was responsible for the hopeless and dire circumstances of the farmers and workers of the world. He became a communist.

Communism came easy to my Dad. In tribal societies such as his, the men discussed their problems openly and arrived at the conclusions that everyone accepted. If an economic catastrophe occurred, they shared what little they had. No one thought of demanding more because of their status. He viewed communism as the natural progression of tribalism and saw no disgrace in being one. On more than one occasion, I saw my Father battered, bruised, and bloodied after confrontations with the police on the streets of New York. As an ardent anti-fascist, he was delighted to serve the war effort by working at the Brooklyn Navy Yard. Since Russia was considered an ally, he was not considered a national threat until the mood of the country changed.

I was about six when my parents divorced. Mother and I would see my father once a year for the next five years when he would come by long enough to drop off fifty dollars and make slipcovers for our sofa.

One day he came by unexpectedly. He was dejected and sad-faced. "Mary, I've come to ask you something but could you send Miki outside first?" He stated somberly.

Mother motioned for me to leave. Anxiously I waited in the anti-hallway where the mailboxes were until my Mother called for me to return. There was barely a discernible trace of emotion in her voice as she spoke. My Mother had been through too much to be shaken by the tribulations of mere mortals.

"Miki, your dad is being deported and he wants you to visit him on weekends until he leaves the country. You will be a good girl when you're with him. Okay? You go next weekend. If you have homework, you will take it with you. Okay?"

"Okay, Mom" I replied.

I knew what deported meant in my head, but it made no connection at the time with my heart. I could be a good girl with my Dad because he was a mystery to me and I was a little afraid of him. I did not know why I was afraid of him. Maybe it was because his looming physical presence made him seem much larger than he really was. Or perhaps it was because when he once shaved his head, I didn't recognize him and screamed "El Kuku", which was "the boogeyman" in Spanish. But I knew how to behave mannerly and respectfully. He was my Father. The issue of being with him on weekends extended itself no further than that.

"Thank you Mary." Dad said every so gently. He shook her hand, gave me his address and directions, kissed me on the forehead, and left.

"He should have kept his butt at home with his wife and child instead of the politics," my Mother said, dismissing the matter with a disdainful wave of the hands.

The following Saturday I commenced my daughterly duty of visiting my Father. As I climbed three flights of stairs to his apartment, I harbored no expectations or illusions. He was an enigma to me. There were men in my neighborhood that I knew better than him. And then only in passing. All that I knew was that I was prepared to spend more time with him on this one weekend than I had spent with him over the previous five years combined.

It was about one o'clock when I knocked on the door of his apartment located in a building at 14th Street and 2nd Avenue. A short, plump white woman opened the door.

"I'm Miki. Is my Father here?" I asked haltingly.

"I'm Eleanor; your father's wife. I've been expecting you." She stated cordially. "Come on in. We'll be leaving to meet him about four or so."

"Wow!" passed through my head as I realized I had a new stepmother. She had a pleasant, round face and wore thick, black rimmed glasses. Her dark brown hair was parted down the middle and formed into a thick braid that was wrapped around the crown of her head. Her breasts were so large in proportion to her body that she appeared to bounce instead of walk. She motioned me into the living room where I sat on an overstuffed chair.

"Would you like something to eat?" She asked.

"No thank you. I've eaten already."

We were both self-conscious and ill at ease. My eyes scanned the apartment. It was small, neat and sparsely furnished. A radio console sat between two windows that faced 2nd Avenue flanked by stacks of newspapers and magazines. The living room faced 2nd Avenue, then a kitchen with a small bedroom behind it.

"We're having a dinner date with some friends who have a daughter named Marilyn who is just about your age." Eleanor offered through the uneasy silence. "We'll pick your Dad up around 4 o'clock at Union Square and go to the Kelsey's from there. In the meantime, if you have any homework to do, you can get it done while I read the Times."

"I've done my math already. I just have some French to study." I said as I picked up my French book that I had placed on the arm of the chair. I opened the book to the passage that I had been assigned to study. French and I weren't on the best of terms. Silently, I began to struggle through the passage.

"Why don't you read to me out loud?" Eleanor asked sweetly as she put the paper aside.

Self consciously, I slowly began reading the passage to her. It was an agonizing effort that I began to resent with every belabored syllable.

"Would you like me to read it to you?" She asked cordially.

I handed her the book as she plopped down on a pillow on the floor beside my leg.

Seamlessly, fluently, effortlessly, Eleanor blew through the passage like a train afire. And then she laughed at the incredulous look that appeared on my face.

"I graduated from Brooklyn College as an English major, but I also had to learn French. Many times your dad and I go to the United Nations. Since I don't understand Malayan, I use the earphones that translate into French. I'll help you with your French as we go along."

She said with a conspiratorial wink.

Eleanor proved to be a Godsend in many glorious ways. She was able to do for me what my Mother could not and yet never imposed herself as my mother. Although she never came across as stern, she also did not come across as affectionate and warm. During the next two years, she instilled in me a value for education and learning. She detested my Puerto Rican accent and labored with me to anglicize my diction and elocution. She also anglicized my last name from Beden to Bidien. Together, we took in the ballet, the planetarium, museums and art galleries. There were symphonies at Carnegie Hall and operas on the radio. There was a delightful outing to the cinema where we watched Bogie and Hepburn in the "African Queen", but she glared at me in red-faced anger when I fell asleep during Olivier's "Hamlet". She spoon-fed me culture as I had never known it. I devoured it and yearned for more. Life for me was no longer confined to a block in Brooklyn.

Union Square was four long blocks from my Father's apartment. We bought hot, soft pretzels from a curbside cart and hurriedly made our way along 14th Street. The park was very crowded. I wondered how we would ever find my Father among this thick milling crowd. My incredulous eyes darted about the park from one frightening, menacing, incomprehensible knot of humanity to the next. The park was filled with small groups of elderly men and women who engaged in vociferous, passionate arguments around other men standing on wooden crates that both berated and exhorted them in words that were incomprehensible to me. The crowds of various sizes were enthusiastic, belligerent, tolerant, and bemused. I had no idea what all of these people were talking about, or why. I felt like I was walking down the midway of a carnival and would somehow be devoured by the unseemly medley of humanity. Eleanor finally tapped me on the shoulder and pointed to my Father. For the first time in my life, I was truly astonished.

His hands were flailing wildly. His eyes were fiercely determined as they were fixed upon a crowd of about twenty men and women.

His dark brown face was intense. His booming authoritative voice condemned them for offenses that I did not understand. Intermittent catcalls and jeers flowed from the crowd. But there were also polite applause. I knew nothing about communism or any other ism and had never heard of Marx or Lenin or Trotsky. All that I knew was that up there on a soap box, with his head above the crowd, was my Father. "How embarrassing", I thought as I watched my Father put on a loud, incomprehensible show for what I regarded as a bunch of unruly bums.

I learned that orating at Union Square on Saturdays was one of the passions of Father's life. Dad had discovered the First Amendment and he intended to use it for all it was worth. His other passion was fighting to free his native Indonesia of Dutch rule. At night he worked as a dishwasher at the Maxwell House Coffee Restaurant for fifty cents an hour. That left his days at the disposal of the Indonesian delegation to the United Nations.

He had no official title or standing with the delegation. But he and Eleanor provided them a service that might have been considered invaluable. Once during an Easter break, Dad and Eleanor took me to a session of the Security Council. The Indonesian delegates spoke only Malayan. The official language of the United Nations was French. While Dad sat near the horseshoe-shaped table to watch the delegates deliberate, Eleanor and I went upstairs where she used the earphones to get the French translation. Afterwards, Eleanor would explain to Dad what the Dutch delegation had said that might have been of interest to the Indonesians. He then took us to the delegation cafeteria. While Eleanor and I sampled the exotic cuisines that were not available in the tourist cafeteria, Dad left us to confer with the Indonesian delegation. He returned in time to eat and take in the afternoon session. He must have realized how bored I was sitting there with nothing to do. He never took me again.

When Dad caught sight of Eleanor and me, he aborted his speaking and leaped from the box. He kissed me on the forehead and gave me a hug. We then started towards the subway station for the trip to 4th

Street and dinner with the Kelseys.

Like Eleanor, Pat and Ruth Kelsey would have special meaning in my life. Both were of Irish descent. Pat was a man of jolly disposition with blond hair and sharp blue eyes. He was in his early thirties and about ten years younger than his wife. I did not know what he did for a living, but Ruth had been a shop steward and union negotiator in a light bulb factory in Ohio. She now worked as a bookkeeper. She was pretty enough to have been a model. Both were diligent activist. Marilyn was Ruth's daughter from a previous marriage. She and I would become almost like sisters. We made the rounds together to all of the Pete Seeger hootenannies, folk dances, and other get-togethers. She was about six months younger than I. She had fuzzy brown hair and green eyes. Like me, she was thin, shy and soft spoken.

After dinner, Pat entertained us with Irish jokes and Spike Jones records. Marilyn and I laughed uncontrollably at the incomprehensible raucous madness that was the Spike Jones trademark. Thus began our "buddy" relationship that lasted until I married and moved to California.

While Dad held court at Union Square, Eleanor and I spent some Saturdays at the office of the Committee for the Protection of the Foreign Born, who were representing my father in his flight again deportation. Although Dad was a communist, many of the committee's clients were not. Some were immigrants who were merely reported to the INS as communists by angry or jealous neighbors. Eleanor did volunteer office work for the committee and I went along to help her. She had no visible means of support. For the most part, she helped my father with his work at the United Nations and most likely served The Party in an intellectual capacity. I emptied the trash, folded fliers for mailing, stuffed envelopes, answered the phone, and was, in general, the office gofer.

The building was located on 26th Street. It contained a basement, three floors, and a penthouse that would be eventually occupied by W.E.B. Dubois, the noted black philosopher and writer. Most of its offices would be later defined as communist front organizations. I was too young to understand what that meant, so it did not matter to me. What did matter was that I had made friends with the people in the building and, whenever I needed to do research for school, I could go to any office and they would give me all the resource material that I could use. In a way, I had my own personal library. I learned about the Spanish Civil War and the Abraham Lincoln Brigade. I even learned "Vive La Quince Brigada", the song the Spaniards sang to the heroic and battered 15th Brigade when they departed Spain after suffering defeat at the hands of Franco's troops. I learned about the struggle of black people to overcome the degradation and oppression of slavery and Reconstruction. I read "This Strange Fruit" by Lillian Smith and I was appalled at the abject cruelty and the horrors of lynching to which blacks were subjected. I saw the movie "Salt of the Earth" and learned about labor unions and their struggle against the exploitation and violence that large corporations perpetrated against the working class in the steel mills, auto factories, and mines. I also read the Daily Worker and tried to make sense of the Czechoslovakian purges. When I asked about it, I was told that the government had to be purged of Zionists, who were described to me as bourgeois Jews who were anti-proletariat. Without realizing it, this was my first lesson in the meaning of "dialectics". Within myself, I wondered if the communists were no different than Hitler's fascists. Furthermore, I began to wonder how my stepmother, who was Jewish, could accept this Party line, when I, who was not Jewish, could not. How could the communists presume to have a better right to persecute or exterminate the Jews than the Nazi's had? Since good little girls do not confront their parents, I kept my questions and concerns to myself. But I had taken my first halting step into the forbidden realm of critical thinking. The first lesson that I learned was a simple one. Any human action, no matter how violent, perverse, or unjust, can be justified by merely relegating it to a twist of semantics.

Sundays were usually uneventful. Eleanor would lie on the sofa and read the New York Times. Dad read the Times at the kitchen table. I would do my homework. Classical music or opera would flow through the radio. I was into Mambo and resented listening to music that had no rhythm but I made no complaint. Dad was a master at making Indonesian dishes. The smells were divine. I couldn't wait for him to finish. I always wanted seconds, but he and Eleanor always cleaned out the pot before I got there. After the dishes were washed, Dad would walk me to the subway station for my trip home to Brooklyn.

My emotions and opinions remained buried deep within me. Not once did I forget that I was supposed to be a good girl and served no other purpose in my father's eyes than an object to be exhibited as an extension of him. I went about my daughterly duties mindless of all except maintaining the unexpressed approval of my father. After all, what was two days a week to give him on his terms? Since I was not expected to have an opinion about anything, I didn't. Not once did it dawn on me to inquire of him how the Indonesian struggle for independence was going until I read about Indonesia's freedom in the papers. To me, communism was a word affixed to some people who were generally nice to me. I had no idea as to my father's status in the Communist Party. I never attended any meetings with him and never heard him speak of attending any. But one of my primary daughterly duties was to accompany my father and Eleanor to the homes of prominent communist members for dinner. We dined and socialized with many of the top communists that the government sought to round up and imprison after the convictions of the Rosenberg's for espionage and treason.

Once we dined with the world acclaimed singer and actor, Paul Robeson. Even in comparison to my father, Mr. Robeson was a huge man. That was all I could think about him. I had never heard him sing nor seen him act. So I had no basis with which to relate to him except that he was huge. Later I saw him in "Emperor Jones" and heard of his acclaim for "Othello". But for that evening my most pressing concerns were not to slurp my soup nor extend my elbows outward when cutting my meat. I did not want to embarrass my Father whose Indonesian culture everywhere entitled him the cultural exemption of eating with his hands. While I was required to sit in a chair with my knees locked together, and to speak only when spoken to, my father usually sat on the floor in a lotus position and spoke with unrestrained animation. When the after-dinner talk began in earnest, I was, as always, sent into another room to watch the goldfish tank or to admire African sculpture or spend the evening playing solitaire until it was time to leave.

Only once during my two years with my Father and Stepmother did I feel a glimmer of hope that I could be regarded as more than just an appendage to his political aspiration. During one of my visits, Eleanor suggested we surprise my dad by making biscuits to go with the stew that she was making for dinner. We followed the recipe in the cookbook carefully, but the biscuits nonetheless turned out as hard as cannonballs and dry as chalk. Eleanor and I watched in astonishment as dad ate two of what we had concluded to be inedible.

"How could you eat those things?" I asked. "They're terrible."

"Well, you made them and I didn't want to hurt your feelings by not eating them." He said self-consciously.

"That's silly, dad. I know I made them right, didn't I Eleanor?" She nodded with a smile as I continued. "They're terrible. Why would you eat these hard rocks just to please me?"

Eleanor started laughing. She looked at me and I looked at her. I shook my head from side to side in disbelief.

"Dad, it was bad enough to eat one, let alone two. I mean I had to force myself to eat the one. Didn't you?"

Dad shifted shyly as he replied. "Yeah; I had to force myself to eat it, but I wanted to show you that I appreciated what you had done."

"You didn't have to do that, Dad. I know you love me. But if they're terrible, I don't expect you to eat them."

Dad grinned and Eleanor started teasing him. She good naturedly threw a biscuit at him. And for the only time in my two years with them, we all laughed together as we made fun of the biscuits.

My Father had one remaining appeal left in his effort to avoid deportation. Eleanor and I took a train to Washington D.C. for a last ditch hearing. The Committee for the Protection of the Foreign Born had arranged lodging for us. But we had to go to a hotel to find out where we were going to stay. When we entered an elevator at the hotel, the operator advised me that I had to take an elevator at the rear of the hotel. I didn't get what he was saying. Since Eleanor didn't move, neither did I. As other people entered the elevator, he repeated his directive. This time, more firmly. Still, I didn't move. I just didn't get it. The elevator got full and the operator became impatient and irritated.

"Please. Will you go to the elevator at the rear of the hotel? I cannot move this elevator with you on it."

I looked at Eleanor perplexed, confused, and a little frightened. She took me firmly by the arm.

"Let's go!" she snapped angrily as we got off the elevator.

As the elevator door closed behind us, I looked at her in askance.

"You've just experienced Jim Crow," she said seething. I finally got it! "Racism!"

The rear elevator was a freight elevator that the black staff used.

Even after we arrived at the room to get our lodging assignment, I was still in a state of dismay as I tried to comprehend the degradation that I had just experienced, and the fear of being lynched for some small infraction like riding a "whites only" elevator.

All of the deportees' families were assigned to lodge at private homes. Most of these homes were those of black people who had volunteered to take us in. In our hour of need and at a time when guild-by-association was running rampant throughout the land, these poor, subjugated blacks agreed to take us in and run the risk of inviting even greater suffering into their lives. Little did I realize that they were taking a stand for freedom. That night, I whimpered quiet little tears of humiliation on my pillow as I gained a moral insight as to the dignity and equality of people that would stay with me for the rest of my life.

My father had exhausted all of his appeals. The I.N.S. gave him the choice of leaving the country voluntarily or involuntarily.

"Involuntarily" meant that he would be locked up in the steerage of any ship going towards Indonesia. Voluntarily enabled him to go anywhere outside the United States. He chose to go voluntarily. Eleanor decided to go with him.

It was in February of 1951 when my mother and I arrived at Pier 14 to see my father off. He was leaving on the "Battory" which was bound for Poland. Many, many people including Pat and Ruth Kelsey, were there to see him off. I was surprised and pleased that my father was so highly regarded. I had painted a picture of a sparrow of many shapes and colors to give him as a farewell gift. It never occurred to me to give him a picture of me. We all gave him and Eleanor hugs and kisses and bade them fond farewells. My stepmother took my mother to the side and they conversed for about ten minutes. Everyone's mood seemed so festive that I still had not realized what was happening. Cheerfully my dad and Eleanor walked up the gang plank and located themselves at the railing of the ship and began waving at us. Dad's face became sad and sullen. Then they walked to the stern of the ship and continued waving at us. Suddenly each of the three stacks of the ship belched thick black smoke into the air. Then the long, deafening blast of the horn came. I waved back to dad and Eleanor. The ship already started to move out.

"Oh my God"! I thought as I now realized what "deported" meant to the heart. "I will never see my Father again."

I was attending the live funeral of my Father.

My stomach churned and knotted. I screamed, but it was muffled by another blast of the ship's horn. I tried to yell "No. No. Don't go." But all that came out was another scream. My knees buckled. I grabbed my mom as I felt myself collapsing to the ground. Pat and Ruth rushed over to me, got me to my feet and held me up against my mom's shoulder as the sobs and tears burst forth. Hysteria had taken over. Everyone was in tears, but they were trying to comfort me. Finally, every part of me committed itself to one last desperate yell at the departing ship.

"Daddy"! I love you! Daddy, don't go! Oh please! Don't go!" I begged hysterically.

Mom, Pat and Ruth tried to move me towards the ladies room. But I wrenched free and tried to run back towards the departed ship. I was desperate to retrieve my Father and kiss him and unburden all of the untold feelings that now swelled up in my heart. Pat's demeanor changed from compassionate to firm as he stared me in the eyes while he blocked my way.

"No, Miki. He's gone."

My heart sank as I stared into the sadness of his eyes. I stood frozen until I allowed Mom and Ruth to pull me into the bathroom where they wiped my tear-drenched face. The tears would not stop, nor would the agony in the pit of my stomach.

As I wrestled to compose myself, I realized that I had done my Dad and myself a great disservice. I should have never tried so hard to be a "good daughter". Now he would never get to know the real me, with my affections and hates and obstinacies. Never again would I see my Father and the only image he would ever have of me was the one I thought he wanted. But it was as phony as a three dollar bill. And I couldn't take it back.

CHAPTER TWO

# *Spiritual Faith*

Mom's life in Puerto Rico indicated far greater possibilities than she came to realize in America. Her mother had blue eyes and blonde hair and was of French heritage and her family was socially prominent and financially sound. But when she married a man who was part black and part Bringer Indian, the family disowned her and turned her away. As the town undertaker, my grandfather overcharged the rich in order to provide free burial for the poor. Each morning he left the house with fifty pennies in his pocket to distribute among the beggars at his door and those he encountered on the street. Although not wealthy, my grandparents did well enough to have rugs on the floor, and a piano in the living room to provide music lessons for their children. They were Seventh Day Adventists and adhered to a strict interpretation of the scriptures. Radio and TV had not yet been invented, so church was the social entertainment of the evening. Excitement mainly consisted of mom inviting the neighborhood children into her home to watch puppet shows. Inevitably, one of the children would claim that an especially unappealing puppet looked like someone's mother and a fight would ensue. The kid designated as lookout would warn them of my grandparents approach and a frantic cleanup effort would commence. Eventually my Mother became so adept at playing the piano that the Catholic Church selected her to play the organ for Sunday mass.

Mom never told me why she left her safe and secure home in Clayey, Puerto Rico. I knew only that she was sixteen when she arrived in New York. Within a month of her arrival, she met and married a man whom she at various times portrayed as a numbers runner, pimp, pretty gangster and practitioner of voodoo. His brutal and surly approaches to the affairs of the streets were also the means by which he chose to manage his home. She assumed that the mastery of housekeeping and cooking was the sole responsibility of servants. Her husband's means of critiquing her efforts at cooking was to hurl the whole pot at her when the meal fell short of his satisfaction. Her mother died before she reached puberty without imparting to her the knowledge that marriage included sex. She believed that marriage consisted totally of two people living together. He consummated their marriage by brutally raping her on their wedding night.

She was terrified of him and wanted desperately to get away. But she became pregnant. No sooner than she gave birth to Vincent, she conceived again. This second son lived for only a short time before succumbing to pneumonia. She finally left with her son and went to work. For two years she rejected his pleas for reconciliation, believing that his ultimate intention was to kill her. Mom suspected that the fruit baskets he sent to her were filled with voodoo poisons. To save enough money to get away Mom found work in a commercial laundry during the week. On weekends, she and a cousin danced the tango and Charleston onstage in Harlem theatres. In an attempt to force her to reconsider, her husband kidnapped their son; Vincent. Mom was devastated. In her mind she had no place to turn. Tradition had embedded in her the belief that the male had complete authority of his son's welfare and concluded that the police would take his side. Having no reason to fear for the child's safety, she decided to leave her son with his father and move to Brooklyn. Eventually, her husband died of sclerosis of the liver, a consequence of severe alcoholism. Almost thirty years would pass before she would see Vincent again.

It was while playing the piano for silent movies at a theater that my Mother met and married the projectionist. He was from India and obsessed with cleanliness. If the house was not spotless when he came home, he would rant and rave incessantly before leaving, not to re-enter the house until he was convinced that it would meet with his approval. My half-sister, Gracie was born of this union. During the early Depression, mother gave birth to another son who died within days from malnutrition. It was about this time that she claimed to have come home one day and saw the picture of her mother that was mounted on the wall blinking at her. Mother pulled out the Bible and began to pray. She then went back to the picture. As she stood there, the voice of my grandmother flowed from the picture.

"Take down my picture and your father's picture, and throw them away," the voice said. "Your father will be passing away soon. We will be with you always in spirit."

The eyes on the picture of her mother closed and never reopened. Mother did as she was told and threw the pictures away. About three months later, her brother informed her that their dad had died in Puerto Rico.

Mother flung herself into religion. Although she continued to observe Friday sundown to Saturday sundown as the Sabbath in ac-cordance with the Adventist faith, she joined a Pentecostal church because she believed in the physical manifestation of the Holy Spirit that the Adventists didn't sanction. She fasted about three times a year. For three days and nights, she sat in a wooden hard back chair taking neither food nor water, getting up only to use the bathroom. Every hour-on-the-hour the alarm clock would go off and she would pray three "Our Fathers".

Dad had not expected that the extent of Mom's religious fervor would conflict with his social agenda. The agenda for his life did not include spending much time at home. As a leader of the Indonesian community in New York, he had to appear at various diplomatic functions. Mom would accompany him wearing neither makeup nor jewelry, and assume the austere deportment of a lady entering a nunnery instead of attending a banquet. Knowing my father, I can only assume that he was embarrassed and slowly lost interest in her.

When I entered school, Mother applied for welfare. She received forty-six dollars a month, of which twenty-three went for rent. From time to time the butcher would give us liver and chicken at no charge. Our ancient manual sewing machine worked well enough for us to make our own clothes. All of the men in the building whether Irish, Jewish, Italian or Puerto Rican saw it as their responsibility to protect us, even at the point of a gun. Every few years Mom would finagle the landlord into giving her free paint. She would then buy beer and make bologna sandwiches and invite the men in the building to drop by. She and I would start joking and clowning and the wives would join in so that the evening would end up being a paint party.

Everyone referred to Mother as Dona Mary, which was a sign of respect. She was a sweet-tempered, compassionate, jovial person even in the face of adversity. One night during her hospital recovery after giving birth to me, Mom recalled a comment Gracie had made regarding a neighborhood dog.

"Paulino has eyes, ears, nose and mouth?" Gracie began in earnest innocence. "But where is his face?"

A nurse entered the hospital room and found mom laughing hysterically under the covers. She called the orderlies and had Mom whisked off to the mental ward of the hospital. During the seventy hours that she spent there for observation, the harsh and brutal treatment of the inmates at the hands of the staff that she witnessed so horrified her that she grew to despise violence in any form. Sometimes when men fought in the street, she would rush into the middle of the fray and beg the men not to fight as she rained kisses on both of the combatants. It never ceased to amaze me that no matter how fierce the confrontation in which she imposed herself, never once did a blow strike Dona Mary. But what made my Mother appear ten feet tall in my eyes was the compassion she showed towards the displaced or unemployed women that she would take in without question or compensation. She fed them, took them dancing with us, and gave them a place to stay until they were able to get on their feet.

Mom soon despaired of being alone and on welfare. She concluded that the only reasonable solution to her problem was to find a husband. Since the men at her church were married, she decided that there was no other recourse than to set aside her austerity and hit the social circuit. The Indonesians had formed a social club for their families and held dances every Saturday night. Eventually they opened to the general public and played Latin music which made the dances popular with the Puerto Ricans as well as the Indonesians. Because of my dad's standing, we got in for free. I was nine years old when I started making the rounds with my mother to the clubs, and eventually to the community bars to watch the various "conjuntos" or musical trios that circuited New York. This lasted until I had to spend weekends with my father. Mom was light complexioned, plump, but an attractive and vibrant woman. She found lots of boyfriends, but would angrily discard them when she realized that they were married, dull, gadabouts or otherwise incompatible. It would take her ten years to hook up with her fourth and final husband.

It was during this period of bar hopping, something happened to Mom that brought me face to face with my first experience with spiritual reality. One evening I came home and found my Mother lying on the floor unconscious. I shook her and tried to talk to her. Her eyes were closed and she wouldn't come to. But she began muttering: "Mary, Mary" over and over. I was in a state of panic. My sister lived too far for me to get her. All that I could think of was to run down the street and get Mrs. Acevedo. Her son had been a classmate of mine. Like my mother, she was Pentecostal. Desperately, I asked her to come and see about my mother. She stopped her cooking, grabbed her Bible, and ran with me to my apartment. When we arrived she opened the Bible and placed it on the floor. She knelt down beside my Mother and began to rub my Mother's forehead as she spoke in a gentle soothing voice.

"I command you in the name of Jesus to answer me. Who are you and what do you want?" When she received no answer, she repeated her command.

"Mary knows who I am," my mother answered in a strange voice.

"Maybe she does. But please, tell me who you are. I don't know you," said Mrs. Acevedo as she continued to rub mom's forehead in slow, gentle circles.

"In life I did Mary an injustice and I cannot rest. I have seen her life and she needs peace. I've come to stay in her body until she passes to the other side."

"Please tell me. What injustice have you done?"

"I kept her first child. I shouldn't have but I kept her son. She's suffered so much and I want to give her peace."

"But you can't do it this way." Mrs. Acevedo stated firmly. "Only God can take her life. It is wrong for you to do this. Besides she has a daughter who needs her Mother. And now you want to take her away from her child? You have already taken one of Mary's children. And this is the way you think you're going to help her? You must leave Mary's body. If you don't leave, you'll go to hell. You must have been a good compassionate soul that you want to end Mary's suffering. But if you leave this child without a mother to raise her, Mary will have no peace on the other side."

"It doesn't matter if I go to hell as long as Mary doesn't suffer anymore!" the voice lamented.

"No! No! No! It doesn't matter what Mary has suffered or will suffer," Mrs. Acevedo said insistently. "That's up to God. You must leave her body. She has a daughter to raise".

"I guess you're right. She must raise her child. But I don't want to leave her to suffer anymore."

"Only God determines whether she'll suffer more or not. You must trust God. Let me help you to come out."

The silence seemed eternal as I stared anxiously into my mother's placid face.

"Okay, I'll come out"; said the disembodied voice.

"Are you ready?"

"Yes. I'm ready."

Mrs. Acevedo stood up over my Mother. She raised her arms and spoke in a firm, loud voice. "Before God and through the power of the Holy Spirit, I command you to leave Mary's body. In the name of Jesus, I command you to come out of her body right now."

Desperately we watched my mother for about a minute. She finally opened her eyes and looked around in dismay. "What am I doing on the floor?"

"Thank you, Jesus," exclaimed Mrs. Acevedo.

Mrs. Acevedo introduced herself and explained to my Mother what had happened. Mother understood and was very grateful. I was relived, but still frightened. I had heard stories of the occult, but I had never before witnessed an exorcism. I was thankful that Mrs. Acevedo tried whatever she could do to save my mother's life.

That weekend, mother and I paid a visit to my aunt and uncle who owned a restaurant called the "Nuevo Gardel" on the corner of Lexington and 110th Street. I was able to stuff myself with delicious Puerto Rican food which my Mom didn't know how to make. Mom hoped that she could locate the spirit's family and consult with them about the spirit of the woman who had raised her first son, Vincent. The following weekend my aunt gave my Mother the address of the spirit's sister who was also mom's ex-sister-in-law. It was not very far from the restaurant, so we walked to her tenement. A short, dark lady in black opened the door to us. While I sat in the living room and watched the flickering candles, Mother and the woman went into the bedroom to talk. When mom emerged from the bedroom she instructed the lady to leave a prayer of forgiveness for the spirit on the altar on her behalf. When we left, she told me that the woman who had raised Vincent had died a month earlier. She also told me that spirits are not aware that they are dead for two or three weeks after death. Six months later, Vincent came by to visit my Mother after an almost thirty year absence from her life. He was a merchant marine and spent most of his time on ship. On his third visit, he asked mother for money towards his wedding. She told him that she had none to spare. He departed, never to return.

Mom tried to return to the Pentecostal church. However, she would not relinquish her Sabbath of Friday to Saturday evening. She generally devoted Sundays to washing, sewing, and ironing to get me ready for the next week's school. One Sunday the pastor came to invite us to a Sunday evening service. He was horrified to see her hard at work on the Pentecostal Sabbath. That evening he devoted his sermon to chastising and castigating my Mother. It would be years later, after she had moved to California, that she would set foot in another church. But she never abandoned her spiritual faith.

# CHAPTER THREE

# *Forgotten Tradition*

I was fortunate that Mom had accumulated a wealth of sayings and aphorisms to apply to my every mischievous and obstinate inclination.

"Look with your hands and touch with your eyes unless I give you permission to do otherwise." She would admonish whenever we went visiting or were in public. "As you travel through life, take two bags with you: one from which to dish it out; the other to take it in." She offered to remind me that the world was essentially a contentious place and that I will have to be prepared for whatever it had to offer.

She believed that words of wisdom spiced with love should always prevail over punitive measures.

Dad divorced Mom shortly after my sister married an Indonesian and moved out. Mother and I were alone. She sold all of the jewelry and most of my toys when we moved to a smaller and cheaper apartment. My joyful world of toys had been shattered. But I would be starting school in September and in my mind, that meant that I had become a "big girl".

I was ecstatic about going to the first grade. I was too old for kindergarten. My environment had provided me a distinct advantage over my classmates. Spanish was the primary language in my household.

But Mom and Dad spoke to each other in English. Dad and the Indonesians spoke Malayan. Although I spoke only Spanish, all of these languages and sounds were swirling in my head. I suppose that in having managed this ménage of languages, I developed a mental dexterity that made the first grade considerably less than a worthy challenge, but I loved it. After breezing through the first half of first grade, I was skipped to second grade. When I reached the first half of fifth grade, I was skipped again to the second half of the sixth grade. I was ten years old when I entered junior high school.

P.S. 48 was so crowded that additional classes had to be created to accommodate a wide range of abilities and interests of the students. I was hoping that I would be assigned to the "special" class for accelerated children. But it filled up quickly and I was shut out. Then the administration hit upon the brainwave that the streetwise, tough girls and boys could greatly benefit if placed in a class with us "smart" kids. Our first teacher had been a sergeant in the army who had seen extensive combat in Europe. But he proved to be merely a petty annoyance to a class of twelve year old Puerto Ricans and Italians for whom authority was a synonym for "enemy". He spent much of his class period dodging and parrying missiles such as chalks, erasers, pencils, and books that were hurled at him with uncommon accuracy. He would quell a pocket of disturbance in one part of the room only to have an eruption occur in another.

From the very first day, we "smart" kids never had a prayer. Survival, not A's, became the primary goal for those of us with a desire to learn when thrown in with those who regarded the classroom as just a place to fill in the day. I had made up my mind that I would not be intimidated or bullied out of my education. My recalcitrance did nothing to improve the quality of my education. Because I had to run or fight my way home sometimes as often as three times a week, I was not shortchanged in the area of physical education. My complaints to the principal accorded me my first of many lessons in the insensitivity of the majority and the ineffectiveness of authority.

The principal listened to my complaints patiently. I did not realize at the time that he had devised the program and that it had his unqualified support. He was certainly not about to allow his experiment to be scuttled by a ten year old who hand not yet mastered kids' English. He concluded that my problems were social rather than educational. But he knew that he had to do something. Rather than resolve the issue himself, he put the issue to a vote of the class. He merely asked all who wanted me to stay in the class to stand up. Since my not getting chased home or beaten up would have undoubtedly created an unbearable void in their lives, everyone stood. The principal, having found a way out of his dilemma, left me in the class. When I appealed to Mom for help, she thought it best to commend the entire matter to the will of God. The new replacement teacher saw my potential and gave me special research projects to fill my mental needs but I remained subjected to the indignities of my classmates for the next two years, until I met Poppy.

Poppy was Mr. Everything at P.S. 48. He was captain of the basketball team, the boys' representative on the student council, and far and away the most popular boy in the school. He was muscular and agile with sharp, dark features and large, smoldering black eyes. Our first meeting was fairly simple and to the point. We were between classes. He and his friends were walking up the staircase. I was walking down. He blocked my way. When I tried to get around him, I dropped my books. He grabbed me and kissed me. Astonished and delighted, I didn't know what to do. So I kissed him back. It was my first kiss. I liked it. It was wonderful. We met after school and he walked me home. No one every bothered me after word got around that I was Poppy's girl. My popularity in the school soared.

The following Friday, Poppy asked my Mother if I could go to the movies with him Saturday afternoon. My Mother told him that I had to visit my Father on Saturdays. But she offered that if my father agreed to cancel the visit, it would be alright with her. Since dad had no phone, I would have to go to his apartment and ask in person. I went early Saturday morning so that I would be back in Brooklyn in time for the 1 o'clock show. I could think of no reason why he would not allow me to miss on Saturday visit. After all, what was one Saturday to miss?

"Dad, I came, but I can't stay." I informed him apprehensively as I stood with my back against the door.

"Why not"; my Father asked, mildly curious.

"I have a date and we're going to the movie this afternoon. Since you don't have a phone, I came to tell you so you wouldn't worry."

A beet red anger flared through my Father's dark brown skin. I couldn't believe what I was seeing. My knees started to knock from fear, but I stood my ground as dad struggled to control his mounting rage.

"How dare your Mother allow a twelve year old girl to go dating"! He shouted furiously. "It's bad enough that your mother takes you dancing. What the hell is your Mother thinking"!

I said nothing. But I wondered how he knew that Mom took me dancing.

"This is all your' Mother's fault." He muttered despairingly as he sat down in a chair at the kitchen table and plopped his head from side to side in his hands.

"I'm sorry, Dad." I said firmly. "But this is my first date and I'm not going to miss it."

Eleanor stood stunned into helplessness as she stared at me in shock. Neither of them had expected this of me and both were taken totally by surprise. She wanted to console dad, but did not know what to say or do next except to pat him on the shoulder. Still shaken and confused, I grabbed the doorknob behind me for support. "I'll be back next weekend, Dad." I said assuring as I opened the door and left.

It took a long time for me to realize why my Father had become so angry. I did not just shut the door to my father's apartment. I shut the door on thousands of years of Indonesian tradition. I was not just daddy's little girl. I was a plot of land, a dozen head of cattle, a chest of jewelry and gems, perhaps in alliance between two warring tribes. A well raised daughter was often the only collateral a man needed to insure a higher station in life. In America, a twelve year old girl going to the movies with a sixteen year old boy would, at best, be questionable. But for a twelve year old well raised Indonesian girl to be in the company of a boy to whom she had not been betrothed would be unconscionable, and downright scandalous. After all, Dad had been banished for his indiscretion. Heaven only knows what happened to the poor girl who was receptive to his advances.

Dad blamed Mom. What Dad did not know was that Mom had matters well in hand. Unlike my Father, she harbored no lofty illusions or hopes as to the nature of the marriage that I would make. She only hoped that I would marry a decent man who would be a good provider. To that end, mother cut to the chase. She simply assured me that if I set foot in her house burdened with child and no husband to support it, I would be dispatched immediately to a home for wayward girls. Whether or not such a place existed, I did not know. Nor did I not want to take that chance to find out. I was not above petting, necking, or heavy foreplay. But Mother's threat was a thick iron wall that stood steadfastly between sexual desire and sexual fulfillment.

It was pretty much taken for granted around the school that Poppy and I were sexually involved. Poppy did try to press the issue more than once. He soon came to realize that I was not like the other girls. Since I had been around so many adult men, I was not intimidated by the desires of schoolboys. I had also begun to physically grow quite nicely. I was tall for a Puerto Rican girl, and my breasts had rounded out well enough to where I did not have to stuff my bra as many of the other girls did. By the time I was 13, I could easily pass for 16 or 17. As flattered as I was by the attention that Poppy paid to me, and as grateful as I was for his part in my meteoric rise in the school pecking order, I realized that I had no shortage of admirers and that no one but me would have to bear the responsibility for the choices that I let other people make for me.

A few weeks after Poppy and I began going steady, his jealous nature got the better of him. He found out that another boy walked me home while he played basketball. Rather than listen to my explanation, he grabbed me in a headlock and started choking me. When he loosened his grip, I broke free and told him that it was finished between us. Since virtually no one believed that Poppy had not "gotten into my panties", open season was declared on me by the boys as they vied with one another to take up where Poppy had presumably left off. I quickly learned the art of terminating relationships the moment a sexual ultimatum became an issue in maintaining them. Only one relationship lasted longer than two weeks.

Tony and I had been involved well beyond the usual two weeks before I learned that he was Poppy's cousin. He was my first love—at least as a thirteen year old could understand love. He was very different from Poppy. Whereas Poppy had straight black hair and was handsome and aggressive, Tony had curly brown hair and was cute and somewhat shy. What I loved most about Tony was his wonderfully infectious sense of humor. He loved to make me laugh, and I loved laughing.

Like Poppy and many of the other young men in Brooklyn, Tony was a member of the National Guard. One evening he invited me to be his guest at a unit review. He escorted me to the balcony and then took my coat and scarf into his unit's locker room.

After the review was over, I joined Tony and his squad in the room where a buffet table had been set up. We laughed and talked and enjoyed sandwiches and soft drinks before Tony and the others went into the locker room to change. While I awaited Tony, I heard the sound of a scuffle from inside the locker room. And then Tony ran out carrying my coat. He grabbed me by the arm and pulled me along with him. I asked about my scarf.

"Forget the scarf." He spouted angrily.

As we waited for the bus I kept asking about the scarf. But all he would tell me was that there was about to be a fight in the locker room and that he wanted to get me out of there, since he had promised my Mom to bring me home in good shape and on time.

The next day at school, I could sense that everyone knew what had happened at the armory and that it had something to do with me. I was getting a lot of snickers and smirks, but no answers. Finally, I cornered a girlfriend and insisted that she tell me what happened. She teased me along for awhile before telling me that everyone knew that Poppy had ejaculated into my scarf. It was his way of conveying to Tony that he was not finished with me and intended to get me back. Tony and some of his compadres had taken issue with him. Although Tony and Poppy were cousins, they belonged to different gangs and both sides were well represented in the locker room. Rather than touch off a full scale gang war, Tony hustled me and himself out of the armory.

The matter of my virginity had been conclusively settled in the minds of my classmates. There was nothing I could say or do to convince them otherwise. Nor could I understand their preoccupation with my sexuality. As my time in junior high school came to an end, I realized that the vast realm of socialization required far more resources than I was willing to muster. I learned that being the "exception to the rule" was fraught with many perilous consequences. Even in junior high school, boys and girls who could not even legibly write their own names somehow managed to develop rules of order and normalcy that they enforced with cruel and relentless dispatch. It mattered not to them what the truth was as long as they had some story to turn into gossip that enabled them to feel superior to those they regard as mavericks to their social order. All that mattered was that my resistance to conforming to their rules required punishment, if only at the very least the ruination of my reputation. Somehow I managed to survive as a minority of one. I would not succumb to sex, drugs, gang activities or peer-pressure. I was the exception the abhorred. I graduated from junior high at thirteen, and did so as the virgin they were determined that I would not be.

Then the time came when I had to select the high school that I wanted to attend. I had fallen in love with Math and English. And my artistic ability had begun to manifest itself. My teacher suggested that I would do well on the Hunter High School entrance exam, which would have enabled me to pursue a college prep curriculum, or attend an art high school in Manhattan as an alternative. When my mother wouldn't sign, the teacher invited my Father to a teacher's conference with the hope of persuading him that I had potential worth exploring. He insisted that any decisions concerning my future were totally in the hands of my Mother.

My Mother refused to consider either of the alternatives that the teacher offered. She could not conceive of my making a living in math or art. Once I graduated from high school, our welfare would be terminated. She could envision no way of supporting me through college. Her primary concern was that I should be prepared to go into the job market as soon as I finished high school, but she didn't want me to go into a sweatshop. So I signed up for Central Commercial High School to prepare to become a secretary.

Once again I found myself caught in the cultural wedge at a key juncture of my life. Dad had written me off as the heir apparent to his lofty aspirations. A son would have undoubtedly conjured up in his mind visions of a Beden matriculating at Columbia University and then evolving into a major force in the world politics or at the very least, a major defender of the rights of the masses. He would have turned himself inside out and backward to help a son achieve that goal. The supreme irony of it all was that Eleanor, his wife, was a college graduate and an indispensably ally in his part in the struggle for Indonesian independence. I guess it never dawned on him that Eleanor had once been a little girl like me, with hopes of exploring her potential just like me, and that someone may one day have need of my abilities just as he needed hers. It both angered and hurt me that my Father would not utter one word of support to my Mother that might have afforded me my best possible chance to reach for whatever golden rings that life might have placed within my grasp.

Both Mom and Dad saw me as becoming a woman of tradition. Women of tradition were encouraged to only dream the dreams of their husband's. And their husbands dreamed only dreams for themselves and their sons. Somewhere inside of me, Grandpa in his silence had given me a license to dream. But there were no precedence of rebellion in my life and it would not have mattered anyway. I could not go against my Mother, even if every part of my being screamed that she was not considering my best interest. And besides, what chance would a thirteen year old girl have in a city like New York who had alienated herself from both her Father and Mother?

One night I had a strange dream that a woman with long, glowing, golden hair took me through the cosmos in a spaceship. She appeared to be about thirty dressed in a short gold lame' toga with gold arm shields. Somehow I realized that she was queen of the cosmos as she had complete authority everywhere she went even though she had neither army nor subjects. After a long excursion through a firmament of pitch darkness during which she stopped at indeterminate places to pick up other passengers, she dropped me off on the moon so that I could catch a shuttle back to earth. I was so disturbed by this dream that I asked Mom what the dream meant. "Someone you know has died and was going to keep you on the other side of life, but changed their mind and brought you back to this life." She said solemnly. I knew of no one who had died and dismissed the dream from my mind. Two days later, I encountered the granddaughters of an old lady whom I met during my stay in the hospital.

At first the doctor thought I was pregnant. When he discovered that I was not, he explored the possibility of appendicitis. Unable to determine the source of my pain, he served me a dose of castor oil and told me he would check back in the morning. After an urgent visit to the bathroom during the night, the pain was gone. The doctor concluded that I had suffered from food poisoning and that he would keep me a few days for observation. But in the ward across the hall from mine, an elderly woman was causing the doctors and nurses considerable difficulty. Because they needed someone fluent in Spanish, I was recruited. As a result, a hospital stay that should have been about four or five days was extended to twenty one.

The lady was afflicted with gas pockets in the lining of her stomach. The doctors were trying to build up her strength for the operation that was necessary to save her life. But the old lady would not permit anyone to treat her for anything. In her semi-conscious state, she always knew what was going on. Somehow, she had established lines of resistance as to what she would or would not permit the doctors and nurses to do. Our first encounter was to get her to cooperate with the doctors to insert a Wasserman. Patiently and gently I would explain what the doctors were going to do and what I wanted her to do. Once we succeeded with that, she would only cooperate if I was at her bedside to reassure her. I felt especially sorry for the lone female doctor at the hospital. Each time that she came by to draw a sample of blood, the lady would insist in a feeble, but firm voice: "No norsa. No norsa." She could not accept the idea that a woman at a hospital could be anything more than a nurse. To compound the problem, whenever the doctor tried to take the blood the syringe would never fill up. After the fourth or fifth attempt, she would have to relinquish her attempt to a male doctor who would get the blood on the first try. The nurses despaired of bathing her and left the task to me. Afterwards I would unwind her long grey hair gently and slowly comb it.

She was as unresponsive to her own family as she was to the nurses and doctors. The family would have to come and get me. I would whisper that her children and grandchildren had come to visit her. She would then open her eyes for a few minutes to acknowledge their presence. The family came to trust the care that I gave her and brought me all kinds of fruits and pastries to show me their appreciation.

I had no knowledge of what became of the old lady until I encountered her granddaughters. They told me that their grandmother had been given the choice of possibly dying during the operation or going home to die in the care of her family. She chose to go home. The granddaughters were on their way home from her funeral.

Mom had been right. I came to interpret the dream to mean the old lady had so valued our short relationship that it had transitioned with her into the spiritual realm and had become a part of the eternal remembrances of her sojourn on earth.

I began to see that there were spiritual dimensions beyond human understanding and that they constantly interacted with us. I concluded that God would take care of me as long as I lived by the Golden Rule and the gospels of the Bible. Hopefully, I too would secure a place in heaven in which all the inequities of life would balance out.

I also realized that although Dad and Mom left me a concern for my fellow man by their example, they succumbed to the traditional purposes of me as "wife and mother". I was too young to realize that in accepting my gender base traditional role, I had accepted the denial of my personage. I had little recourse but to surrender the very essence of my existence with little more than a blink of an eye.

# CHAPTER FOUR

# Ideology Of Love

Even though I was an honor student in my first semester of high school, my grades plummeted to failing after Dad was deported. I could not think beyond my grief. The ship had taken both my Dad whom I never got close to and Eleanor who had become my role model. For me, it was worse than if they both had died. I was morose in my aloneness and life was empty for me. It seemed like nothing mattered and worse, I did not care. My teachers knew what had happened and passed me with C's so I would not have to repeat the semester. Mother took no particular interest in my distress or my grades. Her response to my grief was to explain that, because I was not a boy, I was not an asset to my dad and that he did not care about me enough to give up the politics and make a home for us. And then she entrusted the matter to the will of God and resumed her quest of ferreting out a husband.

Evidently, my father had asked Pat and Ruth Kelsey to look out for me after his deportation. My mother consented to their offer that I continue some of my weekend visitations with them. My relationship with them was much better than with my dad and his wife. They were friendly, affectionate and understanding of my emotional needs. Ruth was wonderful towards me as if she was my real mother. I did not feel like I had to be a "good girl" around them. I could express my silly and giddy thoughts and not have to stand in judgment because of them. Of course they hoped that I would eventually become active in party politics, but they knew they had no control of that. On weekends, Marilyn and I attended hootenannies and parties where we danced and sang folk songs. Sunday afternoons were wonderful as we would all meet in Washington Square and play folk songs in the open air. They were very different from the Latin dances and events, but I enjoyed them equally.

My weekdays were much too hectic to give much thought to dialectics and politics. In the mornings, I was pursuing my secretarial studies. I had a part time job as a typist for an insurance agent that consumed my afternoons. At night I attended Washington Irving High for math and art courses. Theses were my loves and I couldn't get them at the secretarial school. From time to time I sat in at Jeff School and listened to the adults discuss the science and economics of communist doctrine. It was really called Thomas Jefferson School of Economics and was established to oppose the National Association of Manufacturers. Most of what they spoke of was encoded in party jargon that was only understood by party intellectuals. Pat and Ruth encouraged me to adopt the communist ideology and expressed their hopes that I would one day attend the school. Since they expected me to follow in my dad's footsteps, I embraced communism passionately. However, it still remained inconclusively lodged within my every discriminating realm of critical thinking. I learned early on that the communists had no intentions of evolving into clones of their Soviet brethren. They enjoyed civil rights that they would never relinquish to a totalitarian state. Whether they were called subversive, un-American or pinkos, they had rights that were guaranteed by the Constitution. They were much too small a faction to have any meaningful impact on our society, but they had the right to try. Their intent was never to overthrow the government, but to expand the rights we already had into cooperative unions of individuals rather than adversarial factions dedicated only to advancing their own interests.

I attended meetings that were designed to recruit and educate young communists. What actually drew me to the meetings were the parties afterwards where we danced and sang folk songs sometimes until three in the morning. I even tried to play the guitar, but my fingers would not callous. All of the communists were very nice, well-intending, and friendly towards me. But there was a compassionate and distraught Jewish comrade, who unwittingly forced me to question the presumptions and self-righteousness that ideologies impose upon humanity.

I only knew her as Dorothea. She owned a fabric shop near Greenwich Village. Since I made my own clothes, I would stop by her shop on Friday evenings to look over the new fabrics that she had in stock. When she closed her shop for the day, we would go for coffee. When I arrived one such evening, I could see that she was deeply troubled. I asked her what was wrong. At first she was reluctant to tell me. I started to console her as she fought back the tears. When she realized that my empathy was sincere, she told me the story.

Dorothea was a dedicated party member. But her finances were in such bad shape that she could not pay her party dues. Her accountant advised her to no longer extend credit to anyone and that she had no choice but to collect the money that her credit customers owed her. Dorothea began making the rounds of the comrades who owed her money. Most were understanding of her plight and paid what they could. But there was one comrade, a black woman, who not only claimed that she did not have the forty-five dollars that she owed, but told Dorothea that she had no intentions of paying the bill. Dorothea threatened to report her to the party council, the woman countered by threatening to accuse Dorothea of racism. A charge of racism was a very serious matter in the party. Even the stigma of having been accused of it would leave questionable doubts as to one's loyalty and dedication to its doctrine of equality. To be found guilty of it would mean expulsion from the party all together. Dorothea was alone in the world. All of her friendships, as well as her purpose for living were tethered to the Party. Dorothea was devastated when the woman then cursed her viciously and ordered her from her home.

To Dorothea, nothing was more repulsive than racism. She suffered through the virulent anti-Semitic fervor instigated by people like Henry Ford that was rampant during the Great Depression. The reports that she read describing the atrocities of the Holocaust tormented every aspect of her gentle being. She resolved to find a way to fight this dreadful evil. She became a communist not because she was against capitalism, but because she was fiercely anti-fascist. In her mind capitalism was a road that led directly to the doorstep of fascism. She had no idea of where the communist road led, only that it led away from fascism.

In certain ways, Dorothea was like my mother. Through adversity, both had become knowledgeable about the ways of the world. Yet they both chose to challenge its ills and evils with gentle ways and beatific smiles. Both invested the full sum of their faith and passions in forces from which they received, at best, vague and cryptic assurances. For mother, eternal peace would be her reward for faithful devotion to the scriptures of the Bible and the communion of the church. She believed that the fate and salvation of man rests solely in messianic deliverance by God. Dorothea believed that man was the ultimate master of his fate. It was up to him, not God, to build and maintain a world of peace and harmony. Towards that end, she totally immersed herself in the ideals and doctrines of communism.

I felt sorry for Dorothea as I watched the tears roll down her face. She dared not take the woman before the council to claim her money. And yet, not to take her would belie her unwavering faith in the fairness and integrity of the Party. She decided not to pursue the matter. But I could tell that doubt had now breached her faith in the Party and that meant that her hope that humanity might one day achieve peace and harmony became even more remote. She was stuck in her dilemma. Her pain reached into my heart. I could not rationalize away the injustice she was suffering. Unbeknownst to Dorothea, I later presented her case before a group of communists in hypothetical form. Their responses evaded the issue by focusing upon irrelevant party rhetoric. That meant to me a conclusive verdict was not forthcoming and that justice would be at worst denied and at best deferred to some vague and distant Utopia. Dorothea had been right in dropping the issue if she wanted to stay in the Party.

I was drained of all interest in communism after that. From my admittedly developing realm of critical thinking, I concluded that there was no such thing as a pure or perfect political or religious system. Committing myself to any of them would betray my own sense of truth. Ultimately such systems, no matter how well intending, become onerous burdens upon the masses and tools of deceit, oppression, and manipulation in the hands of vain and arrogant men. For me it all boiled down to one's ability to survive whatever system one happens to find oneself and at the same time try to grab a bit of happiness along the way.

Nonetheless, the young communist meetings were fun to go to. The trick for me was to arrive at the meeting in time to listen to just enough of their diatribes so that no one would think I came just to the party. It was at one of these parties that I met Benny. He was one of the many Jews who had entered my life. There were men at the synagogue down the street from where I lived. At about the age of nine, I was asked by them to come by on Friday evenings and turn on the lights. It was their Sabbath and they weren't permitted to do any sort of work, not even turning on the lights in order to study their scriptures. They usually collected ten or fifteen pennies and gave them to me. They were very pleasant men and I was always happy to do the favor. There was a Jewish tenant in my building who was very handsome, but much too old for me. One night though I accepted a date to the movies. He caught me by surprise and kissed me. He rammed his tongue so far into my mouth that I thought I was about to die from suffocation or get and instant tonsillectomy. Then there was the plumber who came by our apartment from time to time to fix our leaky kitchen pipes. He was very cute and I flirted with him shamelessly. My long, shapely legs distracted him haplessly from his work. Whenever he would return to work in earnest, I would reveal more leg and the work would stop. Sometimes it took him three trips just to change a washer. It tickled me to watch him squirm while the beads of sweat popped out on his forehead. From time to time he would drop by to check on his handiwork and, of course, my legs. Although there were times when all that me and Mom had to eat was a bowl of oatmeal, but we had the best kept pipes in the city of New York.

Benny was a rather shy, but very attentive companion. He escorted me to the dances and then saw me home. I knew that he had a crush on me, but he ignited no sparks in me whatsoever. His mother was in seventh heaven. Her greenish-blue eyes jumped alive at the prospect of her son bringing home a nice communist wife. Being a dedicated communist, she gave no thought to my not being Jewish. Several times a week she visited my mother, presumably to enlist her aid in the matchmaking. One day she gave my mom a wringer-type washing machine. No more washboards. No more hand wringing the water laden sheets. No more mopping of water puddles. Mom was ecstatic, but she did not commit herself to the issue of my marrying Benny. It would not have mattered anyway. As destiny would have it, Benny's primary purpose in my life was not to provide my mother with the first washing machine she had ever owned, but to inadvertently bring me together with the man who would become my husband.

It was toward the end of a young communists meeting that Benny gave me the choice of him taking me home or me accompanying him to a party that he had promised to attend. Since to me a party is a party, I went with him. The party was being given by a group of black soldiers who had recently returned from the Korean conflict. The soft dreamy, soulful music from the phonograph greeted us as we entered the dimly lit railroad flat. Benny knew some of the soldiers from school and was trying to recruit blacks for the party. None of the soldiers were members, but they had maintained a friendship with Benny and were glad to see him. I just wanted to party.

Amidst the sea of dark faces in this very dimly lit flat, a white soldier sat in the kitchen conspicuously alone. I watched him with interest as Benny and I danced. He was cordial and friendly to those who spoke to him, but was mostly uncomfortable and ill at ease. The mother of the soldier for whom the party had been given felt sorry for him and told me that his name was Chuck and asked me to invite the man to dance. Self-consciously, he joined me on the dance floor. He was tall, with gentle blue eyes and blonde hair. In his uniform, he was gorgeous. On the dance floor he was a klutz. He told me that he and the black soldiers had served together in Korea and that they were stationed at Fort Dix in New Jersey. Since he had nothing to do at the post, his buddies persuaded him to attend the party with them. He then asked if I would show him the sights of New York. I gave him my home address. Benny was furious, but he realized that he had no claim on me. He grabbed me by the arm and hustled me out the door. He huffed and sulked as we rode home on the subway, but spoke not a word.

To my surprise, Chuck showed up at my door the next afternoon. He met mom and took dinner with us. Mom liked him. So did I. He had a very charming and mannerly way about him. Having met him at a black party and noticing how comfortable he was with me and my mother, I concluded that he was generally free of racial pretentious and prejudices. That afternoon we went to the movies. The moment Benny's mom laid eyes on Chuck; she knew that her son did not have a prayer. I never saw her or Benny again.

I gave Chuck the grand tour of New York City. We went from Coney Island to the top of the Empire State Building. We took in a St. Patrick's Day Parade and ferried out to the Statue of Liberty. Since his corporal's pay was about sixty dollars a month, I happily picked up the checks at the Hindu, Greek, and Japanese restaurants where we dined. We visited Pat and Ruth who quickly dismissed him and eventually me as communist material. I did take him to a few young communist meetings. We usually arrived between the end of the dialectics and the beginning of the dancing. He never suspected that those young people who spoke so passionately against worker oppression and racism were communists. He was impressed with their concerns for the well being of the people of the world. Whenever one of them sought to engage him in conversation, he would listen cordially, smile agreeably or shake his head reprovingly. I would then whisk him off to the dance floor before he realized that he had just returned from fighting a war against the very ideology that his hosts intended to solicit his support in advancing.

During the week, I was in school and working. But on the weekends, Chuck and I spent all of our time together. For about seven months I was on a grand and euphoric emotional glide. I fell in love with him and he with me. He also informed me that he would be mustering out of the army soon and returning to his home in Michigan. He then suggested that I use my vacation time from my job to go home with him to meet his parents before he mustered out. Ecstatically, I accepted.

# CHAPTER FIVE

# Flickering Light

It was night when the Greyhound pulled into the Detroit bus depot. Chuck's father, William, was waiting to meet us. He was a stocky man with grey-brown hair and dark friendly eyes. He and Chuck bore no resemblance. He greeted me jovially as though it were the way he greeted everyone. He moved hurriedly to place our baggage in the trunk of the car, mentioning that he had just enough time to get us to the house before going to work. As we made the thirty minute drive to Wyandotte, Chuck and his father engaged in intermittent conversations about family and friends. To me he only inquired as to the bus ride and told me to call him Bill.

A thickset, white haired woman opened the door to Chuck's anxious knocks. I could tell right off that this was Chuck's mother. Except for gender and age they were the spitting image of each other. She stared at me aghast. I could think of nothing to say or do except to stare back at her numbly until Chuck returned from the car with our luggage. Even as she and Chuck embraced her eyes were transfixed upon me. Chuck introduced me to her as "Miki" with no other explanation. She forced a "welcome" through a reluctant wisp of a smile. I was too tired from the bus ride to concern myself with her frosty reception. Bill rushed off to work at a steel mill where he was a machinist. Chuck and I went up to bed.

Chuck's mother and I said very little to each other the next day. But each time that I looked towards her, I would catch her staring at me. It was as though I were some strange and incredulous apparition that she hoped would transform into something familiar and acceptable. She flew into a rage when she learned that her husband had taken Chuck and me to a neighborhood bar to meet his friends. She thought it inappropriate to take a sixteen year old into a bar. Bill dismissed her outburst with a shrug of the shoulders. He was far more grateful that his son returned alive and well from war than concerned about his wife's adherence to social proprieties. This was especially true in light of the fact that Chuck was wounded in the face when General Dean was captured during the evacuation of Puson.

The unalloyed contempt that Chuck's mother heaped upon me were almost unendurable pin pricks that I was powerless to ward off. She was not only contemptuous of me because I was dark in color, but in her eyes I was now promiscuous because I had not rejected Bill's invitation to meet his friends at the bar. I wanted to tell her that I started going to bars with my mother at the age of nine and that I knew how to enjoy myself around men without being promiscuous. It would not have made any difference. Whatever notions that entered her bigoted mind were trapped inside and had achieved the status of gospel. Chuck's dad abandoned the issue and went to take a nap before going to work. Chuck took me on a tour of the town.

A foul, pungent odor was the salient feature of Wyandotte. Chuck told me that it was emitted from the salt processing mill that dominated the town. The odor hung especially thick and heavy during the summer months, but was present all year round. It was a quiet, peaceful town. Maybe I could have gotten used to a small intimate place, such as Wyandotte. Certainly the rolling green hills and clear blue lakes would be a vast improvement over the grime and crust of New York City. When I mentioned that I saw no other people in town but whites, he spoke of a race riot that had occurred in Detroit during the 30's and how the blacks had been confined to a place called Ecorse. Suddenly,

New York became very appealing.

It was on my second day that Chuck's mother brought her true thoughts and feelings out into to open. Chuck and I had returned from a stroll in the park. We were upstairs in the bedroom when the sound of a violent argument poured through the laundry chute. We could not make out what was being said, but we could tell that it was between Chuck's parents. Chuck told me to stay in the room as he ran downstairs to the basement. About fifteen minutes later, Chuck returned to the bedroom and grabbed me by the hand.

"Let's go!" He said angrily.

I could feel the intensity of his rage as he drove back to the park. He pulled over to the curb and banged his fist furiously on the steering wheel.

"Why! Why! Why is she doing this"! Chuck shouted as the tears streamed down his face. "I can't believe this is happening."

I was frightened. I could only watch and wait helplessly for his rage to subside to find out what had caused it.

"I didn't think my mother could be this way!" Chuck said.

"What is it Chuck?" I asked softly.

"It's my mother, Miki. She thinks you're too young for me and since you're not Catholic, she called you a heathen, a black heathen. She condemned us both to roast in hell. She wants you out of her house immediately."

I sat quietly trying to get past the surging feelings of rage and hate towards his mother, that I knew were morally wrong. How dare she presume this judgment based on my color and religion? Who does she think she is? God? But I knew that two wrongs don't make a right. So I calmed myself rather quickly. But Chuck couldn't. He was being torn between the women that he loved. And I could understand how his rage was knocking at the doors of heaven asking for mercy and yet this was hell. I pulled myself together and gave him what he needed.

"I didn't come here to start family trouble." I began somberly. I was feeling his hurt, as well as his anger. "I still have enough money to take the rest of my vacation in the Catskills or just stay at home if I feel like it. If I'm not wanted, I don't need to stay."

"I just don't know what to say to you." Chuck stated desperately. "I never expected my mom to act this way."

"Let me go back and let me pack. You have a good time with your family. I'll see you when you come back to New York, if you want to."

I had let Chuck off the hook. But what else could I do? It would be his choice as to whether or not he would allow his mother's bigotry to become a wedge between us. He was relieved that he would not have to confront his mother further. Chuck put his arms around me and kissed me. Silently we drove back to the house.

"Come here, Dolly. Come sit over here." Chuck's father said in a friendly voice as he motioned me to join him at the dining table. I later learned that Dolly was a pet name that he called all women. He took my hand in his and patted it gently as his wife glared fiercely at me from the kitchen doorway. I looked at Chuck but he just shrugged his shoulders.

"Dolly, you're going to have a good time while you're here on vacation." He began in a thick Irish brogue. "Chuck will take you around to meet the family. And you'll have nothing to bother yourself about. If anybody says anything to you to make you unhappy, they'll have to answer to me." He concluded sternly. From where I sat, I saw the red faced anger and searing eyes of his wife's face before she disappeared into the kitchen.

Bill's assurances did not quell my apprehension about staying. Even without its reeking, pungent odor, Wyandotte, Michigan was proving to be no compelling attraction for me to want to spend another hour there, much less five more days. And meeting the rest of Chuck's family would undoubtedly be a crapshoot. Chuck's father had served in WWII and learned from the experience that, on the whole, people were pretty much the same no matter what their race. I was a guest in his home and the beloved of his son. To him, nothing else mattered. To his wife, I was a black heathen who was bent on leading her son straight into the roaring fires of hell. Somewhere between these poles, lay the remainder of the Bissett clan.

Chuck was adamant that I spend the week as I had originally planned. He was proud of his father for sticking up for him and didn't want to insult him by whisking me off to the bus depot for my trip back to New York. As Chuck and I made the rounds to meet his family, I became somewhat sympathetic towards his mother's concerns. Chuck's family was an old and prominent one that had entered the New World through Nova Scotia. They had been mainly sailing captains and doctors. They were all of Scottish, Irish and French ancestry, and by all that I saw, intended on keeping it that way. I was introduced to the chief of staff at a hospital, vice president at a steel mill, a town mayor, and an assortment of other professionals. The men of the family were friendly and cordial towards me. One uncle even pressed a twenty dollar bill in my hand. To the women, I was a vague and inferior curiosity that had to be tolerated but, hopefully, would disappear. With the exception of a very pleasant aunt, they talked through me, around me, but not to me. I could not envision myself being included in this portrait of Aryan respectability. There will most certainly be a meeting of the Bissett clan at the earliest opportunity and I figured that Chuck will most emphatically and forthrightly be shown the error of his ways. After he mustered out of the service, I figured that he would resume his life in Michigan without me.

When we returned to New York, Chuck asked me to convert to Catholicism as a concession to his mother's greatest opposition. It was not a proposal of marriage at this point. Since I had no religious affiliation to convert from, one religion seemed as good as the next. I enrolled in a catechism class and was assigned a nun. Even after Chuck mustered out of the Army and returned to Michigan, I remained faithful to my studies. I had no problems with the saints, sins and sacraments of the Catholic faith. But I could not accept the concept of the infallibility of the pope. "Had not the pope sanctioned the Spanish Inquisition and the burning of so-called witches and heretics?" Conscience screamed in protest. "Did not the Pope Pius XII sanction the Holocaust by his passive accommodation of Nazism? How could such persons be infallible with so much blood on their hands?" I could in no way accept the doctrine and refused to be a hypocrite just for the sake of a potential marriage.

Chuck wrote me twice from Michigan. In neither letter did he express a commitment about our future together. I more or less resolved within myself that he would resume his life in Michigan and that I would soon become a faded memory. But Chuck did return unannounced to New York and asked me to marry him. The Catholic Church would not marry anyone except their own members, and I refused to convert. As a compromise to Chuck I agreed to permit the children to be christened in the Catholic faith. So a month after Chuck's proposal, we were married in a Protestant ceremony at my mother's apartment. A total of five people including the minister constituted my entire wedding party.

While Chuck took a job at a shop that made blueprints, I completed my last semester of high school. It was an inordinately stressful time for me. I was pregnant and the jostling on the train ride to school made my morning sickness almost unbearable. I kept the job, but gave up night school. I could not reveal my pregnancy to the school or I would have been expelled. Along with the stress of the pregnancy, morning sickness, and settling into married life with Chuck, there was the matter of a term paper that gave me a two-month case of the blues.

All that was left for me to graduate from high school was for me to turn in a term paper on the difference between civil rights and civil liberties. I returned to the house on 26th Street and made the rounds to gather as much information as I could. And then I pored over materials from the Anti-Defamation League, N.A.A.C.P., ACLU and the public library. The more I delved into the project, the more confused I became. When the teacher collected the term papers, mine was conspicuous by its absence and apparently, so was my chance of graduating.

The teacher invited me to come to his office after school to explain why I had not turned in the term paper. I told him where I had been, who I had seen, and what I had read, only to conclude that a civil right was guaranteed by the Constitution and a civil liberty was a right or privilege not covered by laws or statutes. I figured that any paper that I wrote to explain this would have been such a mess and I would have gotten a bad grade anyway. He pondered my explanation for a fraction of a minute and then opened his grade book.

"You're absolutely right," he said and then entered an 'A' as my grade for the course. "That's exactly what it is."

To this day, I don't know if he said that because he just wanted me to graduate or because I had maxed all of my other tests and he didn't want to fail me.

And so my school days were about to come to an end and, true to my cultural heritage, I anticipated settling into the life of a dutiful wife and mother. But there remained one last heart rending irony for me to confront before I closed out my life as a student.

My English teacher, Mrs. Fetcher, called me to her classroom just before I was to graduate. She and I had become Shakespeare buddies. We usually read the major roles in the plays that she assigned to the class. She greeted me with a radiant smile and then informed me that she had arranged for me to receive a full scholarship to Barnard College, the women's auxiliary to Columbia University, to major in English Literature. Since I had not studied a college preparatory curriculum, she must have had such a high regard for me that she went out of her way to secure a scholarship for me. Her face dropped in utter dismay when I informed her in an anguished voice that I could not accept the scholarship. I could not tell her that I was married with child or she would have had to expel me one week before graduation. I told her that I was going to California and the plans were firm. I could do nothing but thank her for her efforts and leave to be alone with my sorrow as I rode the subway to my job.

Wistfully, I stared out of the window of the subway train as the clankering of its wheels accompanied the fading away of most likely my last hope at achieving my ambitions. There was an angry voice in my soul that kept repeating, "Why didn't she tell me her intentions in February or March? Maybe we could have figured out a way for me to afford to go to college. Why didn't she tell me? Why was life playing this sadistic trick on me?"

For a tiny moment in time, someone had expressed their love for a part of my inner personage that life's circumstances had caused me to abandon. I could only hope that whatever light within me that beckoned Mrs. Fetcher would somehow flicker the rest of my life. In the meantime, my responsibilities to my unborn child took precedence over any plans and ambitions that I would have wanted to make for the future.

# CHAPTER SIX

# *Critical Thinking*

A majestic and awesome revelation of the glory of God filled my vision and unleashed a tidal wave of terror within me. Silently I prayed that we would scale the panoramic white pristine caps of the Rockies and press safely onward to Burbank. Chuck told me that a thermal caused the plane to bounce and wake me from a sleep that I hoped would last for the duration of the flight. It seemed so powerful and invincible when I boarded it at LaGuardia. But against the looming, intimidating presence of the seemly endless range of the mountains, the DC7 seemed little more than a flea of steel. If we were to crash, I didn't want to know about it. I closed my eyes and returned to the safe haven of sleep.

It was hot as hell when we landed. Fumes from gasoline overpowered me, causing me to gasp. I held my nose and mouth as Chuck and I made our way to the Burbank terminal where my brother-in-law, Raymond, was waiting to pick us up. Mother had visited Gracie and Raymond for a month the previous year and returned with glowing reports of Southern California. Chuck had a sister, Jean, who had married an airline pilot and was living contentedly in Los Angeles. Transitioning from a quaint and personal town of Wyandotte to the intimidating and suffocating metropolis of New York City had become too daunting a project for Chuck. He concluded that California was teeming with opportunities and possibilities. It seemed an ideal place for us to start our married life.

'You're pregnant, too?" I asked laughingly of my sister Gracie when we arrived at she and Raymond's duplex in Hollywood.

"Yeah, I flunked three rabbit tests". Gracie said jovially. "But I am pregnant."

Gracie was very generous with us. They had made a unit available for us. Raymond helped Chuck find a job at Lockheed where he worked. Chuck and I began what I at least hoped would be a life of modest respectability.

About four months after our arrival, I gave birth to Rodrick. He was born prematurely. That gave rise to speculation in Chuck's family that Chuck had been compelled to marry because he had gotten me pregnant. I suspected that it was Jean who dispatched her husband, Ray, all the way from Redondo Beach to Hollywood to visit me at the hospital and confirm the speculation. Ray and I were hardly on the best of terms. In fact, he was probably the most obnoxious person I had ever met. He was an irredeemable white supremacist who made no secret of his contempt for those segments of humanity that were not Caucasian. Soon after our arrival in California, Chuck took me to meet his sister and her husband. Jean had been an airline stewardess before marrying Ray. She was gracious and accommodating. We had barely finished saying grace over dinner when he pointedly informed me that there were only two kinds of people: those who are Irish, and those who wished they could be.

"Well, I'm certainly not Irish and don't want to be." I responded hotly, when I saw that Chuck made no effort to stop his insults. "Because the ones I met in New York, I wouldn't even wipe my ass with." Of course, I didn't mean it. But he was the sort of person who had to be slashed to the marrow before he felt the point.

I was, therefore, very much surprised when Ray and his flight engineer turned up at my bedside. It was not until he saw the baby in an

incubator that he became convinced that the baby was indeed prematu-
ture and that inferences of a "shotgun wedding" were unwarranted.

Jean was also pregnant and gave birth to a girl about two months
after my son Rodrick was born. Chuck's mother flew out to help her.
I dreaded seeing both Ray, and Chuck's mother. But of course they
were family and we had to visit. Once again Chuck's mother opened
the door and we stared uncomfortably at one another without saying a
word. This time her eyes were not aghast. They now reflected an apology that she could not bring herself to state. Not knowing what else to
do, I shoved the baby into her arms. No doubt she had heard that the
baby was more the complexion of her son and not of his wife, and that
her son had not been compelled to marry me. With those concerns
arrested, she playfully tickled the baby's chin. For the very first time
since I had known her, a smile formed on her face. During our visit,
Rodrick soiled his diaper. I wanted to change him quickly as little boys
have a tendency to spray everything when the diaper is removed. I
asked Chuck to empty the diaper in the toilet and deposit in the diaper
bag. As Chuck headed to the bathroom, Ray yelled out to Chuck that
emptying diapers was woman's work. Forgetting that Chuck's mother
and sister were in the room, I flew into a tirade.

"You motherfucking male chauvinist pig". Who the fuck do you
think you are to tell my husband what to do when I talk to him? This
is his child too. If I want him to go to the fuckin' moon, you ain't got
nothing to say about it. So you keep your fuckin' opinions to yourself.
You white supremacist asshole!"

Ray flushed red and slouched anonymously into his seat. Chuck's
mother and Jean said nothing, but their eyes gleamed with joy. Where
I expected condemnation from them for my vulgarity, they were both
ecstatic. It was as I had reasoned all along. Beyond the petty pretensions
of race, religion, and the quests for power and wealth, there exists the
human bond—eternal and inviolate. Once she held baby Rodrick, she
had to respect my motherhood. I was the mother of her grandchildren
and they would carry her genes as well as mine. There was no sense

carrying on a race war. The frosty reserve between me and Chuck's mother began to thaw. After she returned to Wyandotte, we began to exchange warm, friendly letters. Ray spoke to me no more for six years. But Jean and I developed an intellectual and emotional respect for each other that I still cherish.

Mother had landed husband number four and flew in from New York to live with us. His name was Arcelio. He was a kind, soft spoken Puerto Rican who was about ten years her junior. Chuck and I slept on the Murphy bed in the dining room and gave them the bedroom so that taking care of the baby would not disturb their sleep.

It was one of those hot, smoggy, arid afternoons that made even taking a nap seem like a day's work in a salt mine. Chuck had tossed and turned himself to sleep. I was hoping to soon follow. But Rodrick was just beginning to teethe and could not sleep comfortably. No matter how I walked him, he kept whining. Finally I placed him between me and Chuck, hoping he would fall asleep. But he kept waking up whining. As I was trying to quiet Rodrick and lull him to sleep, Chuck turned over with a pillow in hand and brought it down angrily; onto his son's face. Instantly, I hurled myself onto Chuck's chest and began furiously gouging at his eyes.

"You son of a bitch, I'll kill you"! I screamed. He tried to cover his eyes and fling me off of him. But from my fury I drew an uncommon strength. I finally heard the desperate wailing of my son. But I was so focused on killing the man responsible for it that I could not stop gouging at his eyes and face.

I was aware of nothing else until my Mother and Stepfather pulled me off of Chuck and wrestled me into a chair. Chuck's eyes darted about in frantic bewilderment. Tiny rivets of blood began to ooze from the network of scratches on his face. He hurried into the bathroom to tend his wounds.

My Mother succeeded in quieting my baby by walking him around the room. I then calmed myself enough to tell her and Arcelio what had happened. I could find no reason within myself as to why Chuck would do this to his teething son. Arcelio attributed it to the heat and stress brought on by the incessant crying. My mother concurred and stated that we have a child to consider and I should forgive him. When Chuck emerged from the bathroom, his face reflected genuine remorse. He said that he had no idea as to what had gotten into him and promised that it would never happen again.

"It had better not." I responded bitterly. "I don't know what's wrong with you. But you better think about it—hard and deep. Because if you ever do that again, I'll kill you with my bare hands, goddammit."

Chuck's inexplicable surge of violence crushed my hopes for a joyful and seamless love. The thought of him being a violent and sadistic man had never entered my head. Now that it had, distrust had driven a wedge between us. Hopefully, it was embedded in his mind that I would not sit idly by and watch him abuse my child and that if need be I would defend my child to the death.

Life returned to a blissful normalcy. Mothers husband; Arcelio found a job near downtown Los Angeles. He and Mom moved to Echo Park to be near his job. A Filipino couple who were our neighbors had agreed to be Rodricks' Godparents for his christening. Chuck had changed jobs and we moved to Venice. It was about this time that I became pregnant with Nathan. Once again, Chuck raised the issue of my conversion to Catholicism. I was surprised one evening when one of Chuck's co-workers brought his wife by the house to baby-sit while he took us to Loyola Marymount University for a Jesuit priest to presumably clear whatever misconceptions I harbored about the Catholic faith. Chuck was convinced that the nun had not properly responded to my queries and that the Jesuits would do better. And his friend concurred.

The priest was a middle age, kind and compassionate soul. He informed us that he could only spare thirty minutes to clarify my misunderstanding of Catholicism. Three hours later, the priest was in a state of amazement at my knowledge and my husband was seething with anger. I began by explaining to the priest that I had concluded that religion was too intolerably corrupt and self-serving to be considered a spiritual verity. I reminded the priest that, according to the very Bible we both honored, we are to call man father in the reverential sense. Even aside from this, I stated flatly that I believed deeply in the sanctity of human life and that no one, papal or otherwise, had the right to condone wars, slaughter, and genocides for the sake of political, economic, or religious advantage. I proceeded to challenge moral precepts as demonstrated by church history. The priest hemmed, hawed, and cleared his throat before tossing congenially contrived rationalizations at me that bounced harmlessly off of my firm and determined wall of conviction. Chuck shifted uncomfortably in his chair and glared at me with menacing anger. But he uttered not a word. It was obvious to me that he thought it unconscionable to question a priest, let alone a Jesuit priest. When the priest asked me how many years I had of seminary training, I realized that he was impressed with the arguments I presented. I told him that I had none and had only completed high school. Since Chuck had no knowledge of my affiliation with the Communist Party, I was not about to divulge that it had inadvertently set me on a course of critical thinking as a means of defense against its self serving dialectics. I was now prepared to apply to any "ism" that came along. No longer was I a little girl who only spoke when spoken to. I was an adult who was no longer afraid to speak my mind.

Chuck had been born and raised in the Catholic faith. For him, its theology loomed beyond any possibility of rational inquiry. I had hoped that he would have been just as proud of me as the priest was impressed that I had a well-functioning mind and was not afraid to use it. It had not occurred to me that if he had wanted an incisive and aggressive mind, he would not have married a "Puerto Rican" from Brooklyn. Instead, I took the tight-lipped silence that accompanied us all the way home as an indication that I had achieved a clear and decisive over the priest in our debate. Never again did Chuck broach the issue of my conversion to me. And none of our subsequent five children were ever christened.

It was not long after the birth of my second son Nathan that I found myself under psychiatric care. With my predisposition to allergies, exposure to smog and the stress of my pregnancy, I began to experience bouts of depression where I would cry uncontrollably for no apparent reason and skin lesions that were diagnosed as eczema. My case was assigned to Dr. Knox at a newly opened psychiatric clinic in Hollywood. He moved back there after Chuck took a job at Flying Tigers as an instrument technician. Dr. Knox was a patient and compassionate man. He had a ruddy red complexion and white hair. He reminded me of Santa Claus, even his disposition.

"Tell me about your relationship with your father," he said at the outset of our first session.

As I began reflecting upon my relationship with dad, tears welled in my eyes and cascaded down my face. Each time I tried to speak, the words would become lodged in my throat. Dr. Knox would hand me a box of tissue and then return to indulging Rodrick's two- year- old curiosity. He never pressed me to respond to his questions and gave me all the time I needed to cry through my pain. He scheduled me for three sessions a week. During the first three weeks there were only tears and screams, but I couldn't get out any words. My son Rodrick would get frantic when he saw me crying and rummage through the drawers in the office until he found the box of tissues and wiped my tears. Dr. Knox took a special liking towards him because of his depth of sensitivity at such a young age and indulged his energetic play. It was his fondness for my son that drew me beyond the tears and hysteria to where I could comfortably reveal my thoughts to him.

I told him about my father's deportation and of the feelings I was never able to express to him. We also went into dream analysis when I told him of a nightmare that I had had of a huge black gorilla furiously coming after me. It was "El Kuku". Dr. Knox made me realize that it was time to confront my fears of my father. Eventually, I came to see my dad in a dream as he really was—proud, looming, and yet smiling, dressed in a beautiful beige soft camel hair coat and a velvety black fedora. He was not a crackpot on a soapbox. He was not "El Kuku". He was a chief's son who was raised for leadership, but that now seemed an elusive possibility. As the son of a chief, it was his duty to put his community's concerns before his own. He had envisioned that the principles of his tribal upbringing would somehow prevail in 20$^{th}$ century New York. But he was overwhelmed by the ideological warfare's of the Great Depression. His good intentions allied themselves with political factions who played upon his ego needs. He could not let go. He would have to surrender the princely pride of his upbringing and that was all he had left.

In my heart, I came to respect his courage. He came from a jungle, learned to read and write in a foreign language, juggled complex ideas and debated them. He spoke his beliefs to whoever would listen. None of this responded to my nagging fear of him. It took many sessions with Dr. Knox to raise the source of my fear to the surface and offer me the possibility of putting the issue to rest.

It was for my third birthday that dad took the family to Coney Island. For reasons that I have never understood, he insisted that I ride with him on the Cyclone, the world's highest roller coaster at the time. The car moved slowly to the top and then zoomed down the first dive so fast that the rush of air pressure almost suffocated me. It then clipped along at a 55 mph pace. But before I could catch my breath, the cars rounded a curve causing the full weight of my Father to fall against me. I felt as though I was going to die from either suffocation or being crushed to death. We were moving so fast that I could not scream. We plunged into a dive so harrowing that I envisioned myself being flung over the crossbar and lying dead on the ground. I crunched low into a corner, held on tight to the crossbar and refused to open my mouth. By the time we got off, my stomach was in knots, my vision blurred and the world was a maddening spin. Through it all, I received not a word of assurance from my Father. Even as I stood there trying to gather my bearings, he did not even have the sensitivity to pick me up. Instead, he yanked me from the platform of the roller coaster.

From that day forward, I hated my Dad with a passion. Now I knew why I could not get close to Dad. Being close to my Dad meant being crushed by him and possibly dying. Dr. Knox helped me to forgive his errors in judgment and get over my hatred of him.

However, he remained an enigmatic figure in my head. I was no longer threatened by him. Finally, I could now lay the issue of my Father to rest.

For reasons that I did not understand, Chuck began pelting me with verbal abuse. To him I became "bitch" or "slut". What should have been discussions between man and wife, turned into insulting abuse? Once I hurled a steaming pot of peas and carrots that missed his head by a few inches. The most crushing blow I received was the morning that my three year old son, Rodrick, called me a bitch when I would not permit him to run out into the street. I turned to Dr. Knox for help.

"Why don't you leave him?" Was his response to my desperation.

"Don't you see how my dad's leaving affected me? I don't want that for my children. I want them to have a Father. If I can get well enough to cope, I won't tear up this marriage. But he's got to make an effort too."

"Why don't you bring Chuck with you to our next session? Maybe, I can talk to him and get him to lighten up."

Chuck accompanied me to my next session. He and Dr. Knox conferred alone for a long time. As Chuck was leaving the office I heard Dr. Knox speak to him admonishingly.

"Don't be such a master sergeant."

At home that evening Chuck attempted to convince me that Dr. Knox had given him a clean bill of mental health. In a voice that was both malicious and contemptuous, he flatly concluded that it was I and not him, who was mentally afflicted. I lost control of my temper and cursed him out soundly. The next day I advised Dr. Knox that his consultation did not yield the results he had hoped and that Chuck had distorted what the doctor had told him to suit his own needs.

Our relationship more or less limped along at a fairly tolerable clip. After I flung the pot at Chuck, the verbal abuse stopped. Our arguments became mostly about money. Being an apprentice, Chuck's paycheck barely made ends meet. I had no problem with that. My problem was with Chuck's new love. Ray had told us that during one of his flights, a UFO stopped in front of his plane and then darted off into points unknown. Chuck became almost obsessed with the possibilities of extraterrestrials flying in American airspace and joined a club to hunt them down. For Chuck and his friends to confirm their suspicions, certain equipment was essential. So money that was needed for household went instead towards the purchase of telescopes, cameras, and camping equipment. In no way could I comprehend his obsession with flying saucers and aliens; especially since it was creating hardship for his family.

One Friday, Chuck came in from work and announced that he and his friends were leaving that night to spend the weekend in the desert searching for UFO's.

"You're not going anywhere until I get some groceries." I responded angrily as I grabbed the car keys from the table.

"Oh, yes I am." Chuck stated defiantly. "They're leaving at seven and I'm going with them."

"You expect to leave me all weekend without any food for the children?" I retorted. "You must be crazy!"

"Crazy or not I'm going and you're not going to stop me." Chuck yelled in a voice that slammed the door on the argument.

Chuck gathered his equipment and made his way down to the car. To his surprise and anger he found Rodrick seated in the back seat and me holding Nathan in my lap while triumphantly dangling the car keys. His only choices were to drag his family out of the car, take us with him, or take us shopping for groceries. He left his gear in the hallway and with a sigh of indignant resignation started the engine.

He was still smoldering as we approached the stop sign at the bottom of the hill of our street. He was not slowing down.

"Chuck, what are you doing?" I yelled.

He jammed on the brake. Rodrick rolled out of the back seat onto the floor with a loud thud. He began crying. I reached back over the seat and picked him up. His mouth was covered with blood. He had bitten a hole through his bottom lip.

"Chuck, take me to Children's Hospital right now." I demanded.

The emergency room was crowded when we arrived and we had to wait our turn. We ended up spending the night at the hospital while the doctor x-rayed Rodrick's' jaw for unseen fractures and stitched his lip. Chuck's weekend of saucer chasing was gone. That next week, Chuck learned that his UFO hunting buddies did in fact see some strange and distant lights through the desert darkness. Fearing that they had been sighted by aliens bent on kidnapping them, they fled to their cars in masse and drove back to town with not one photo to substantiate their claim. Concluding that his friends were flakes, Chuck forsook UFO hunting and took up soaring in motorless gliders.

With our third child on the way, we needed a larger place. We moved out of our apartment and into a small house in Panorama City. I had given birth to my daughter Julie and was beginning to feel happy and contented. It was on a Saturday morning, about four months after I gave birth to Julie that I had to confront Chuck's impulsive nature again. I was nursing her under a quilt when I asked him to see about Nathan who was trying to get out of his crib in the next room. To my extreme horror, Chuck brought Nathan into the room dangling by an arm and leg and then flung him at me. He landed on top of Julie. Panic stricken, I pushed Nathan off of Julie and pulled up the quilt. She was gasping for air and then she began crying. After I reassured myself that she was safe, I started dressing Rodrick and Nathan. I said not a word. I then called my Mother to pick us up and then dressed Julie. Like a determined whirlwind, I began packing as many diapers and clothes as I could carry while Chuck watched in desperate astonishment. He then slumped down into an armchair in the living room.

"I guess I must be going crazy." He said softly as he held his head in his hands. "I don't know why I do these things. But please, Miki, don't leave. Give me another chance. I'll go for therapy."

I loved Chuck and didn't want to leave him. I concluded that he was a sick man. I would not abandon him if he had a broken leg. Then why would I abandon him because he had an infirmed psyche? He pleaded with me not to leave. But I heard it as a cry for help. Perhaps he had finally seen how monstrous he can be. As long as he was willing to submit to therapy, I resolved within myself not to walk out on him.

Chuck's therapy lasted about three months. It ended through no fault of his own. He started getting overtime and his employer expected him to work. I could see that he was making a concerted effort to control his violent eruptions. My own therapy had ended a month earlier.

"You know you're a pioneer and pioneers always get shot at by the Indians. Sometimes they make it and sometimes they don't. Good luck." Dr. Knox said as he ended our sessions with a pat on the shoulder. Little did I realize what Dr. Knox was implying until much later in life.

When the overtime ended, we had to adjust our budget accordingly. We moved back to Hollywood. Nathan started kindergarten and I became pregnant with Victoria. Having another baby did not concern me. I loved children and had hoped to have three or four close together. I had reduced housekeeping to a virtual science. By ten in the morning I was finished with dishes, diapers and cleaning. I would relax until it was time for me and the kids to pick up Rodrick from school have lunch and settle in for our afternoon naps.

Chuck left Flying Tigers and accepted a job as a technical artist trainee for a company in Hollywood. After only three weeks he became an instructor. A short while later he accepted a position with yet another company as a technical art director. Because the company subcontracted with the government, he was required to get a security clearance. It was then that I was compelled to tell Chuck of my father's communist affiliation and deportation. What was supposed to have taken one month, took three. While waiting for his clearance, Chuck would become very upset with me that I had cast doubts upon his patriotic loyalty. When the clearance came through and he felt secure about his employment, we moved to the Marina to be near his place of work. Later I learned from my brother-in-law that an Indonesian had told him that an FBI agent had been dispatched to Indonesia to confirm that my dad was in Indonesia and had never met my husband. It was about this time that I began receiving letters from my Father.

From his letters, it was obvious that Dad found it considerably easier to espouse communism from a soapbox than to live under it in Poland. He could not comprehend the reality that just as freedom of expression may be vital to the establishment of totalitarian regime, it is an anathema to maintaining it. He and Eleanor were expelled from Poland for reasons that Dad did not state. They moved to France and used it as a base to undertake their mission of reforming communism. Hungary, Czechoslovakia, and Russia were no more receptive to them than Poland. They were asked to leave and never return. Dad did not tell me whether Eleanor remained in France or returned to New York. But he went home to Indonesia alone. According to his letters, he was honored with status equivalent to knighthood for his part in his country's movement for independence. Unfortunately, his elevation to "Sir Rodrick Beden" did little to help his financial circumstances.

Somehow he had learned that I had married a white man and naturally assumed that I was well off. His letters began with the warmest of salutations and apologies for any hurt that he might have caused me, and then abruptly shifted into requests for funding for projects ranging from starting a duck farm to setting up a washing machine factory. In one letter he assumed that Chuck was an airline pilot because he had worked for Lockheed. He claimed that he had arranged for Chuck to fly over a Lockhead Connie that his government had purchased and drop off a thousand dollars to help him launch an assortment of enterprises. When I wrote suggesting that such funds would find their way into the black market, he was furious that I should infer that he was a crook. I wanted to send him a little money each month, but my fourth child, Victoria, had been born and I could not afford it. I did send a bank draft and a box of dry foods. I never heard from him again.

Chuck and I had been married about six years and it had not yet dawned on him that just because two loves can merge and function as a single heart, it does not necessarily follow that thoughts and ideas should merge to function as a single brain. Chuck was not one given to independent thought. I attributed it to both the domineering influences of his mother and autocracy of the nuns and priests at the parochial schools that he had attended. Dyslexia was unheard of during Chuck's school days. Both the nuns and his parents assumed that his inability to spell was due to laziness or obstinacy, and punished him severely. The dyslexia and punishment undoubtedly forced him to seek the refuge and safety of the inherent power and authority of being a male. He naturally assumed that his word was law, especially where his family was concerned. We never discussed politics, religion or any other issue that would generate debate. That was fine with me. I did not marry him for his mind. I married him because we loved each other.

Now that Chuck was bringing home a larger paycheck, I was able to return to one of my loves. I began taking art classes once a week. When the co-workers that Chuck brought home for lunch indicated how impressed they were with my novice talent, he stopped bringing them home for lunch. One of them invited us to a party at which some Argentineans began a spirited, animated debate regarding Castro's reign over Cuba. Me and my Spanish waded into the debate arguing passionately that Castro will evolve into no less a despot than Batista. The Argentineans were impressed with my arguments. Although Chuck did not understand Spanish, he could see the intensity of our discussion. Having no idea that this is how Latinos argue, he grabbed me by the arm and took me home. In the car he unleashed his fury.

"Why can't you act right?" he gushed furiously.

"You mean I can't express my opinions?" I retorted defiantly.

"Why can't you act like a lady and quit arguing with men?"

"Are you trying to tell me that arguing with men means that I'm not a lady? You're full of shit! And you know it!"

"I can't take you anywhere because you don't know how to act." He went on oblivious to anything I had said.

"Well, it's too bad. God gave me a mind and a mouth and I'm going to use them whenever I please."

"You goddamn slut! I ought to knock the shit out of you."

The contempt in his word stunned me into silence. Hate rose within me like a serpent determined to pounce upon its prey. That horrible word was back in my life. Chuck didn't know how to attack ideas, and was threatened by even the presumption of independence on my part. Instead, he attacked my personage. The question was could I take it and for how long? Any mother considers the needs of her children first and readily sacrifices herself for their sake. I had made my bed and was perfectly willing to lay in it even if it turned out to be a bed of thorns. But from the contempt in his eyes, I realized that I was no longer the wife he wanted. Yes, I was the mother of his children, but I would have to resign myself to being in this marriage alone.

# CHAPTER SEVEN

# *Alone In A Marriage*

As Chuck and I began to save money for the proverbial rainy day, brochures about lots for sale in Hawaii began to appear in the house. I felt that Chuck had a right to pursue his dreams as long as they contributed to the betterment of his family. But I objected to the fact that the lots were too close to a volcano and we would have to build a huge tank to store rain water. And what would we do to earn a living? He had changed jobs at least seven times and we had moved more times than I care to count. Some part of me questioned this man's stability of mind. But there was an inherent decency about Chuck that permeated his most impervious faults. He had fathered four children that neither frustration nor inner turmoil could compel him to abandon. None of this prepared me for what I labeled the "Chuck's Hawaiian Fiasco".

A lot of people thought the world would come to an end that week. According to some Hindus in India, a peculiar planetary alignment foretold eminent doom. Khrushchev moved to install nuclear missile sites in Cuba. Kennedy was determined not to let that happen. Both sides postured for a doomsday war. As I prepared to give birth to my fifth child, Chuck was about the task of creating a disaster of his own.

Not long after I had thought Chuck had given up on the idea of transplanting his family to Hawaii, he announced that he had quit his well paying job at General Dynamics in order to accept employment in Honolulu as an instrument technician. While we packed everything that we would take with us and sold or gave away those things that we couldn't, Chuck went ahead to Hawaii to start work and to prepare for his family's arrival. The kids and I were to join Chuck there on a Sunday. The day before our scheduled departure, Chuck returned home sullen and depressed. To his astonishment, he had arrived in the midst of a longshoreman's strike and nothing could move in or out of Hawaii by ship, including the materials and equipment that were vital to his job. Chuck was now out of work in both Hawaii and California. If this wasn't a fiasco, I don't know what was. The nine of us crowded into my Mother and Arcelio's two bedroom house. I began to seriously contemplate divorcing Chuck, but I was in such a dependent position that I had to put it out of my mind. I convinced myself that as long as I remained a dutiful wife, he would somehow manage to see what was important and what wasn't.

A few days later, we were in downtown Los Angeles shopping for baby things when I had an urgent need to use a restroom. Fortunately, the proprietor of a newsstand allowed me to use his. The baby figured that this was good a time as any to make her entry into the world. No sooner than I entered the restroom, I began to hemorrhage profusely. I shouted for Chuck to get me to the hospital. Through the bumper to bumper rush hour evening traffic, Chuck rushed me to Queen of Angeles Hospital. About an hour after our arrival, my daughter Anita was born.

The much fabled "luck of the Irish" was with Chuck. The Monday after Anita was born, Chuck was reinstated at his job at General Dynamics with no decrease in pay or status. We moved to an apartment in Culver City. It was there that our marriage began to unravel beyond any hope of repair.

My son Nathan was six years old and seemed destined for a career as either a vandal or a pyromaniac. During that year, he roasted his live pet turtles in a coffee can, disconnected the refrigeration units at a drug store, set fire to the air conditioning unit at a grocery store and trashed a gardener's entire stock of gardenias. He also indicated problems in controlling his bodily functions. A thorough medical workup at UCLA hospital revealed no physiological problems. In my desperation, I returned to UCLA and registered Nathan for psychotherapy. As part of the program, Chuck and I were required to attend family therapy sessions. Chuck was incensed and pleaded that we could not afford it. But his resistance squelched when he learned that it would cost $2 a week for all of us. I realized that our only hope in salvaging our marriage lay in our attending therapy together.

His violent outbursts had become more frequent and intense. During one two month period, he angrily hurled a vacuum cleaner into the midst of Julie's birthday party because he felt that the kids were making too much noise. He threw Nathan into my bed causing his head to knock a hole in the wall, and he began choking Rodrick because he drank his orange juice before he had been served his breakfast. After each incident he would stare at me bewilderedly as though oblivious as to what had transpired. I would threaten to leave and take the children with me. He would plead with me to stay and promised that he would control his violent impulses. Calm would prevail, sometimes for many months at a stretch, before some seemingly innocuous incident would set him off.

While Nathan underwent his therapy, the rest of the family was to meet with the analyst. At the outset of our therapy, it became apparent that our sessions would be too heated for the children to attend. There was one condition we had to meet. Chuck and I were not to separate or Nathan's therapy would be terminated. The analyst knew that he had his work cut out for him.

Dr. Walters was a large, imposing man who wore a bow tie to no doubt accentuate his qualities of professional concern. For me the sessions were a welcome catharsis where my mind was cleansed of its illusions of happiness. What remained was the glaring, unblemished truth. I no longer had to torture myself with a litany of "what ifs" and "maybe I should haves". I flung my deepest, heartfelt emotions on the table. Nothing was held back. Chuck could no longer portray the role of the saint. I was there to confront his insidious lies that were destroying this marriage. He labored under the absurd presumption that his mere presence at the sessions somehow exonerated him from any blame for the eminent disintegration of his family. Dr. Walters became so concerned with my well being that he allowed UCLA to transfer my calls to his home 24 hours a day. After a few sessions, Chuck displayed his first interest in our discussion.

"How come you're always on my case?" He asked challengingly of Dr. Walters. "Why don't you get her to quit talking that stupid stuff?"

"What stupid stuff is she talking?" Dr. Walters responded after making an almost seamless transition from surprise to concern.

"Well, she keeps talking that people need each other. They're supposed to share with each other instead of being so individualistic. Why does she need to talk that stupid stuff? And worse, people believe her and then they're all talking that stupid stuff." Chuck explained in a voice heavy with exasperation.

"Chuck, have you heard of Jean Paul Sartre?" Dr. Walters asked.

"No."

"Have you ever heard of existentialism?"

"No." Chuck responded irritably.

"Jean Paul Sartre wrote a whole theory called Existentialism. And it seems that your wife believes in some of his ideas. Why don't you buy the book and maybe Miki won't seem to be talking such strange stuff."

Chuck began to fidget uneasily in his chair. I sensed that he felt abandoned, if not betrayed. After all, why wasn't Dr. Walters giving credence to his complaint? Shouldn't Dr. Walters be putting me in my place instead of siding with me? Dr. Walters did not realize that Chuck was not disposed towards critical thinking and that any 'ism', existentialism or otherwise, would be a betrayal to his religious upbringing. Chuck regarded the sessions as a magnanimous gesture towards helping his son's recovery and quelling his wife's talk of divorce. He dismissed both me and Dr. Walters as insane for even suggesting that he may somehow be responsible for the turmoil that raged in his household. Chuck perceived himself as the lord of the manor with absolute autonomy over his five children. To him it was intolerable that anyone would question his actions.

From my previous experience with therapy, I knew we were not there to affix blame, but to resolve those issues within oneself that manifest themselves in the form of harmful and destructive behavior. I could see that Chuck construed each session as a blatant assault upon the integrity of his manhood that had to be repulsed at all cost. I decided to resort to whatever means a woman has to breach the weakest point of a man's defenses to get him to express his caring. One evening, I decided to pull out all of the stops.

It took me most of the day to get ready for our afternoon session with Dr. Walters. I restyled my hair and perfectly applied the make up I had bought that day. A few months earlier I had made a white and royal blue silk dress that would have been the envy of the finest boutique in town. I accessorized it with white freshwater pearls, blue earrings, blue velvet pumps, and topped it off with a royal blue beret.

"My God, you're beautiful!" Walter gushed as we started the afternoon's session.

"Thank you Walter," I responded flirtatiously.

"What's the occasion?"

"I wore this for you. I just wanted to show you that I don't have to look like the wreck of Hesperus, just because he calls me that," I said with a poised and seductive wink.

"I can see. Don't you think she's beautiful, Chuck?"

"Yes of course," Chuck answered, entranced with my transformation.

"Then how come you don't take me anywhere? Even when you take me to church, you take me late," I scolded.

"Well, what do you like to do?" Walter asked.

"I like to go dancing. I haven't been dancing in years." I replied.

"Chuck, how come you don't take her dancing?" Walter asked.

"Because, I get an erection."

"If I turn you on, you're supposed to get an erection." I retorted. "How stupid can you be?"

A look of shock appeared on Chuck's face that waned into a blank stare as he squirmed in his chair.

"How in hell do you think men know when they want a woman? They get an erection and jiggle it in their pants!" I fumed into that blank, vacuous stare of his that signaled his retreat from the issue that he did not understand. Dr. Walters extracted a promise from him that he would take me dancing. But this promise, like all the others he had made to me, was promptly forgotten and I never bothered to press it.

For all intent and purposes, my marriage was over. I could tolerate living with him for the sake of the children were it not for the fact that there seemed no end in sight to his abusing them. Three months into our session, I learned that there would be a sixth child on the way. I wished that I had not gotten pregnant. But I had and that life within me consumed all of my thoughts. I shared my concerns and apprehensions with my sister, Gracie. I told her that I was thinking about having an abortion. I asked her if she knew a competent American doctor who performed abortions in Tijuana. It was against the law to perform abortions in California and I had no intentions of risking death in a back alley operation. The next day my Mother called me. She was livid.

"Gracie told me that you're thinking about having an abortion."

"Mom, I know how you feel about abortions. But I'm not going to bring a baby into this mess. It's just not right."

"And you think that killing a baby is right? You can give it up for adoption and not have to kill it."

"Mom. If I have the baby, you know I'm not going to give it up for adoption. I'll just wind up keeping it, and we really can't afford it."

"What do you mean you can't afford it?" Mother shouted. "Don't you think that God knows you got five kids and a sixth on the way? If He's provided for five, why won't He provide for six? Where is your faith? Miki, I don't believe in psychiatrists, but you sure need to see one 'cause you sure are crazy." She punctuated her tirade by slamming down the phone.

I sat by the phone for a long time as I tried to think through my alternatives. I then started to cry. Mother was right. Could I really live with the guilt of aborting a child? Had my panic consumed my sanity? When Chuck came home from work, I announced my decision.

"I knew you couldn't do it." He said.

"Chuck, you mean you know me well enough that I couldn't do it and yet you said nothing to stop me?"

He didn't answer me, but kept on to the bathroom. Why didn't he answer me? Did he want the abortion, but not the responsibility for the decision? In my mind, the divorce was final.

"Well, how's it going?" Dr. Walter's asked jovially, as he did at the outset of each of our sessions. For me it became almost like a call to battle. Things I could not get across to Chuck during the week would gush forth in torrents of contempt and disgust.

"Not too well." I responded during one session that would become especially galling and violent. "It's eating me up alive. I can't cope with this shit." I burst into hysterics. It took about five minutes for me to stop crying long enough to tell what had happened.

"Julie told me that on the night I went to school, Anita kept crying and whining in her sleep." I began tearfully. "Chuck came into the bedroom and picked Anita up by one arm—one arm, mind you—and spanked her so hard that she was blue and no sound would come out of her mouth. And then he threw her on top of Julie. Julie said that Anita's heart was racing so fast that she was scared that Anita was going to die. When Anita started crying, Julie consoled her to sleep. What do I say to Julie about her father?" I asked belabored. "I can't trust him with his own children."

Dr. Walters glared contemptuously at Chuck as he spoke to me with an intense, seething anger. "Miki, if he does anything like this again, Goddammit, you call the police. Do you understand?"

"How could you do that?" I continued. "How can you do these

things to your own children?" I screamed through my hysteria. "Don't you understand that one of these days you're going to kill one of your own children? "Doesn't that mean anything to you?"

I waited for a reply for about three minutes. While I waited, his anger stricken eyes waned into a blank stare. His silence triggered a surge of rage through my soul. Suddenly, I lunged towards him and began flailing him with my purse. "You son of a bitch!" He covered his face with his arms and sank down in the chair. "I'll kill you!" He made no attempt to fight me off. Even worse, he said nothing to acknowledge my rage or his remorse.

"Miki. Miki, please." Dr. Walters whispered pleadingly. "Please sit down. I don't want to have to have you confined."

I stood over Chuck, panting breathlessly and fighting to control my rage. Dr Walters handed me some tissues to wipe my tears and then gently guided me back into my seat. I searched Chuck's face for some clue of comprehension or remorse. He simply recomposed himself and stared at me as though he were awaiting an apology from me for attacking him.

"This has been eating at me for three very long days." I began disconsolately into the uneasy silence. "How do you think I feel? I don't want to kill him. But I will defend my kids. Can you see my kids telling people that their mother killed their father? What kind of a heritage is that to leave the children?"

Chuck finally spoke. "Well if that's how you feel, then you're right to get a divorce." He said as though he were washing his hands of the entire matter. My anger began to surge once again. But Dr. Walters intervened just in time.

"Chuck your wife isn't talking about a divorce. Can't you see what she's saying?"

Chuck's eyes darted bewilderedly from me to Dr. Walters. I sensed that he felt he had magnanimously given me my victory and was at a loss as to what I wanted from him.

"Chuck, you've got a war going on with Miki." Dr. Walters

explained sternly into Chuck's incredulity. "But the kids are the ones getting hurt. She can't love her children and let you hurt them. Can't you see what you're doing to Miki? You're backing her into a corner. What she's asking you is: "don't you love your kids enough to keep them out of your war?"

"Of course I do." Chuck retorted defensively.

"Then why do you keep doing this to your kids?"

Chuck stared numbly at Dr. Walters and shifted uncomfortably in his chair. The few minutes that Dr. Walters and I waited for a response seemed like an eternity.

"This is hopeless." I interjected in despair when I could see that an answer was not forthcoming. "He just doesn't get it."

On our way home we stopped off at a market to pick up some groceries. Chuck turned into a parking slot. The kids streamed out of the car and ran into the market. All that had transpired gathered within me to form a thick, sappy wave of sentimentality that swept over me. I turned to Chuck and spoke to him in a low, humble voice.

"Sometimes, I want to love you Chuck, but you make it so hard."

"You slut!" He shouted fiercely as his harsh blue eyes glowered at me as though I were something loathsome and despicable. "I hate you and I'm going to get even with you for this."

I stared at him in shock. It was incredulous to me that the man I had married could be so devoid of soul that the pain and humiliation that I set aside to share with him what morsel of love I had managed to hold onto was regarded as no more than the pathetic offering of a slut or fuel for revenge. Back I plunged into that depthless rage that had flooded my sense of reason and any hope for happiness.

"You son of a bitch." I raged as my hands lunged toward his face. "You rotten, filthy, prick." I wanted to tear his eyes out. I wanted to rip that imperious face to shreds. I wanted to kill the motherfucker with my bare hands. Cursing, flailing, scratching, I was an unceasing tide of maniacal passions that at best would be capable of inflicting only a fraction of my pain upon the cause of it. Chuck covered his face with his arms so that I could not get at his eyes. So I sank my teeth into his arm as hard as I could. The taste of his flesh in my mouth disgusted me. I let go and then looked up to see the expression of shock on the face of my daughter Julie as she stared at me through the car window. She then began to scream and stomp the ground. I knew that I could never explain to her what was happening. Anyone looking in could only see me as a violent person and Chuck the poor innocent victim. I reached over Chuck and opened the car door.

"Get out!" I screamed as I pushed Chuck out of the car. "Get out!"

I was in a panic. I had to get away. I started the engine and drove off. I raced back to the clinic. Thankfully it had not closed and Dr. Walters had not left. He sat quietly as I told him what had happened. He managed to console me to the point that I could return to the market and finish shopping with my family. The following week, Dr. Walters prescribed Librium for me.

While Chuck and I attended joint therapy, I also attended individual therapy with Dr. Walters. During one such session he attempted to tap more deeply into the roots of what he diagnosed as my "predisposition towards submitting to such unhappiness."

"Well, I can't think of what that could be." I replied.

The thought stayed in my head though. Mom would probably never tell me what she may well be trying to conceal or want me to forget after all these years. Only Gracie could tell me. Whether she would or not was another story.

# CHAPTER EIGHT

# The Strength Of A Woman

At first Gracie was reluctant to fill in the precognitive years of my life. But when I asked what life was like for her when I was born, she unfurled a story that gushed forth a stream of remembrances from regions of my consciousness that I had not known existed.

I was sent home with my father a week after I was born. Mother kept hemorrhaging and remained in the hospital an additional two weeks. In the midst of the Depression, dad was not about to turn down work with the WPA to baby-sit. So he decided to leave me in the care of my ten year old sister. Gracie, however, was on summer break from school and her mind was on playing outdoors. Oftentimes she would become so engrossed in her play that she would lose track of time. Dad would come home and find me starving, soiled and chafed. When Gracie finally made it home he would be waiting for her with belt in hand.

Chills of anguish surged through me as I listened to my sister re-count the story of my first week at home. Through my ears flowed a stream of remembrances that sent me to the verge of fainting. Visions unreeled inside my head of me screaming myself into exhaustion was the overwhelming hunger gave rise to a fear of dying. The summer heat burned the urine and feces into my skin trapping me in a blanket of terror and helplessness. The terror of my Father's deep, booming angry voice and Gracie's screams embedded themselves into my psyche so intractably, that years of therapy had not dislodged them.

After Mom was released from the hospital, Gracie told her of the horrors she had endured. Mom committed her to silence by threatening to put her in a home for wayward girls until she was twenty-one. That day, Gracie came down with the first of many asthma attacks. Now bits and pieces began to fit. Mom always claimed that Gracie had sibling rivalry. I now realized that it was Gracie's hatred for my dad that she took out on me. Fearing that her children would be taken away from her, mom applied gels to the welts and kept her out of school.

Within a week of our conversation, Gracie came down with an asthma attack that caused her to spend three weeks in an oxygen tent. Mom called me angrily accusing me of trying to kill Gracie by dredging up the past. The outrage that surged within me forced me to go to her house and confront her.

"Mom, how could you let my dad beat Gracie and not do anything about it except to put Vick's on the bruises and keep her out of school?" I brusquely asked my mother as I entered.

"I did do something about it. I prayed to God."

"But it took God six years to get rid of my Dad. It would have taken you six minutes." I retorted.

"Don't you talk to me like that. I had to give you a name and I put up with a lot from your dad to try to maintain a home for you and Gracie."

"But God gave you a brain. Why didn't you use it? If you married dad to give me a name, then five minutes after he did so, why didn't you get rid of him? Why did you threaten to put Gracie in a home?"

"I don't want to talk about it, and if you insist on talking about it, I'll have Arcelio throw you out."

"So what? If Arcelio throws me out the door, I'll butt the windows and come back in. And I'll still ask you the same question. How could you let my dad do this to Gracie and do nothing about it?"

Mom was furious that I had the temerity to question her actions. I kept sitting there waiting for some kind of explanation, anything, even just a simple apology, but it never came. I would have understood. After all, child abuse was also a part of my own household. But perhaps had I known about my father's abuse of Gracie, I may well have been better able to handle my own. Were we not women of tradition? Were we not conditioned to inwardly contain and rationalize away our suffering for the sake of our husbands even to the detriment of ourselves and our children? Mother had lost three of her children and was determined to hold onto the other two anyway that she could. I could not fault her for that. Self-righteousness did not become mother. I had always regarded her as a woman of great humanity; an ideal I earnestly wanted to preserve. How could mom think that I could possibly want to hurt my sister, let alone want to kill her? How was I to know what Gracie would reveal? Had she not suffered enough? Instead of accusing me of such a heinous act, I expected mom to tell me of her fear and how she would tolerate any hell in order not to lose Gracie and me. We could have shared our fears and it would have lent me support in my situation. As I sat across from her, she glared at me in silent hatred for about twenty minutes. It was killing me to watch the ever thickening wall of hatred that mom was erecting between us. Unable to stand it any longer, I left.

It had not dawned on me that the best I could have derived from my confrontation with mom would have been a victory of the ego. Cognitively speaking, my father never raised an angry hand to me, mother or Gracie. The worst I could recall was a furious argument between mom and dad over a lawsuit he hoped mom would bring against the church she attended. It seems that while caught up in the throes of spiritual fervor, the pastor leaped from the pulpit and pounded mom senseless. She steadfastly refused to permit the sanctity of the church to be impugned by the dissension that a day in court would cause. The matter was resolved to the satisfaction of all concerned, when she prudently chose to change churches.

In my obstinate rush to place judgment upon my mother for that over which she had no control, I permitted Chuck to persist in his brutal ways while I continued to delude myself into believing that it was an aberration that could be overcome with therapy and tolerance. I had become resolute in my decision to divorce him until that fine March day when he gave me cause to hope that our marriage could somehow be salvaged. He had me dress the kids, loaded us in the car, and then announced that we were going house-hunting. Perhaps Chuck was beginning to understand. I had already made the decision to divorce him. But the marriage wasn't counted out until I walked into the courtroom. I had nothing more to lose and a marriage to gain—so why not?

We settled on a house in a newly developed tract of no down payment, VA approved homes located north of Los Angeles in the city of Camarillo. It had four bedrooms, a complete built-in kitchen and two complete bathrooms. For me it was a dream house.

Chuck and I continued our weekly therapy sessions with Dr. Walters. It was during the last session that Chuck and I attended when the appalling and numbing reality upon which our marriage had been based came crashing down upon me. It began with an incident that occurred a few days earlier.

My son Rodrick joined us at the dinner table as usual. For some odd reason, Chuck sent him to the bathroom to wash up. When Rodrick returned, his father ordered him back to wash again. For a third time, Rodrick was forced to wash because Chuck claimed he was still dirty. Chuck then scolded him severely for not washing his arms properly.

"This is my color!" Rodrick screamed on the verge of tears. "I'm just brown!"

"Chuck. Are you trying to turn your wife into a white black person?" Dr. Walter asked in astonishment.

"What do you mean?" Chuck asked.

"Well, you knew that she was black and your kids are brown. So why do you keep wanting them to wash so much unless you expect their skin to turn white?"

For the first time in twelve years of marriage, I was forced to confront the demon of racism that had been lurking menacingly about our marriage.

"Is this why he calls me a slut?" I asked incredulously of Dr. Walters. "Because in his mind I'm a dirty, black whore? So now I understand his shame in my talking, laughing, or expressing my opinions. My God! How could he be prejudice and marry me? He wasn't blind when we got married." Even as I said this, Chuck made no attempt to disavow the implication. And then the entire sickening, sordid spectacle of a union that had produced six children and, for me, a lifetime of heartache streamed through my mind in a lurid procession of deceit, revenge, and manipulation.

Oh my God! It all fits. He married me to get even with his mother who punished him severely for getting dirty. So he married me to get dirty. I am the "slut" that he used as a weapon against his mother's compulsive cleanliness. Now that I am a mother, I too became a target for his rebellion. Wow! This is too much! To further aggravate his mother's wounds, he married outside of his religion. Nice freakin' touch! So now I am also the evil seductress that led poor little innocent him down the path of perdition. He desperately tried to escape to Hawaii so that I wouldn't be so conspicuous. When that fell through, he decided to take his ever glaring inadequacies out on his family. He could only handle extremes. There was no middle ground. Things were either good or evil, male or female, white or black, dominant or submissive, up or down. I realized that it was much too simplistic to judge him a racist. There was what I could only describe as a psychosexual element that dominated our relationship. He had his life to live and I was an appendage relegated to the role of housekeeper, child bearer and whore. He had hoped that by converting me to Catholicism, I would be compelled to accept a state of bondage that had long been sanctioned by the traditions of the church. Then he would no longer be in a state of sin for marrying a heathen. We had never been equal partners, but I resolved to stay in the marriage until Sarrah was born. But now that I understood the nature of his goddamm war, I realized that there was virtually no possibility of a truce.

Because of the distance between Camarillo and El Segundo, Chuck decided to stay with his sister in Palos Verdes during the week and come home on weekends. My weekdays were blissful. I settled into a routine of laundry, baths, dishes, naps and everything else that went with motherhood. But weekends with Chuck became nothing short of nightmares. The abuse reached a point that the children dreaded the sight of him. By noon on Saturdays they were fear stricken and terrified. The slightest provocation would result in slaps and verbal abuse. In one instance, I returned from shopping at a supermarket to find that Chuck had beaten my son Rodrick with a garden hose leaving a red stripe down his spine from the nozzle. I became hysterical and jumped into the car and drove back to the market. From there I called the minister of a nearby Presbyterian church to meet me. He consoled me before driving me home. Chuck greeted us warmly, as though nothing had happened. The minister involved himself no further in our troubles, other than to invite us to join his church and participate in its activities. He hoped that Chuck might learn better solutions than violence by making new friends. The children had already lost respect for him and were losing respect for me because I was powerless to protect them. I was eight months into my pregnancy with Sarrah. Any physical confrontation with Chuck would have endangered her unborn life. Besides, things had long ago gone beyond that point. I concluded that I had no other choice than to divorce him or kill him.

Not long after Sarrah was born, I came down with an asthma attack which put me in bed for a week. About the same time, my daughter Victoria suffered such a severe bout of eczema that I had to wrap her arms and legs in diapers and rock her to sleep so that she wouldn't tear at her skin. Arcelio and mom cared for my older children while I recovered. Nothing would deter me from getting free of Chuck. When he gave Rodrick two black eyes, I gave him the irrevocable choice of arrest or divorce. Since arrest for a felony would insure the loss of his security clearance, he chose divorce. We located a lawyer to set the process in motion.

In the meantime, Chuck and I settled into lives of quiet detachment. Chuck was home on the weekends. The brutality gave way to appeasement. He had been taught that divorce was a sin and was confident that I would come to see the error of my ways. All I needed was a little time to come to my senses. For me, the issue of divorce had been settled and I had no intentions of turning back. It was during this time that Chuck's mother called from Michigan.

"I hear that you're going to divorce my son." She stated in a voice laden with sadness and disbelief.

"You better believe it." I retorted defensively.

"But why? He's such a good boy."

"Don't tell me what a good boy he is. I live with him and he's a monster."

"But you can't divorce him. Why the children are so lovely. And you're such a good Mother." She offered pleadingly. "What has he done that has been so bad?"

"Why don't you ask him?"

"He's such a good boy, I don't think he could do anything so bad for you to divorce him. Maybe I'll pay for some lawyers to go out there and keep you from divorcing my son."

"You better not do that. I mean it. I'll have Chuck put in jail. You don't know what the kids and I are going through. If you want to do something, you better talk to him. Why don't you tell her what we're going through? Here." I shoved the phone into Chuck's hand.

"Mom, please don't worry. Everything will be okay. Please, Mom, stay out of it." Chuck kept repeating reassurances to his Mom, but he wouldn't tell her what the problems were.

I could hear the whimper in her voice and the helplessness in her questions. What she had long ago feared had now come to pass. But it was her son who was the heathen and not me. She had long ago given up all pretenses and had grown to become tolerant and sincere. She was seeing all of her hopes and dreams for her grandchildren dismantling before her eyes.

In order to effectuate the divorce, I would need a witness. Like Chuck's Mother, mom believed in the sanctity of marriage and that we were obliged to reconcile at all costs. Neither mom nor Gracie wanted to get involved and refused to testify. I could not bring myself to ask my neighbor Cynthia. But as the Day of Judgment approached, she became my only hope.

Beatrice De Clune and her family had been living next door to us for about five months. During that time she had seen and heard more than enough to exonerate me from any insinuation that I was some sort of ungrateful tart intent on abandoning a good and long-suffering husband. She and I were soul mates in more ways than one. We shared an island heritage in that she was Hawaiian. We believed that children were a blessing from God to be nurtured and encouraged to be free and self-reliant rather than chattel to be abused and degraded. We had both married white men whose passion for exerting absolute authority and control over their families could not accommodate the love they professed to have had for them. When my son Rodrick entered the kitchen while Beatrice and I were talking, he was sporting two black eyes. Beatrice was horrified and asked what had happened. Rodrick responded that his Father had punched him a few nights before. I confessed to her my intentions to divorce Chuck, but needed a witness. She readily agreed to testify on my behalf.

I watched with both relief and anticipation as Beatrice made her way to the stand and took the oath. She could have easily backed out at the last minute. She was taking a big chance testifying on my behalf. Were her husband to somehow find out, he would undoubtedly make her life a living hell. I could tell by the stern resolve in her dark eyes that she would be a steadfast ally in my cause.

"Have you seen incidents of mental cruelty by Mr. Bissett?" My attorney asked.

"Yes. I have." Beatrice responded resolutely.

My attorney then dismissed her from the stand. I stared at him in askance as he took his seat beside me. I wanted her testimony on record. I wanted the world to know what a brutal louse he was.

"This is a no-contest case." He responded to my look of dismay. "We just need a witness for the record."

He then turned his attention to the judge. "Your honor. Since this is a no-contest case, can we make this short?"

The judge nodded. "Call the plaintiff." He ordered.

"Mrs. Bissettt. Are you requesting this divorce on the grounds of mental cruelty?" My attorney asked after I was sworn in.

"Yes."

"But Mrs. Bissett," the judge interjected with an expression of disbelief on his face, "look at the amount of child support Mr. Bissett is willing to provide, I mean. Mr. Bissett seems like a good and generous man."

I almost leaped out of my chair in rage. But I knew that I had to control myself.

"Your honor, don't tell me what a good man he is. I'm the one who is going to therapy. My children are the ones who bare the scars of his brutality. Are you trying to tell me that the amount of money he gives me makes him a 'good man'?"

My lawyer sensed my agitation and quickly interceded.

"Your honor. My client is under a lot of stress and is on medication." He said pleadingly to the judge as he motioned me to calm down.

The judge was still in a state of disbelief and heard neither my attorney nor me.

"Not too many men would give this much for child support under a no-contest." The judge stated.

"They're his children. Why shouldn't he?" I retorted. I was livid.

He looked up from the financial settlement report that he had been reading and into my smoldering eyes. "What do you think you are going to do with six children alone?" He asked me contemptuously.

"I'm going to try to raise them!" I stated emphatically. "My children need some peace and perhaps we can find it now. There can be nothing worse for these children than what's going on in our home. The standard for a home cannot be money. There must be some love. And if there isn't any love, they are at least entitled to have some peace."

My eye-to-eye contact with the judge was determined. His expression softened. He got the point.

"Decree of interlocutory divorce granted."

The words from the judge were not the gongs of doom that I thought they would be. Instead, they were like the insistent tolls that signal the end of a prize fight. No more punches to be thrown. No more strategies to be explored. All that might have drawn victory from defeat now resided in the archives of the mind to be scrutinized and examined during moments of reflection, but never to know the light of certainty. I was naïve. I had really believed in "happily ever after". But it was over and I would have to content myself with whatever "happily" meant to me. Never again would I allow appeasement to be disguised as reconciliation.

I walked Beatrice to her car and watched as she drove off. I was in no rush to go home. I sat on a ledge of the short brick wall outside of the Ventura County courthouse and stared despondently across the park as my mind tumbled with alternatives that emerged from the crossroads of my life. Relief from the brutality and abuse gradually began to yield to trepidations about the future. It then dawned on me that my ex-husband had an income of eighteen hundred a month. Of that, he agreed to provide three hundred and fifty dollars subsistence. Anger rose in my mind. How could that judge really think that three hundred fifty dollars a month for six kids was "generous"?

A gentle ocean breeze kept the feeling easy instead of hot. I was going to enjoy this wonderful feeling for as long as I could. Mrs. Bissett, the wife, no longer existed. However, I decided to carry the name for the sake of the kids. My ego was shattered now. I had to resurrect the personage who had been shunted off into some oblivious corner to make room for the woman of tradition who had been fashioned and molded to conform to the specifications of Mrs. Bissett. That subservient, dependent Mrs. Bissett with six kids had virtually no chance of making it alone. I needed to reclaim the child of passion and intelligence who had begun to nurture a faculty for critical thinking that had been short circuited in the name of love. I would have to plunge deep into my soul to find her and hope that my time spent as Mrs. Bissett, the wife, had not altered her beyond recognition. From time to time she had raised her head in defiance. This time I was determined to grab hold of her in earnest and go wherever she led me.

# CHAPTER NINE

# *Adrift*

There were no manuals to read or dots to follow that could show the way for a woman cast adrift with the lives of six children to manage. She may be subjected to all manner of blame and re-criminations, but tomorrow is least sympathetic to those tethered to the concerns of yesterday. Wagging tongues produced no food. Self-righteous judgments paid no rent. And impersonal bureaucracies provided no clothing even as protection against its own wintry blasts.

The transition from "wife and mother" to "single parent" gave me no peace. I was faced with the overwhelming bitterness of a failed mar-riage and the extreme loneliness that began to envelope me. Chuck had provided me no emotional support, but he did give me his pres-ence. Whatever feelings of re-attachment that welled up inside me were quickly dispelled when confronted by the knowledge of the violence and it's insensitivity that brought me to this point in my life.

Since our house in Camarillo had built up no equity, Chuck rented it out to cover the mortgage and we agreed to sell it later. I got the car. He assumed responsibility for all the bills that we had accumulated during our marriage. I had no choice but to move to Los Angeles and find a rental and a job. The three hundred and fifty dollars a month that the judge thought so generous, was well short of what was required for a woman with six children to rent a place. There was a house listed in the newspaper that rented for a hundred dollars a month in Santa Monica. As I negotiated the winding street in a rundown part of town, I girded myself for what awaited me on the cul-de-sac that I turned onto.

The house was unbelievable—not in filthiness, but in decrepidness. There was a large gap between the door and the top of its frame. A pernicious crack highlighted the floor-to-ceiling window. All of the window frames and jams were badly in need of repair. The discoloration in the floor boards indicated recent repairs. The cabinets in the kitchen needed total replacement. The bathroom reeked of water rot, but the fixtures worked. The three bedrooms were very small but each was large enough to accommodate a set of bunk beds and a chest of drawers. And there was a small service porch leading to the back door.

My nearest neighbor occupied the house to the rear of mine. There was a family of "Texicanos" or Chicanos who had moved to California from Texas. With eight in their family, there was no shortage of playmates for mine. Our surroundings were essentially very private given that the Santa Monica City dump was located on one side of us and a freeway under construction was on the other. Behind us was the Santa Monica Rifle Range.

As Chuck helped us move into the house, he kept shaking his head in disbelief. Now that he had attained a firm grasp on his middle class aspirations, he could afford himself the luxury of forgetting that we once lived in a shanty next to the Venice railroad tracks that was so decrepit that he had to sweep out the dead mice every morning before I would get out of bed. I had no value for his opinion. This was the best I could do. All that mattered to me was that the kids had a fair chance to grow peacefully.

My landlady was named Angie. She was a Chicana who inherited the property from her father and lived there during the early years of her marriage. We became good friends. She understood my plight. My neighbor's eighteen year old daughter, Maryann, agreed to Angie's request to baby sit my children while I searched for a job.

Rodrick, Nathan and Julie had been enrolled in school for only one day when I was confronted with my first major crisis as a single Mother. I happened to look out of my window and saw a mob of kids accompanied by two ladies and Rodrick approaching the house. I opened the door to find out what was happening.

"I'm Rodrick's Mother." I announced bewildered.

"Oh, Mrs. Bissett, it was just bedlam." One of the ladies said desperately. "We just can't have this at our school."

"May I ask who you are?"

"I'm Mrs. Pelham, the principal. It was just bedlam. It took four teachers to break it up. Three must have been at least twenty children."

"Rodrick got in a fight with twenty children?" I asked incredulously.

"Oh no, it was just he and one other boy."

"How old was this other boy?" I asked somewhat relieved.

"They're both in the same grade."

"I thought you said there were twenty kids."

"Well, they were watching the fight." She admitted sheepishly.

"And it took four teachers to separate two eight year olds?"

"Oh, yes Mrs. Bissett." She replied emphatically. "I just sent out a memo last week about fighting. Any child caught fighting would be expelled. This fighting has to stop."

"Rodrick was not at your school last week and he has no way of knowing that. It might be better if Rodrick comes in and I'll explain it to him. "I'll bring him to school tomorrow. We'll give him a one-day expulsion", I offered hopefully.

"I hope you can make him understand. We'll give him another chance since he's new. But this kind of bedlam will not be tolerated. It was just terrible."

"Thank you for bringing him home. Mrs. Pelham. I'll try to explain it to him."

I shut the door.

"Oh, it was bedlam." I mimicked her and we all laughed. I could not believe that his so-called intelligent woman thought two kids fighting could be regarded as "bedlam". And these are the people who run our schools.

"Rodrick; we can't have bedlam at school. They don't understand it, ok?"

Rodrick nodded knowingly.

"Now, tell me what happened?"

"I told him I didn't want to fight." Rodrick insisted. "But he kept hitting me and calling me chicken." Rodrick concluded still huffing and puffing from the rush of adrenalin.

"Did you have a good fight?" I asked gently.

"Yeah, I gave him a bloody nose."

"I guess Rodrick isn't too chicken. Right, Rodrick?"

In light of all the many changes that heaped upon the children, on upon another, they all needed to gather their self esteem as best they could. Although I did not condone fighting, my value, there and then was for Rodrick. How could I have explained to this woman that Rodrick was finally beginning to behave normal? If anything, she would have become more paranoid. How could I have made her understand that it would serve no honor for Rodrick not to fight at age eight and wind up in jail by age eighteen.

I considered myself very lucky to find a clerical job at U.C.LA. Though still bitter, I looked forward to getting my life together. Just as I thought that it was beginning to turn the corner onto a positive direction, things turned the other way.

I had to hurry if I was going to catch the bus before it pulled away. With my first step onto the bus, my leg collapsed. I grabbed hold of the door to keep from falling to the ground.

"Hey, wait a minute." Something just tore my foot open." I cried as blood poured from a gash at the top of my foot. "It's that piece of metal sticking out of the ground." I concluded pointing to the bus stop that had been sheared to about six inches above the ground.

"I'm sorry lady." The drive said in a voice that was sympathetic, but insistent. "I have a schedule to keep lady. You got to get off."

I shifted myself off the bus and grabbed hold of a lamppost. As the bus pulled away, I tried to stop the bleeding with my hand. "What do I do?" I thought to myself.

"Help, help"! I yelled out loud to no one in particular.

Some students emerged from a nearby fraternity house and ran towards me.

"I tore my foot on that post. Can you guys bring me a towel or something?"….. "And call me ambulance."

A couple of the guys ran back into the house. Two of them tried to help me to the bench to sit down.

"What's going on?" a man asked as he joined us from across the street.

"Do you have a handkerchief so I can tie my foot?"

"Has anyone called the ambulance?" he asked as he began wrapping the foot.

"I think the fellows at that frat house are calling for some help,I replied.

"Well, I'll go to the hospital with you."

"I don't see what for," I stated irritably.

"To get a tetanus shot, of course."

"I'm the one who needs the tetanus shot. Are you implying that you're gonna catch something from me? There's no such thing as bad blood and unless you get cut you sure can't catch tetanus for wrapping my foot."

He shifted himself about uncomfortably as he cleared his throat.

A gray Volkswagen stopped for the light. One of the guys asked the two girls to take me to the hospital. They agreed. Hobbling on one leg, I was gently placed in the car and take to the medical center.

Once again I became dependent upon Chuck. He came by after work to see that the children were fed and bathed. He took pictures of the scene of the accident and I submitted them to the transit company for settlement. My anger was on again full blast, but I had to cool it. To compound my circumstances, I received a termination notice from my job. As I recovered from my injury, a daily wave of despair reminded me that I was confronted with the same problems with which I had begun.

After Thanksgiving, I found a part-time job wrapping packages at a department store that lasted to Christmas. That Christmas was not one of plenty. Each child was allowed to select a toy from a Blue Chip stamp book. We wrapped the toys in large boxes and wrapped them with fancy ribbon. We made an elaborate affair of decorating the little two foot tree on the sewing table. This had been the most austere Christmas that I had experienced since my own childhood. We were, however, very joyful.

Of all the annoyances that plagued my efforts to build at least a tolerable sense of being, Chuck proved to be the most daunting obstacle. It was obvious to me that my foot injury and then my having to work implanted in his mind the notion that reconciliation between us was inevitable. Like a confident buzzard, he circled above my efforts at independence awaiting their demise. He had taken care of the kids during my recovery and babysat them when I worked in the evenings. I guess he figured that I owed him at least one indulgence. He came by the house to collect.

"The guys at work are giving a New Year's Eve party and I don't have anyone to go with. Miki, please go with me." He asked plaintively.

"Chuck, you're not serious". I responded in disbelief.

"I promise I won't get upset. I know it's over between us."

"I don't think I should, Chuck."

"It's just for one night. Please. I promise. I won't get upset. I just don't want to go alone."

"Okay, Chuck. But you must remember that I'm not your wife anymore."

"Yeah, I know that."

The party was in Manhattan Beach. I knew most of the guys from those times that Chuck brought them by the house for lunch.

They were surprised to see us together. We all sat around drinking and talking, mostly about work. The party was very boring and I felt uncomfortable. I had been stupid to even go. I was glad when, after a few drinks, Chuck suggested that we leave.

We said nothing on the way home, but Chuck's driving frightened me.

"Why are you driving so fast, Chuck?"

"How do you think I felt in front of my friends?" Chuck stated angrily. "You embarrassed me."

"You promised not to get upset. And, besides, this was all your idea."

"But it wasn't my idea to get divorced." His face was turning red as the light we were approaching. "I ought to beat the hell out of you; you slut!"

I jumped out of the car at the light and started running. He turned the corner and drove after me. I ran onto a vacant parking lot. There was no escape. He slammed the brakes on, with the car up beside me, jumped out of the car and came at me with clenched fists. He swung hard at me. I ducked. The blow landed on my shoulder.

"Chuck. Stop. Help"! I screamed at the top of my voice.

He got back in the car. I started running towards the first house I saw.

"Please. Help me"! I yelled as I banged on the door. No one answered. I ran to another house with the same result. Chuck pulled up and began yelling for me to get in the car. I ran to anther house. A police car stopped beside him. They got out of the car. One stayed with Chuck. The other climbed the steps to me.

"What do you think you're doing?" The officer asked as he reached me.

"I was trying to get some help. He tried to beat me and I got away."

"If you bother another house, I'll run you in for disturbing the peace. Do you understand?" He stated as he glared at me angrily.

"Why me"? He's the one who was trying to beat me."

"I don't care." He said as he directed me towards the sidewalk. "Don't bother these people anymore. You understand"?

"Yeah; can I have the car so I can get home to my kids"?

"No".

"No! The judge awarded it to me".

"I don't care about that. The registration is in his name. As far as I'm concerned, it's his car".

"How do I get home"?

"I don't care how you get home lady, walk for all I care but don't bother anybody or I'll run you in".

Chuck pulled away and so did the police. I stood alone angered and confused. I could not understand the attitude of the police. It seemed that as long as the residents of Westchester were not disturbed, they would not have cared if Chuck had killed me. I recalled that Loyola Marymount University was nearby and headed there. The attendant at the parking lot would not disturb any of the priests, but did allow me to sit inside the small booth out of the cold. I reconciled myself to waiting until 5:30 in the morning when the priest would be up. Chuck must have watched me walk to the booth before pulling up.

"Miki, I'm sorry, I'll take you home".

"No Chuck. I can't hack anymore of your shit".

"Miki, I promise. I know you have to get home to the kids. I'll behave. I promise".

I took my chances and prayed he wouldn't wind up killing the both of us in the car. No sooner than we stopped in front of the house and I was about to get out, Chuck swung his arm so hard across my face that he broke my glasses and shattered the lenses into my eyes. I was blinded and could feel blood coursing down my face.

"Chuck, stop". I screamed. "Maryann, Maryann".

"You slut, I'll fix you". He said viciously as he banged his clenched hands on the steering wheel.

I bounded out of the car and blindly made my way to the house. "Maryann, Maryann, call the police". I cried as I reached the door.

Maryann opened the door, but stood there unable to move. Chuck came running in after me. He trounced around the living room like an enraged bull.

"Maryann, call the police." I yelled at her as I tried to get little pieces of glass out of my eyes.

She was petrified and still could not bring herself to move. Chuck kept pounding on anything he could find. Surely he must have realized that it was over between us—and over for good.

"Chuck. Get out of here." I screamed. "Get out and don't ever set foot in my house again. Maryann, give me the phone I'm calling the police."

The fear in Maryann's eyes must have startled him into the awareness of what he was doing. His eyes darted wildly about the room. Realizing that nothing could be achieved by any further outbursts, he left in a huff.

Maryann brought me a pan of cold water and a towel and helped me wash the broken glass from my eyes. Now I hated Chuck more than ever. The next day, Chuck brought back the car. The day after New Years I went to the optometrist to see about my eyes. Fortunately, the damage to my eyes was not as bad as I had thought. I was fitted for a new pair of glasses. After a few days, I resumed my job hunting.

I was in dire financial straits and hoped to instigate a quick settlement from the bus company. I received thirteen hundred dollars. After paying all my bills, I was left with $8.42.

Towards the end of January, I found a job at a rubbish removal company. The office where I worked was dirty beyond all hope of cleansing. For an entire eight hours a day, I stared into the rubbish yard and the smell permeated my very being. The entire surroundings were filthy. My job was to type billings, and dispatch trucks to collect rubbish that had been missed. Because the trucks were old, there were frequent breakdowns, and I was required to dispatch trucks to complete their routes. The men worked long days, especially when a truck broke down. Since the county contract required that each route be completed by 6pm, I had to dispatch trucks to pitch in to meet the deadline.

To me throwing trash seemed like one of the most unrewarding jobs in the world. In addition to the arduous task of managing all sorts of filth and refuse, the men were forced to endure the ever nagging nuisance of ants and maggots crawling all over them. Most of the men drank all day, every day, just to get through the day. But they respected Lloyd, our boss. Because he was astute enough to never look down at them, Lloyd had the lowest employee turnover in L.A. A tall, powerfully build man with Nordic features, he gambled, drank, and cursed with his men. He bailed them out of jail, paid their rent and car payments. He felt nothing about decking a recalcitrant employee at the slightest provocation. But he knew that the men could do the same to him. The fact that the men needed to work and Lloyd needed the men to work created an atmosphere where everyone felt self empowered including me.

Despite my dismal surrounding, I was strangely happy. Lloyd supported me whenever I had confrontations with the men. I endeared myself to the men when I stood up to Lloyd on those paydays when he wanted to take off early and did not want to prepare their checks. We would compromise. He did the calculations and I made out the checks. I worked six days a week and made very little money. But my self esteem began to rise quickly.

The men were very much men. They made passes at anything in skirts and I was no exception. There was the "payday promenade" that I found both flattering and funny. Each of the men would attempt to convince me that I should go out with him because he knew how to treat me right. They were rough, earth hewed men who displayed little tolerance for even the most elementary social amenities. I watched their strutting and primping with great amusement. I knew better than to take the men seriously. But there was one who proved to be too irresistible to ignore.

Wilbur Jefferson was the sexiest man that I had ever met. He was tall with deep dark brown skin that was tinged with subtle reddish tone. He was all muscle-sleek and taut. His large, brown eyes evoked within me desires that seemed beyond my control. His deep, sensual voice enthralled me. He sometimes spoke in jargon that made no sense to me, but left me straining, oftentimes unsuccessfully, to keep me from laughing. He was well aware of his effect on me and was determined to break down my resistance. For about three weeks we played cat and mouse until I agreed to meet him one night in the parking lot of the Culver City hospital after work.

I spotted his bad-ass Pontiac convertible by the Continental kit that contained the spare tire. I pulled into the stall next to his and got in beside him.

"I was wondering if you was going to show." He said with a knowing grin.

"I didn't know whether I should show up or not." I replied rather sassily.

"You know, I like you. I watch how you handle the guys at work. You don't go for the oaky-doak."

I wondered what the "oaky-doak" was, but I decided to let him talk and not ask questions.

"You're a beautiful woman and I see them clowns trying to get into your pants. But you just jive them along and don't fall for their "oaky-daok."

"I fell for your oaky-doak." I answered self assuredly.

He shook his head a couple of times and stared at me reprovingly.

"Ya know, you're smart." He continued. "Maybe you're too smart. Maybe I should just take you home."

Inside, I panicked. I had not played cat and mouse for three weeks just to go home. I had no intentions of flinging myself at some self centered super stud. But nor was I about to be dismissed at his whim and certainly not without at least a peek at his game.

"Why? Are you afraid of me?" I asked playfully.

"Me? Afraid of you?" Wilbur asked in disbelief. "You see this here?"

He said pointing to a long scar that extended along his head like a part that was concealed by his thick reddish black hair. "There's a plate in my skull form World War II. You think I'm afraid of a weakling-ass woman!"

"I didn't mean it that way." I responded with a tremor of trepidation that passed quickly. I had no idea as to the hand I was being dealt, but I could not bring myself to throw it in yet. The plate in his head was not my primary interest. "I meant you are afraid I'll get under your skin and you'll fall in love with me."

"If I do fall in love with you, I'll be serious. I don't go for no oaky-doak. I can't take none of that pressure. I'll go ape shit. You're too beautiful and I get too jealous. I don't want to hurt you."

His words were tough and stern, but there was a gentle sincerity in his voice that completely disarmed me. "I understand." I said softly as my hand shifted to his leg. "None of us can really take pressure. And I think you're wonderful."

Wilbur leaned back against the car door as if to get as far from me as possible. But his large eyes drifted dreamily into sensuous horizontal slits as his mouth slowly drew close to mine. A surge of ecstasy consumed my entire being. It was the middle of February but our passion fogged up the window works of the Pontiac. We both yielded to our rapture and abandoned all thoughts of where we were. We began to undress each other in the front seat and then shifted about to make ourselves comfortable. Even the sweat from his taunt, agile body fueled desires. It wasn't until I happened to catch sight of a large, red light through the rear view mirror that I realized the jeopardy love had gotten us into.

"Wilbur, it's the police!" I blurted out desperately.

He slid down on the floor and started handing me my clothes.

"Tell 'em I was raping you." He said as he slid on his shirt.

"I'm not going to tell them that." I said as I rushed to get my skirt and blouse on.

"You tell 'em that, or do you want to go to jail?" Wilbur stated firmly.

I was in a state of panic. I rolled down the window and looked into the side view mirror. Now there were two red lights. So I braced for whatever would come next and waited.

"It's not the police." I reported with a sigh of relief. "It's one of those cars with big round tail lights. It was just backing out."

Silently we sat collecting ourselves and considered what might have been had the police in fact come upon us. I could not believe that I had been so foolish. I had permitted myself to be swept up into a whirlwind of passion without as much as a thought about the six children whose lives depended upon me. But it was not the police. It was just some guy backing a Ford Galaxy out of a parking space. Our eyes met as the thoughts of our respective predicaments passed through our minds. And then we spent the next ten minutes in fits of uncontrollable laughter.

"How come you wouldn't tell the police that I raped you?" Wilbur asked. He was genuinely perplexed.

"Because it ain't true."

"Yeah. But I told you to tell 'em that so you wouldn't have to go to jail."

"Then we both would have had to go to jail, because that wasn't true. They would have sent you to jail for a long time for that."

"I don't understand you. You'd rather tell the truth and go to jail?"

"I don't want to go to jail. I'm not that crazy. But I'm not going to send you to jail for something you didn't do."

"You don't know the first thing about jail." Wilbur insisted. "You'd never survive. At least I can handle that better than you. Why there's all kinds of murderers and bull daggers in there. And you're noting but a little kid. And you got kids at home to take care of."

"Wilbur. What kind of woman do you think I am?" I asked irritably. "What makes you think you'll survive? You can't take pressure. Ain't that what you told me?"

Wilbur shook his head in bewilderment. "You're something else."

We sat quietly while he tried to figure me out. I could not

understand why he was so troubled by what I considered a matter not even worthy of mention. I could not believe that the only women in the life of this warm and passionate man were the sort who would allow him to spend a long term in prison for a crime he did not commit.

"The night's shot." Wilbur offered gently. "Why don't we go out some other time and pick up where we left off."

"We better. I ain't ready to go to jail." I replied jovially.

"Howda like to go to Jefty's on Saturday?"

"Okay." I answered although I'd never heard of Jefty's.

"Why don't I come pick you up about nine o'clock?

"You better not stand me up. I might be the one who'll kill you." I said smilingly.

"Listen sweetie, I'll be there."

Visions of ecstasy gushed in my mind when he kissed me good-night. I held them at bay as I got into my car and allowed them to gambol wistfully as I drove home. For me, two days was going to be a long, long time and I'd have to cool it on the job to boot.

Helen, Maryann's teenage sister, did a masterful job of Frenchrolling my hair and making up my face. I wore a shirt coat dress with black embroidery. I rounded it out with a black and white fake fur beret, a short black jacket and black pumps. I had almost forgotten what it felt like to look beautiful. It had been almost a year in Dr. Walter's office since I had gotten myself dolled up. Even the children were impressed with their mother's transformation and rallied around me as if I had punted a game winning field goal.

As a trash man I thought him handsome. But the man standing in my living room dazzled me with his manly elegance. In his royal blue sweater jacket and beautiful silk shirt of gold, black dress trousers and black narrow brimmed hat, he tantalized the very core of my woman-hood. He and the kids exchanged cordial greetings. I could tell that they were as impressed with him as I was.

Jefty's was what some people would refer to as a hole-in-the-wall. The cavernous hall was dimly lit by fluorescent fixtures that hung precariously from chains that seemed to be wearying of their task. Tables had been arranged on the dingy green floor about the wooden pillars around the dance floor. There weren't many people in the place when we arrived. A waitress took my order of rum and coke. Wilbur ordered scotch on the rocks. Someone turned off the jukebox and the band assembled on the stage.

The band began to play "The Jerk" a few couples made their way to the dance floor.

"Would you like to dance?" Wilbur asked as he swayed rhythmically to the fast tempo of the music.

"Baby, I don't know how to jerk." I stated apologetically. "But I'll take a rain check on a slow number." A trace of disappointment passed across his face. I felt sorry that I did not know how to do the "Jerk".

Wilbur paid the waitress for our drinks. I had sipped most of mine before I realized that the bartender had not added the coke. By the time Wilbur informed the waitress of the mistake and she retuned with the coke, the rum had done its damage. My head became woozy and heat wave flowed within me. The band finally played a slow number and I decided to chance a dance.

"I'll dance this one if you like." I said offering my hand.

"Okay, sweetie."

He was a beautiful dancing partner. For me, it was heaven being in his arms. The band then played an up tempo number.

"Why don't we try this one?" Wilbur said as we started towards our seats.

"Okay. But don't say I didn't warn you." I said spiritedly as we returned to the floor. I must admit that it felt good to kick up my heels again albeit some of my best moves were powered by rum.

"I thought you said you didn't know how to dance." Wilbur said as he escorted me to the table. I acknowledged his compliment with a smile, but concluded that he was just saying that to make me feel good—which I did.

Wilbur ordered another round of drinks. The jukebox was turned on. As we nursed our drinks and listened to the music, I grew more and more tipsy. I was not used to drinking. The band returned to the stage and opened the set with a slow number. The place was now alive with people. When we got to the dance floor, it was so crowded that we could scarcely move. The heat from our grinding bodies and the drinks began to take a toll on my stability.

"Why don't we go somewhere alone?" Wilbur whispered softly into my ear."

"Yes. Let's go," I replied from the warmth of my passion.

We drove to a nearby motel where our love feast began. I couldn't tell who was the wolf—him or me. Passion drenched the small motel room. He and I emerged as king and queen of our realm of love. It was about six in the morning when we were awakened. Our time for the room was up.

"I'm hungry." Wilbur said as we checked out of the motel.

"I sure don't know where to go to eat around here."

"Well then what we gonna do?"

"Do you want to go out to Burbank for breakfast?" I offered haltingly. For me it was a long drive to Burbank from southeast Los Angeles. But for a truck driver like Wilbur, it was a mere hop, skip, and a jump.

"What's out in Burbank?"

"My mom. How about it? Come on, let's go to Burbank."

"It's six in the morning." Wilbur stated emphatically.

"So what. She's my mother and she'll feed us. Besides, you'll get to meet her.

"If she's sweet like you are, you got a nice old lady."

The traffic was light so we traveled quickly north on the Harbor Freeway to Burbank. All the way my mind flittered back to the motel room and how I wished it had never ended. My hand responded to my imaginings by gliding slowly along his thigh.

"Ain't you got something better to do?" He said rather annoyed by extremely controlled. "This ain't the place. Or do you want me to have an accident?"

"I'm sorry." I said, as I was trying to control my laughter. I had never experienced anger that made me laugh, but he did that to me every time he got mad. I slid over toward the door as the temptation to touch him was too great.

"I think we get off here." I said as the Riverside Drive off-ramp sign came into view. We got off the freeway and traveled the few blocks to mom and Arcelio's house.

"You sure your momma won't mind?" Wilbur asked pointedly.

"I told you. It'll be okay. I stated assuredly as I got out of the car. "Besides, we're here already."

A tired groggy eyed Arcelio opened the door to my calls and knocks. He told me that mom was in bed and then had me invite Wilbur in as he left to wake up Mom.

Arcelio came back and greeted Wilbur cordially. I then directed Wilbur's attention to an oil painting mounted prominently on the living room wall.

"I did that." I stated proudly. It was a landscape that I had done during the earlier days of my marriage.

"Did she do that?" Wilbur asked Arcelio in disbelief.

"Yes, she made that." My step-dad nodded admiringly.

Wilbur regarded the painting with childlike fascination. Wilbur seemed incapable of containing an emotion. For me it was a refreshing quality. The looks of amazement and delight that rose in his eyes came straight from his soul. He could not bring himself to believe that people actually created paintings and that I was one of those people. There was a strange and inspiring innocence in his face that drew me closer to him. It was glorious to me that I had met a man who was so secure in his masculinity that he could stare in childlike wonder at a simple painting without feeling the slightest bit threatened.

"Baby, that is beautiful. How'd you do that? Did you really do that?"

"Yes, I did that."

"That's beautiful. Why you're an artist." He gushed in admiration.

"No baby, I'm just trying to be. To a real artist, that's kindergarten stuff. But you gotta start somewhere."

Wilbur became so engrossed in the painting that he did not notice my mother when she emerged from the bedroom.

"Ma. This is my boyfriend, Wilbur." I said as I went to greet her.

"Hello." Mom said to Wilbur's back.

I drew Wilbur away from the painting and repeated my introduction.

"Pleased to meetcha." Wilbur said warmly as he approached her with extended hand. While Wilbur returned to his affair with the painting, mom and I sat down at the dining room table to chat.

"What are you doing bringing that Negro in my house?" Mom asked angrily in Spanish.

I stared at her in shock. I had never in my life heard my mom make a racist remark. In Brooklyn, mom had two black friends who were not Puerto Rican. One was Alma and the other was Helen. So it never passed my mind to question it before bringing Wilbur to the house. Besides, one of my uncles was married to a very sweet and gentle black woman named Esther.

"Ma. You are a racist?" I responded incredulously.

"Blacks were cursed by God. I want that evil man out of my house."

"But mom, you're part black."

"No I'm not." She retorted emphatically. "I'm Puerto Rican!"

"And what do you think Puerto Ricans are?"

"I don't care. I want that devil out of my house!"

"Well. I'm not going until we eat." I began defiantly. "I promised him that and I'm not going to tell him that you're not going to feed us because you're prejudiced."

Arcelio heard the argument and hurried in from the living room.

"He's behaving himself Mary, and I'll make them breakfast. Please, take it easy you two, he pleaded. Arcelio loved to cook and was happy for the chance to whip up something for someone other than his wife. Arcelio returned to the kitchen.

Mom sat tight-lipped at the table struggling to control her rage. I walked over to Wilbur, hoping that he didn't sense that we were having an argument.

"That's really something," he said shaking his head in dismay without looking away from the painting. "I ain't never seen nothing like that in my life".

"You really like it?"

"Yeah baby."

We talked about the painting as I fought to recover from the shock and anger that I felt. Arcelio informed me that breakfast would soon be ready and began setting the table. As we sat, he returned to the kitchen and appeared with plates of scrambled eggs and hot dogs. He then turned his attention to Wilbur who was eating heartily.

"Do you know Jesus?" Arcelio asked in broken English.

"Yeah man. Jesus is the Lord." Wilbur responded almost off handedly.

"Jesus died on the cross for our sins and we must repent." Arcelio pressed on realizing that he had a captive audience. "We must repent from all works of the devil. Jesus came to save us from the devil." Arcelio continued staring at Wilbur with a vacant consumed look in his eyes.

"These are the best eggs and hot dogs I have ever eaten. This is terrific." Wilbur enthused as he patted Arcelio on the shoulder.

"My kids think their grandpa is the best cook in the world." I offered.

"Do you want some more?" Arcelio asked Wilbur.

"Okay."

I took Wilbur's plate to the kitchen for a refill while Arcelio seized the opportunity to resume his sermon.

"Yes, you gotta call on Jesus to deliver you from sin, and to resist temptation. Why the devil is all around us."

"Right." Wilbur nodded and dug into the plate I put in front of him.

My mother sat rigidly silent throughout breakfast. All I hoped was that he did not notice, or that he would consider whatever he saw as our way of communicating in Spanish. But I knew better than to bring him back again.

As we made the drive to Santa Monica, I was hard pressed to understand my mother's attitude towards blacks. I grew up around black Puerto Ricans in New York where they would come to the point of fighting when they were mistaken for being American blacks. I was both surprised and confused to learn that mother had become so Americanized. She had forgotten that her own Mother had challenged racism by marrying a black Indian in Puerto Rico.

I thought about Wilbur. He was not into subtleties. He took life as it came; casting aside the superfluous while scrupulously maintaining at arms length those variances that would incite his impulsive nature beyond his control. For me the difference between a man and a devil had nothing to do with race or pedigree, but his humanity. Wilbur was well aware of the difference between right and wrong, good and evil but by being black in America, it required all of his coping skills to walk the fine line between them. It made me sad that my Mother was so blinded by ignorance that she had now become ungracious and intolerant. I was ashamed that Mom used the Bible to justify her bigotry.

# CHAPTER TEN

# *Betrayed*

It was Easter vacation and the kids had no school. Both my neighbor's kids and mine were very independent and set about exploring everything in sight. Since there were all sorts of mischief they could get into, I would call from work around 4 o'clock every day to see if the kids had gotten home alright. Jovita, my live in babysitter, answered the phone one afternoon.

"Ay, senora, la bebita se perdio." She said in tearful Spanish.

"What do you mean the baby got lost?" I asked in alarm.

"I was washing the diapers in the back room." Jovita began. "When I came into the living room, she wasn't there. So I looked throughout the whole house. And then I went outside and called but she didn't answer."

"Didn't you get the other kids to look for her?"

"The older children wanted to go to the park. You know, P.O.P. and Anita started to follow them. They brought her back into the house and told me to shut the door and not let her out. So I shut the door and started washing the diapers. When I came back, she was gone."

Jovita was now sobbing heavily and apologizing profusely.

"Jovita. What time did they go to Pacific Ocean Park?" I asked firmly.

"Around 12:30. Right after lunch."

"Jovita. Take it easy. I'm going to the police. When Rodrick and Nathan get home, tell them not to go out. I'll be there as soon as I can."

I could appreciate the desperate dilemma in which Jovita found herself. She was a wetback and spoke no English. She told me that she had been engaged to marry a man in her native Mexico. But when her mother died, she broke off the engagement in order to care for her invalid brother. After he died, she made her way to America. She was 32 but looked much older. Despite the ravages of time and circumstances, Jovita had maintained a caring touch. She drew from a seemingly depthless reservoir of humility and patience. The kids responded to her kindness and affection and always saw her as the wonderful person that she was. Julie began to understand her Spanish commands and interpreted them to others.

For me, Jovita had been a Godsend. I figured that finding a live-in babysitter for six kids while living behind the Santa Monica Dump would be next to impossible. I could only pay her thirty dollars a week, but she was grateful for whatever she got. What the hell did I care if she was an illegal alien? I needed to work and she needed to work. And besides, "wetback" could hardly be a dirty word to a "spic" like me.

I was consumed with panic and fear as my mind flashed a rotary of horrors that could beset a year and a half year old toddler wandering about the least hospitable section of Santa Monica. I envisioned her wandering helplessly among huge trucks and entering and exiting the dump or the lumbering flow of earth moving equipment on the uncompleted freeway or possibly being kidnapped. Frantically, I organized my desk, grabbed my purse and headed towards the door. Wilbur pulled into the lot from his trash run. I hurriedly explained to him what had happened. He agreed to watch the office until Lloyd returned.

"Pick me up at Howard's place after you get through and I'll come back with you." Wilbur called me as I headed for my car.

"Okay."

As I started the car and pulled onto the street, I only knew that the rush hour traffic had better look out. I was desperate to get my baby back and every minute seemed like an hour in limbo.

I dashed into the police station and rudely shoved my way to the front desk.

"I want to report my baby missing!" I shouted to the officer at the desk.

"You'll have to see the juvenile detectives down the hall to your right." He pointed.

There was no one in the room when I entered. A detective soon came in behind me.

"What can I do for you?" He said.

"I want to report my baby missing!" I said almost hysterically.

"What's your name?" He asked officiously.

"Elizabeth Bissett "

"What's your baby's name?"

"Anita Bissett, she's about a year and a half."

"Oh, we found the baby on Cloverfield Avenue. We placed her picture in the Evening Outlook and her father came in to identify her already. She's been placed in a foster home overnight."

"I want to pick her up." I stated somewhat testily. "Where is this foster home?"

"They won't release her to you until you've seen Detective Evans. And she's gone for today. Your baby is okay, Mrs. Bissett." He offered to my mounting anxiety.

"What time is this Detective Evans supposed to be here tomorrow?" I asked indignantly.

"Anytime after 8:30."

I was at once relieved, confused, and depressed. I did not know what to do. I thought about going home. But I was too upset. How could I console Jovita and the other children when I'm this upset? I wondered how they got Anita's picture in the evening paper so fast. Calling Chuck had crossed my mind, but I wasn't on speaking terms with him. Emotional support was what I needed more than anything and he was hardly the person to turn to for that. However, I could get it from Wilbur.

Wilbur had been waiting for me at his nephew's apartment. Like Wilbur, his nephew Howard was also a trash collector. Only a few years younger than Wilbur, he was far more contentious, angry and volatile. Burley and snarling, Howard was seldom seen without his gun and no one doubted his willingness to use it.

Wilbur opened the door to my raps on the glass door.

"How'd it go?" He asked with genuine concern as he invited me in.

"She's been found. But they put her in a foster home and I can't get her until tomorrow. Ain't that a bitch?" I responded with venom as I entered the apartment. It was a very small bungalow located at the rear of a single family residence near 41st and Main. A full sized bed, a well worn vanity, and a radio that dated back to the 40's dominated the living room.

"I don't know what I'd do if she was mine. I'd just have to go home and get my shotgun and shoot up the police station until they gave me my baby."

Wilbur's expression of anger always tickled me. He was so emotional that he was funny. Of course I tried never to laugh. I knew that he said what he did because he could think of nothing better to say. It was his show of support and it uplifted my spirits.

"I can't do that." I said graciously. "I'll just go down there first thing in the morning. I have to call home."

"Sure, baby."

Wilbur tried everything he could think of to assure me of his support; even cooked. Given the fact that he was an inveterate male chauvinist, this was a major concession. Our dinner of hamburger, rice and beans looked like hell and was laden with enough salt and pepper to gag two horses. But his generosity of spirit took my mind off of my taste buds enabling me to eat.

Somehow his brusque manner never affected the conveyance of his appreciation of me as a woman. This made me love him all the more. I had been love starved in my marriage and he knew how to reassure me of my personage. Somehow, my children sensed this about us. They knew that something very positive existed between me and Wilbur that did not exist between Chuck and I. Wilbur and I were happy with each other and my children were happy for us. When he came by the house, the kids did everything possible to entertain him. The sound of his deep laughter inspired confidence in them and delight would be aglow in their eyes.

The sun had barely risen when we arrived at the house. I got everybody up and asked Jovita to fix breakfast while I talked to the kids. I looked to my eldest, Rodrick, to tell me what had happened with Anita.

"We decided to outrun Anita. But she kept running and crying after us, Rodrick began pleadingly to my query. "We brought her back and asked Jovita to lock the door to keep her in."

"Well, how in the hell did she get out?" I roared.

"Mom." Julie said sheepishly. "Anita knows how to open the door. I saw her do it once, but I didn't think to say anything about it."

"Oh my God!" I sighed, realizing that this was not anyone's fault. Anita was just growing up.

"Miki, I want to talk to you." Wilbur said.

We went into the kitchen.

"I know you're upset, but I was a kid," He began with his hands placed compassionately on my shoulders. "And kids don't want to have their baby sister tagging along. You gotta understand."

"I know that, but they can't just run off to have a good time and jeopardize everybody else." I said despairingly.

"Listen. Why don't you let me take the boys on the route? I can't take the girls, but they have little friends to play with."

"What if Lloyd finds out? I can't let anything interfere with my job right now."

"Who the hell is going to tell him?"

"Okay. But you're spoiling them; and I know it."

Wilbur's offer was the ideal tonic for the gloom and depression that received us when we returned from the kitchen. The kid's were enthusiastic about riding with Wilbur. Even the girls wanted to go. But I insisted they stay with Jovita.

"Well, if you guys are going, you better move it." I said to the boys. I then smiled at Wilbur as he reassured me that the boys would be in good hands.

With Wilbur and the boys gone, my thoughts turned to Anita as I bathed and set my hair. I wanted to be at the police station promptly by nine. Hurriedly I dressed while giving instructions to Julie and Victoria. Jovita was in a much better frame of mind, and was working diligently at changing Sarrah's diaper and making breakfast. Soon she would start cleaning the house and no one would know that a hurricane of six kids had gone through it.

This time I didn't even bother with stopping at the desk sergeant. I went directly to the juvenile detective's office. A man and woman were sitting at their desks.

"Detective Evans?" I asked of the attractive blonde who appeared to be about thirty-five.

"Yes." She responded cordially.

"I'm Elizabeth Bissett, Anita Bissett's Mother. I was told last night to ask for you. I've come for my baby. I understand she has been found."

"Why don't you sit down here, Mrs. Bissett?' There are some questions we have to ask you before we can let you have Anita."

I plopped myself onto a wooden chair and inwardly attempted to gather myself for what I knew would be the onslaught of a bureaucratic storm.

"This is Detective Morgan. He will assist me with this investigation." She said as she directed my attention to an older man with dark features that I presumed to be Italian. He and I exchanged nods as I began to wonder what there was for them to investigate. I figured that she wanted to know the circumstances of Anita getting lost. But, I was in for the shock of my life.

"We have information that you bring all kinds of black men to your house and perform fellatio with them in front of your children," Detective Morgan stated with his eyes fixed on the table.

"What!" I roared as I jumped to my feed and pounded on the desk. Was I hearing properly?

"Sit down, Mrs. Bissett," he said firmly.

"I have one boyfriend and we go into town to have our affairs." I shouted. "Where did you get stories like that?"

"We have a report that quite a few black men come to your house and leave at all times of the night. He said accusingly.

"So my boyfriend has friends and he brings them by the house. That doesn't mean that I go to bed with them. And why can't I have friends over and party."

"I bet you party." He retorted.

My anger flared. "Are you insinuating that I'm a prostitute?

"Don't tell me you and your boyfriend don't copulate?" Detective Morgan stated after a long uncomfortable moment.

"There isn't a court in this land that would not permit a divorced woman to have a boyfriend. You're a filthy man. You better get a dictionary and read the definition for copulation and fellatio. And then wash your brains out with soap."

"Well, this case is for juvenile court to investigate. An investigator will get in touch with you in a few days." Detective Evans interjected.

"I hope they have more sense than I've seen here."

"We're just doing our job."

"What about Anita?" I asked brusquely.

"We'll go pick her up, then we'll go to your house and I have to make a home visit."

We stopped off at the juvenile center, picked up Anita, and then went home. I felt uneasy even as I was able to return home with her, I didn't know what to expect next. Waiting for us in the living room was Chuck; accompanied by a Hispanic man whom I did not know. I lashed out at Chuck furiously.

"Didn't I tell you to never, never set foot in *my* house?"

Chuck wouldn't answer me nor would he leave. Why should he? He had the police there with him and clearly they were on his side.

"If you don't calm down, Mrs. Bissett, I'll have to arrest you." Detective Evan's interrupted.

"What do you mean, arrest me? This is my house and I don't want him in my house."

"Calm down, just calm down." She said firmly.

"And who are you?" I asked of the man with Chuck.

"I'm the deportation officer. I have come to take Jovita to jail."

"How in hell did you know Jovita was here?"

"Well, Mr. Bissett reported her." Detective Evans said haltingly.

"You son of a bitch!" I screamed. "So you instigated this shit. Get out! Get out before I kill you!"

Both detectives grabbed hold of me as I moved angrily toward him. Chuck sidestepped the three of us and left. But it took the sight of Jovita sitting sullenly on the couch to calm me down.

"Oh Jovita, Jovita." I said as I tearfully embraced her and apologized for what Chuck had done. Even in her sadness, it was she who tried to console me.

"But Senora, what are you going to do about the children?"

"Please Jovita, don't worry about us. God will somehow make a way."

"Jovita has to go now." The Deportation Officer said, as he slapped the handcuffs on her.

"How can you put your own people in jail for nothing more than trying to live?" You're a disgrace to Mexicans." I shouted in fierce anger, and then watched as they led Jovita away in handcuffs.

The circumstances of my life passed before the mirror of my mind. The contrast between Chuck and Wilbur was like night and day. The thought of Wilbur's subdued self-assurances offered me the possibility of peace and stability. His total acceptance of me kept me loving even when I felt trapped in the eye of life's seemingly ever swirling maelstroms of social madness. No piece of paper made my marriage a love affair. How could the law debase my relationship with Wilbur for no other reason than his skin color? It was my marriage that was the source of fear and degradation. It was Chuck who had diminished the humanity out of me and the children to compensate for his inadequacies in achieving what he presumed to be his proper place in the citadel of male-dom. There was no doubt in my mind that I had done the right thing. But it was I who was being condemned for it. If his intent was to use the system to pressure me and the kids into returning to him in a state of grateful submission, he was sadly mistaken. All that he insured was that there could never, ever be any hope of reconciliation between us. I can now only wonder about what will become of Jovita and how to get on with my life and that of my children.

Sarrah's cries reminded me that lunch time was here and that the crisis that loomed before me would not be washed away with tears of self pity. Now I would have to figure out a way to provide for my children without a babysitter.

Wilbur finally returned with the boys. During dinner we discussed what had transpired during the day. The boys had spent a wonderful day with Wilbur sightseeing parts of Los Angeles that they had never seen before. Wilbur offered a possible solution to my babysitter problem.

"You know, Howard's old lady's mother, everyone calls her Grandmother Young, she might be able to help us. Why don't we go into town and ask her?" he said in a reassuring voice.

After dinner, we all got into the cars, and headed to Grandmother Young's on Figueroa and Vernon. The older kids rode with Wilbur; the younger two rode with me. It seemed that once again I was starting over, alone and with six small children. I couldn't seem to get past square one.

Wilbur's nephew Howard had two girlfriends. One was Lillie; the other was Bertha. Wilbur took us to Bertha who took us to see her mother, who everyone around the neighborhood called Grandmother Young. She was a sweet and simple old lady who was a security blanket of love and affection to her own grandchildren. She was reluctant to leave her grandchildren, but realized that I needed her and consented to help me for as long as she could.

Grandmother Young was as dear and patient with my children, just as she was with her grandchildren. The children responded to this grey haired, sweet black woman as though she were in fact their very own Grandmother. I was very much relieved that I could return to work with one less problem to have to cope with. I did not realize that there was yet another problem even greater waiting in the wings to take its place.

Lloyd was a very compassionate employer, and understanding about the various problems that forced me, from time to time, to miss work. I was very conscientious about not abusing his generosity, nor my own integrity. I tried to conceal my discomfort from him, hoping that the itching would soon pass. After awhile I confided in him that I was experiencing what I could only express as "woman trouble". He referred me to his doctor. Dr. Williams who treated me after work for three weeks for what he had diagnosed as "trichinosis". There was no cure for it at the time, but he managed to render the ailment to a level of a tolerable nuisance. Dr. Williams had also ordered a biopsy to test for cancer. Fortunately, it came back negative.

But the trichinosis persisted in multiplying faster than Dr. Williams could eradicate. He stated that if the condition would not adequately respond to treatment, I should consider having a hysterectomy.

"I've got to think about it." I said when he proposed that option to me. "I'm too upset to make this decision right now."

"Listen Miki." Dr. Williams said in a serous voice that reflected his compassion and concern. "I've been into spiritualism. Why don't you get a reading? I know this lady who I have seem make a cripple walk. I know she can help you. Believe me, I'm a doctor and I can't make a cripple walk."

"Do you really think she can give me some direction about this?" I asked skeptically.

"Let me call her."

"It's 10:30 at night. You think she'll see me now?"

"I'll call and find out." He said as he dialed the number.

He spoke to someone that he called "Mother Mary". She told him to send me over. He directed me to a house on the corner of Washington and Harvard in Los Angeles.

A man answered the door and directed me inside to wait in the foyer. When Mother Mary appeared, I stared at her in shock. My hands covered my mouth to muffle a sudden shriek. Mother Mary was older and walked more slowly, but she was the spitting image of my own mother.

"Take it easy dear." She said with a knowing smile. "Come into the other room where we can talk."

It was a dimly lit room full of eerie silences that seemed to swirl about me. We sat at a small table where she stared at me for a long time before she spoke.

"Some doctors are like butchers." She began in a slow measured tone. "Don't let him put a knife to you. Go get another opinion. Don't tell him I said so, but don't let him put a knife to you. Pray dear. Let God take care of you. You have a lot of troubles, but you'll be all right. Call me when you go to another doctor. God bless you my dear."

Mother Mary said nothing about money. As I was about to leave, I offered her five dollars. She gently pushed the hand away.

"No. You need it now more than I do."

The next day, I called the doctor who had treated my foot when I was injured at the bus stop and asked for the name of a gynecologist. He referred me to a gynecologist who worked out of his office one day a week. I called the doctor and made an appointment for the following week.

"He sure doesn't know his business." Dr Michtaskin said after I had told him what Dr. Williams had said and done. "As soon as you get through your cycle, I will be able to cauterize the affected area, and you should heal just fine."

"What's cauterizing?"

"First I'll freeze the walls inside of you, and then burn away the dead tissue. Then the tric can't feed off the walls and multiply. It takes about three weeks for you to completely heal, and you must take it easy. You'll have to abstain from sex for at least six weeks. And Miki, never get a hysterectomy unless you really need it. Your ovaries affect the hormone balance of your entire system and you're too young to go through that unless you need it."

I called Mother Mary to let her know what had happened and that I appreciated her advice.

# CHAPTER ELEVEN

# The Subpoena

I had finally settled into what I felt was a manageable routine that enabled me to both work and function as a Mother and Father to my kids. The kids were an absolute joy to me. They rarely complained about our circumstance. Rodrick, Nathan, and Julie had taken readily to public school. Victoria and Anita were bundles of ceaseless energy that both managed and were managed by the ever resourceful Grandmother Young. Sarrah was such a peaceful baby that, except for feeding and changing, she was no problem, and very content. With a confident sense of well being about home and the children, I was able to involve more of myself with Wilbur. The children had grown to appreciate Wilbur and were always glad to see him. He was easy going towards them and readily indulged them in their mischievous play. He laughed heartily at their jokes. But above all, there was that afternoon that he provided the children something that they had not experienced before.

Wilbur and I had returned Sunday morning from our night on the town. Rodrick rushed into the house in a state of panic.

"Trini's going to beat me up." He stated breathlessly.

"Who's Trini?" Wilbur asked.

"Trini's one of the kids in the back. He's nineteen years old though."

He's too old to beat up Rodrick." I answered fearfully.

Wilbur got up from the sofa and walked determinedly outside. He stood on the curb and waited for Trini as he crossed the street towards him. I was in a panic. If Wilbur decided to beat Trini, there was nothing I could do to stop him. Wilbur grabbed Trini by the shirt collar and hoisted him about a foot off the ground. He glared menacingly at the terrified Trini and he spoke to him through clenched teeth.

"Why don't you pick on someone your own size, like me?"

He turned Trini loose and pushed him away. A shaken and frightened Trini hurriedly headed home. My children were ecstatic. For the first time, they had a sense of being protected that they never felt with their father. After that, there was nothing that Wilbur could ask of the kids that they would not do. Victoria took to calling him Daddy Jefferson.

It was not long before my sky clouded and then threatened to crash down upon me. I was working at the trash dump. I was seated at my desk when a small, officious looking woman entered the office and glanced around bewilderedly.

"Are you Mrs. Bissett?" She asked shyly as she approached the desk.

"Yes."

"I'm Mrs. Ackerman from the probation department. I brought you a copy of the charges against you."

"What charges?" I asked irritably as I accepted a paper she offered me and offered her a seat as I read it. The paper was a subpoena to go to court. The charges against me claimed I needed help and that the children should be placed in a foster home. It required that I appear in court and show cause as to why the children should not be made wards of the court, and taken away from me.

"I can't agree to this." I stated firmly.

"Well, you can tell it to the Judge in court. The hearing is in two weeks."

"I may not be there." I offered desperately. "I've been undergoing medical treatment and may need a hysterectomy. I could use a foster home for a short while until I am well. I might be laid up for three weeks or so and wouldn't be able to afford a babysitter. In that sense, I may need help. But not permanently."

"Maybe the Children's Home Society in L.A. can help you. This is my card. If you go into the hospital, let me know."

The more I stared at the paper, the less I understood what it meant. I knew that it meant the possible loss of my children, but there was no discernible basis that I could argue. I was steadily employed and the children were being fed, clothed, and housed. There were not problems of which I was aware of that for any circumstance would necessitate them taking away my kids.

I can't agree to your charges," I said angrily. "You don't know what you're talking about. You better go, because this is definitely not the kind of help I need. You're not here to help me."

"Well, I'll see you in court," Mrs. Ackerman said noncommittally as she rose and left.

I had no idea which way to turn. There was nothing substantive in the subpoena for me to prove or disprove. A billowing hatred developed within me. If the system and its bureaucrats did nothing at all, I would somehow manage. But hauling me in before some self serving magistrate because of circumstances over which I have no control created distractions that served only to diminish my ability to raise my family. According to Dr. Michtaskin, the treatment for the trichinoses was going quite well and that the chances of me needing a hysterectomy were virtually nil. I saw no need to involve the state in what seemed a remote possibility. If one thing I was certain of was that neither the state nor Mr. Bissett could be relied upon to act in the best behalf for me or my children.

I went to see the pastor of the church I had visited while living in Culver City. I was hopeful that he could help me or at least testify on my behalf. He referred me to a lawyer, who was more concerned with my bosom than my problem. I was forced to remind him that I had been referred to him by the church for legal assistance and would expect me to report back whatever transpired between us. When he realized that I was deadly serious, he apologized and offered his services. My confidence in him was shaken, but I had little time remaining and could only hope that he would not sabotage my case.

When I entered the Santa Monica courthouse, I entered with full sole custody of my children. I was under a subpoena that ordered me to"show cause" why my children should not be made wards of the court. But when the court referee asked me how I pleaded to the charges, I reeled from the impact. He informed me that eight charges were the basis upon which the subpoena was issued. He began with charges that related to accusations of not properly caring for and feeding the children. Medically I had only been in need of a little help. My attorney protested before the Court that we had no prior knowledge of the charges and required a continuance of two weeks to study them. The referee stopped reading and wearily granted the two week delay. In addition, the Court Order "Denied" me the right to "Work" *during* the time all the minor children were in my care."

So I was suddenly confronted with the absurd logic of the judicial system. When I walked into the court I had a steady job forty hours a week and child support ($650.00 a month) to provide sustenance for my family. I exited a court that had ruled in effect that since I could not support them on $650 a month, conditions may well improve on only child support of $350 a month to care for six children. Since the children were not eating to conform to some standard known only to the "Court" itself, the court had now decided to enforce rules that should not allow my children to eat at all. And further more take my right to work to support them.

I was heartsick and crestfallen when I had to inform Lloyd that I could no longer work for him. He was very understanding and assured me that my job would be there for me when the crisis passed. I then told Grandmother Young that her services would no longer be required. The kids and I had grown fond of her and were sorry to leave her. I settled into a day to day existence, dreading the possibility that the lives of my children would be damaged beyond any hope of repair. It was Nathan who dropped the first crisis in my lap and reminded me that no matter what happened I would have to be the one responsible for their guidance.

"What's the matter Nathan?" I asked my fear stricken son after he came running into the living room.

"Georgie says that he has to defend his honor and is waiting to beat me up." He responded ashamedly. "I can't beat up Georgie. Georgie will beat me up."

"Nathan, you have to fight this one alone." I began sympathetically. "If you don't fight him now, he'll be waiting for you until you do. If you hide, all the kids will call you a baby or a sissy and pick on you. I don't know what this honor thing is all about. But if its important to him, you're going to have to deal with him sometime. Wouldn't it be better to be scared and get it over with than to go around scared all the time?"

Nathan pondered his dilemma for a moment and then reluctantly went to find Georgie. I watched him leave with deep seated misgivings as I sat on the edge of the bed sad and anxious. This was a talk a father should have with his son. I was opposed to fighting, but my son had to be encouraged in ways of this violent world. My female sensitivity had to be brushed aside to somehow accommodate the male necessity to strut courage.

My daughter Julie ran in screaming for me to stop the fight. Nathan was not faring well against Georgie who was a year or so older and slightly larger. When I told her that I couldn't interfere she screamed hatreds at me and flung herself into the bed. A short while later Nathan returned home. He admitted to losing the fight but he and Georgie shook hands and were off to celebrate their renewed friendship over ice cream. In the kitchen Julie had taken a brush and black paint and wrote "I hate you" on the wall. I started to laugh out aloud and then called her into the kitchen. She stood sheepishly before me as my laughter turned to anger.

"You will get the turpentine and get this off the wall. So you hate me, so what. The world doesn't stop because you hate me. But you won't ever write on the walls again. Do you understand me?"

Victoria qualified for a newly established program called "Project Head Start " and soon established herself as a bright, assertive child who willingly took advantage of all the arts and crafts programs that it had to offer. In fact, Victoria had so impressed her teacher that she paid a visit to our house.

On the very afternoon that Mrs. Rose chose to come by and talk to me about Victoria, virtually every kid in the neighborhood was running in and out of my living room for what to them was nothing less than the exhibition of the century—tadpoles. Nathan had taken it upon himself to explore a nearby marsh and retuned to the house with mud dripping from his legs and a tub full of tadpoles that he plopped in the middle of the living room floor. Word of Nathan's find spread rapidly throughout the neighborhood. When Mrs. Rose entered the house, she was surprised to behold no less than a dozen kids transfixed in awe and excitement upon the tiny, wriggly, creatures swimming about in the tub.

"Nathan, why do you bring that inside? Take that outside at once and your friends with you." I said irritably. "I hope you don't mind the mess, but kids have a life of their own." I said to Mrs. Rose as I directed her to sit on the sofa.

"Not at all." She said.

"What can I do for you?"

"Victoria is such a lively and expressive child that I wanted to meet her mother. I can see that you've got your own child care center going. Do you always allow this much freedom?"

"Yes." I replied.

"How do you do it?"

"Well, if you provide children with a peaceful environment, their natural joie de vivre makes them curious, expressive, and happy." I stated. "So how is Victoria doing?"

"She's just wonderful. She is such a pleasure. She gets into every activity without fear or apprehension. She's a delight to watch."

"Thank you."

"Mrs. Bissett. Can I come back again?"

"Yes. Of course, and please call me Miki." I said as I walked Mrs. Rose to the door. I was grateful that she had taken the time to visit me personally. I had been a bit apprehensive about entrusting Victoria to an experimental federal program that would entangle her and me in a web of bureaucracies and regulations. With a class full of kids to contend with, I did not expect her to come again. I was very much surprised when she returned the following week.

This time some of the kids brought her in by the hand. It was time for our story-in-the-round. There were about a dozen kids assembled around the dining room table anxiously waiting for me to start a story. Quietly, she sat down to watch.

"Once upon a time there was a unicorn." I began. "It had one horn in the center of his head..." Each child contributed to the story. I was pleased and sometimes even astonished by the depth of imagination that they employed to enhance the excitement of the plot. Of course, I helped them along, too. It was not unusual for squabbles to break out when some of the kids jumped their turn or when someone's offering was deemed especially unacceptable. I always closed out the story with a moral that, more often than not, made sense to no one—not even me. But everyone, including me, had a good time and looked forward to the next time.

"And the moral for today was that two horns are better than one." Everyone roared with laughter. "Okay everybody, story's over." I told them, and then began to shoo them out to play. But some of the children wanted more and refused to leave and pouted until I promised more tomorrow. The boys left to climb into the tree house overlooking the freeway, while the girls went into the bedroom to play with their dolls.

Mrs. Rose's eyes beamed at the gaiety of the children. I picked up

Sarrah and put her on my lap. I surmised that Mrs. Rose had come to determine whether what she had seen on her first visit was a fluke or the way I normally conducted my home.

"That was wonderful." She said.

"I try to end the stories with an appropriate moral, but I don't always succeed. What's important is that every child regardless of age has an equal opportunity to contribute to the story and that the older children learn to allow the younger ones to express their ideas even if it is only foolishness. Even foolishness has a place in the scheme of things. So story-in-the-round serves a lot of life skill purposes. They don't know that's what they're doing. They only know that they love it and that's what matters. Isn't it?" I replied.

Victoria came back in and began tugging at her dress.

"Can you do anything?" She asked.

"Like what?" Mrs. Rose responded.

"Like singing or dancing."

"Well, I can sing." She answered as the other little girls also came back in.

"Let's hear you sing." Victoria challenged.

"It's okay." I said reassuringly. "You don't have to be self conscious. We all let our hair down. I dance with the kids. They know the popular dances and that's how I learn them. Mrs. Rose stood up, adjusted herself, and sang an aria in a voice that was pleasantly operatic. The girls and I rewarded her rendition with a round of applause. She grinned from ear to ear. Mrs. Rose had joined my child care center as Victoria had joined hers.

I needed Wilbur. For me he was a tower of gentle strength that he placed at my disposal during my time of need. Fortunately, marriage was never an issue with us. I needed time for me and the children to heal from the abuse suffered from my marriage, before I could begin to consider committing to a permanent relationship. Wilbur had fathered at least nine children by two women and was deeply affected by his inability to have the sort of relationship with them that he desired. His relationship with his first wife; Angeline was stormy and violent. But he missed the six children he had with her and would take a chance to visit with them. Sometimes he insisted that I go with him in the hope that Angeline would be more gracious in front of company. Within fifteen minutes, the visitation would degenerate into a physical brawl between them. In order to extricate himself from her fury, Wilbur would end up having to punch her. We would then leave, having accomplished nothing but detriment to the kids.

While with Angeline, he met Georgia and began another family. She presumed that her possession of Wilbur's person and the children by him entitled her to engage the beleaguered Angeline in an incessant volley of harassment. Conflicted between the mothers of his children, he took up residence with Georgia. Wilbur's war injury had created intolerance for stress that rendered the taming of two shrews well beyond his capabilities. The first time I saw Georgia was at the funeral for Wilbur's sister-in-law. Her eyes were prominently discolored and she wore dentures that Wilbur claimed that he was constantly having repaired.

After school let out for the summer, Wilbur asked me to let his first batch of children spend a few days at the house to avoid another confrontation with Angeline. They proved to be surprisingly cooperative and well-mannered children who were only too ready to play with my kids. Although Angeline and Wilbur continued their fight-on-sight relationship, she and I developed a cordial one.

About three days before going to court, I received a copy of my file from my attorney. It was obvious by the self serving contrivances, innuendos, and presumptions that the Judge and Mrs. Ackerman were determined to take my children away from me. She even claimed that I did not buy food to feed the children, even though she had never been to the house. How could I defend not having an income when the court had ordered me not to "Work" while the children were in my care? But the most disturbing entries in her investigations were those derived from my mother and Dr. Walters.

I figured that Dr. Walters, of all people, understood what I had endured in my marriage. He knew about the abuse of the children and the racist attitudes. I could not fathom how he could suggest that I was at fault for the dysfunction in our family. He concluded that the husband would not be dysfunctional if the wife submitted to his control. He had dismissed the reason for my insubordination as irrelevant. Hurriedly, I went to the phone to call him. I wanted to understand how he could conclude that I was out of control and said nothing about their Father who abused his kids.

Dr. Walters was annoyed and defensive at what he regarded as my presumption to question his diagnosis. He was abrupt and terse when he closed out the conversation by informing me that the court asked about me and not Chuck. I vowed never to trust another therapist again.

I sat beside the phone for a long time pondering what I might hear when I called my mother. According to her I was "possessed of demons". She told Mrs. Ackerman that is was beyond her comprehension as to why I would leave such a "good man" like Chuck-a man who worked every day and provided for his family. Hoping that Mrs. Ackerman had taken my mother's testimony out of context, I dialed her number.

"Mom, I need to ask you something?" I asked.

"What is it?" She answered.

"How could you tell the investigator that I was possessed of demons? How could you tell her that; when Chuck was the one beating the children?" I asked contentiously.

"Weren't you going to a psychiatrist? Then you're crazy. All insanity comes from the devil. When God is on your side, you don't need a psychiatrist. And if your kids are bad, then Chuck has every right to beat the badness out of them." She responded fiercely.

"But, I'm you're daughter. Couldn't you trust me enough to feel that I know what I'm doing?"

"Why should I feel that way? You're just like your father—you have no common sense."

"What has my father got to do with this?" I asked irritably.

"Well, you were no benefit to him and you're no benefit to me."

"But Mom, don't you care about me?"

"What can you do for me, except to be a burden on me? I couldn't even find a man until after you got married. So tell me, now that you've gotten divorced, what benefit can you be to me? And you brought that Black devil to my house. Why shouldn't I think you're crazy! Well, they should take the children from you. You're not my daughter. You're the daughter of the devil."

"Oh my God!" I gasped as I hung it up. My soul wanted to scream. I felt desperately alienated from all possibility that the torment would ever end. I dropped my head into my hands to keep from screaming. "Mom, how could you do this to me?" I screamed in bewildered anguish.

A compassionate, loving hand shifted my head against her youthful bosom just as I was on the verge of hysteria. Julie sensed the gravity of my despair and came from her bedroom to console me. My teardrops upon her head caused me to tremble as I felt consumed by the thought that Mom's betrayal may cause me to lose my children. I embraced Julie as tightly as I dared, clinging to her as if my life's blood was spilling out on the floor. She tried to console me, but I was inconsolable. Mother could not have inflicted greater pain upon me than if she had knifed me in the back. She was a willing party to a conspiracy to snatch all that mattered to me in the world. I resolved never to set eyes upon her again.

The referee allowed me another month's continuance. Mrs. Ackerman took the opportunity to shore up her case by visiting my house for the first time. She said very little to me. I granted her permission to look around while I returned to washing diapers. Her well trained eyes swept through every room undoubtedly scooping up every gram of evidence that would corroborate her judgment of me as an unfit mother. I told her that I had recently undergone the procedure and was not feeling well. Her eyes jolted. I felt certain that my admission would be prominently distorted in her file.

Mrs. Rose came by two or three times a week. She stayed about an hour to watch the children play. One day she finally got up the courage to ask what was really on her mind.

"Miki, what is your philosophy for raising children?" She asked earnestly.

"It's a gestalt," I answered. "Children are born about three quarters of the person they will become. It's up to the parents to help them to develop the rest. If you force the gestalt, then you have rebellion. I see them as my equal. But I am the final authority. If you allow children a chance to develop within themselves, they will trust you enough to let you show them the way."

"From what I've seen, you have a wonderful philosophy," she said.

"I wish the court thought so."

"Why, what's happening?"

I told her about my case. A look of disbelief formed on her face.

"But you're such a good Mother!"

"They're not listening to me," I responded plaintively.

"Let me see what I can do about it," she offered assuring.

A few days later Mrs. Rose returned.

"Miki, I have some bad news," she said solemnly. "I have been warned that if I testify on your behalf, I will lose my job. This is a pilot project and I can't afford to lose my job. I've been fighting very hard to implement this program all over the country; to benefit all children. I feel so bad that they're giving you a raw deal. But I can't testify. However, there is one thing I can do as an honor to you. We're making a project film and, if it will be alright with you, I'd like to include you and the kids in it."

Towards the end of the semester, she came with a cameraman and filmed me and the kids. I never saw Mrs. Rose again.

As I expected, Mrs. Ackerman's report weighted heavily against me. It claimed that although I was home with the kids, there had been no change from her first report to the court. If it came to a vote for Mother of the Century, Ma Barker would beat me by a landslide. Everything in the report was a skewed to convey the impression that I was dangerous to my children. There were no charges in the report for me to respond to. Nor was there a single syllable offered on my behalf. Their Father was not even made to be present in the court room the day they issued the warrants for my children's arrest. The court accepted the probation officer's report without question. All of the children became wards of the court and Mrs. Ackerman was ordered to pick them up at the house. The ultimate crush that life had to offer descended upon me full force.

My children gave me a small white Bible for my Birthday. Three days later, on July 16th, the court ordered that the children be taken to Juvenile Hall. I reasoned with the Judge to no avail. I told him, if they wanted my children, they were going to have to come and get them. That afternoon, Mrs. Ackerman, two police squad cars, and Chuck came to fulfill the court directive.

The oldest were with Wilbur in the house in Santa Monica and had just gotten out of school when I got the call. The youngest two were hidden with Grandmother Young in Watts. I had hoped as a last stance of sorts they would see at least my infants needed me, and leave them from imprisonment. I rushed to Grandmother Young's and begged for them not to take my babies. They had a worker waiting in the squad car to take them from me. When we pulled up to the house in Santa Monica, another squad car had gone to find Rodrick, he was on his paper route. They chased him on his little bicycle, held him down and arrested him. The children were outraged, and terrified. They screamed to their Father. "Why don't you tell them the truth; she didn't do anything …tell them the truth!" But he only shushed them to be quiet as he and the police gathered them together for the ride to Juvenile Hall. Anguish gathered within me to the point that I could scarcely contain it. The state had already deemed me as dangerous. I could have easily lost control,… and gotten myself shot by the police, I was surrounded. As I cried and begged for them not to take my babies; Mrs. Ackerman regarded the entire affair as no more than a rescue mission that had to be successfully completed. Even with the children screaming, she and the police reflected no concern that things might not be as they appear.

I spent the remainder of the day in bed crying over the injustice of the legal system. After all the things this man had done to his children, the court treated me as though I were the criminal. The next day I had no choice but to begin the slow arduous process of building a life that portended little else but emptiness. I had learned from Wilbur that Lloyd had been involved in a boating accident and was listed as missing at sea. His widow decided to close down the company. There was little option for me except to apply for welfare. From this day long ordeal I garnered a $5.50 a week grocery order—no rent, utility or even gas money to launch a job search. I stopped off to buy a box of instant breakfast and a quart of milk. The sight of people dispatched surges of extreme hostility within me. So terrified was I of what I might do, that I locked myself in the house. And then there were strange and horrible hallucinations such as flames jutting my skin that drove me to seek the refuge of sleep. Each night I cried myself to exhaustion.

On the sixth day of this devastating routine, I had a vision. I saw an image of Jesus on a stage to the right of an austere old man with long white hair and flowing beard seated on an ornate throne. Although I stood behind them as a very interested observer, I also stood before them with my head bowed and my hair parted down the middle. It appeared to me that some form of judgment was about to be rendered concerning me. The man stared into my mind's eye as he spoke in a voice that was stern and clear.

"Go and Live."

The next day I decided to do what the man said and went to the unemployment office to see what I could find. I was in no condition to work full time as of yet. There were suitable jobs available, but I had no cash for gasoline. A sympathetic friend exchanged my grocery order for cash. A job folding clothes at a laundry in Westwood provided a tedious, but useful re-entry into the world of work. About three weeks later the ideal position opened as a part-time nursery school teacher in Santa Monica. The hours were 6 in the morning until 1pm and I ate with the children. How ironic it was that I was deemed competent to care for other people's children, but unfit to care for my own.

Gradually, I gathered my composure sufficiently to where I felt comfortable about seeing my children. I called Mrs. Ackerman to arrange for visitation with them at Mc Claren Hall which was located well east of Santa Monica in Baldwin Park.

"Mrs. Ackerman, this is Mrs. Bissett." I stated.

"What can I do for you?" She asked.

"I'd like to know the visiting hours at Mc Claren Hall."

"The hours are from one to two on Sunday afternoon. But I have noted in your file that you cannot visit the children without a Guard present."

"Why?" I spouted angrily.

"Well, I don't know how dangerous you are to your children. So I'm not taking any chances." Mrs. Ackerman retorted.

"Thank you." I said and rang off in a huff.

It was all I could do to contain my fury. This lady had pulled out all the stops. Now I was compelled to submit to the almost intolerable indignity of visiting my children under "Armed Guard" as though I were on leave from some psycho ward. Most of me felt like not going. But I knew I had no choice except to swallow my pride and submit to the judicial drill.

For me it was a long tortuous Sunday drive along the San Bernardino Freeway. All the way, I tried to prepare myself for what awaited me at the juvenile center. Of course what greeted me upon my arrival was what I did not anticipate. I was informed that the guard was available only Monday through Friday and I could not see the children. An unyielding determination not to be undone seized control of me. The high brick wall gave way to a chain link fence, and at the top Barbed Wire. I stood at the fence and yelled toward the kids romping about in the playground.

"Rodrick, Nathan, Julie, Victoria!"

All of the kids stopped their play, and mine came running to me. I gave them kisses through the fence and tossled their hair. They told me that Anita and Sarrah were doing alright in the toddlers sections. The older children were only permitted to visit them once a day. The yard monitor who promptly rushed over and joined us ordered the children to go back to the others.

"I have to report this." The monitor said. "You cannot do this. You have to leave now."

"I came out here all the way from Santa Monica. I'm going to see them if I don't do anything else." I retorted. I could see that he was sympathetic to my plight. Slowly he walked away so that the kids could still see me wave at them on their way back to the main group.

It was still a worthwhile trip, even though I only spent a few seconds with the kids. They were glad to see me and it filled my heart. Monday morning I called Mrs. Ackerman.

"Why in the hell didn't you tell me that the Guard only works on weekdays?" I railed contemptuously.

"I heard you raised a ruckus out there." She responded unaffected.

"If it were your children, wouldn't you? I can't go out there during the weekdays. I have to work. And then, I can only visit them accompanied by an Armed Guard? I don't know what kind of person you are to set me up this way, but you're sick." I ranted.

"Well I didn't know they don't have a Guard on Sundays." She answered apologetically. "Let's make a deal. If you promise not to create a ruckus, I'll withdraw the Guard."

"I wouldn't have created a ruckus if I could have seen my children. No, but you got to have a Guard there… and not my children. Don't you understand yet? It is Mr. Bissett who's dangerous to his children, not me."

"To be honest, Mrs. Bissett, I don't know you or Mr. Bissett from a hole in the wall. So I went to your mother and after what she said about you, what do you expect me to think?" She stated.

"But my Mom's a religious fanatic and doesn't understand psychology. Don't you understand the language of religious fanatics? How can you take her literally? She doesn't understand about child beating. All she knows is what the Bible says: spare the rod and spoil the child. I don't care what Dr. Walters says, I could not submit to the control of my husband. He's a child beater."

"I have no proof of that. What I have is that your own mother thinks you've gone crazy. And I have to act in accordance to what I find." She replied.

"I know, Mrs. Ackerman. But you believe the wrong person." I insisted.

There was a long moment of reflective silence before she continued.

"You know Mrs. Bissett; this is the first time that we've had a nice talk."

"Thank you, Mrs. Ackerman. But the damage's been done; you arrested and imprisoned my children." I said angrily and then hung up.

The following Sunday I returned to Mc Claren. True to her word Mrs. Ackerman had arranged for me to visit without a guard. I could only see Sarrah, my one year old, through a window as she lay in a crib. Anita was placed in a room of toddlers where I could only watch her play while seated in a child's cold metal chair. The father of one of the other children sat next to me and lamented how dirty the State of California was doing him. He told me how the state had promised him custody of his child so that he and his mother could raise her in Tennessee. After he signed the appropriate consent forms, the state then kept the child and placed her in Juvenile Hall. I was finally permitted to give Anita hugs and kisses before leaving to visit my other four children. It was a fine visit that went all too quickly.

During subsequent weeks, the children were separated. The two boys were placed at the Episcopal Children's Home, or more commonly called ECH. Julie, Victoria and Anita went to a family in Manhattan Beach, while Sarrah was placed with a family in Baldwin Park. My children were now placed all over Los Angeles County. Visiting them was almost impossible. My income was so minimal that I could not afford the extra five dollars for gasoline. And then I always felt guilty about not being able to afford to bring them gifts.

It was in early August, 1965 when I visited my baby Sarrah in Baldwin Park. I sat her on my lap, stroked her hair and kissed her. She recognized me as her mother and did not resist my attentions. As I rocked her and held her close to me, tears rolled down my face. She would wipe them with her tiny little hand. We shared our love in silence. The hours flew by when I noticed it was getting late. I did not want to be on the freeway at night.

The horizon before me was grey with smoke and an orange glow. I figured that either an oil refinery or one of the large factories such as firestone or Goodyear was on fire. The smell of smoke was unmistakable in the air. I turned onto the Harbor Freeway and headed towards the house of Howard's girlfriend, Lillie, who lived near Slauson and Main. Everywhere people were out in the streets running and shouting.

"What's going on, Lillie?" I asked as I entered her house hurriedly.

"They're burning up Watts." She said excitedly with pride. "The police are fuckin' with us niggers and we ain't gonna take it no more. They shoot at us and we're shootin' back.

As violent and formidable as Howard was, he treaded lightly with Lillie. She had bought a .38 special and was not afraid to use it when Howard got a notion to go into his caveman act. It was laying on the coffee table, fully loaded and a box of bullets next to it.

"The police better not come by here," She added defiantly with her hands on her hips. "I'll shoot them suckers in the mother-fucken ass."

"Have you seen Wilbur?" I asked somewhat tepidly.

"Yeah. They went to get some booze. They'll be back in a few minutes."

Her kids flew in and out of the house with all of the gossip about the riot. Wilbur, his brother Alfred and Howard came in. They were so involved in the heat of their talk that Wilbur did not notice me. They took a few drinks and worked themselves up to go out and shoot at the police. Wilbur asked me to drive them around the riot area. I tried to talk him out of this madness. His face clouded. He was in no mood to be refused anything. So instead of a quiet visit with my man, I was drafted to be a gun moll for three whiskey swilling men intent on riding through the riot area to shoot at cops.

As they ordered me to drive along one street and then another, I prayed fervently and constantly to God for deliverance from this ordeal. Fortunately, we encountered no cops and they were relegated to shooting at empty buildings and TV antenna's. We returned to Lillie's and spent the rest of the night drinking and talking. Wilbur took Alfred home and we went to Howard's place on 41st St.

Two days later, I went to see Grandmother Young and Howard's other girlfriend, Bertha, to see how they had been faring during the riot. They were glad to see me. Only because they needed someone to look after the children while they went out to join the looters. I sat frightened and apprehensive waiting for them to return. Intermittent sounds of gunfire drew a spontaneous "Lord have mercy" from me as I clutched the crying children close to me. An imposed curfew had come and gone, but Grandmother Young and Bertha had not returned. I was getting nervous. They returned empty handed and angry that they had gone out too late. I rushed out of the house and hightailed it onto the freeway to Santa Monica.

For some inexplicable reason, I was drawn back to riot torn Los Angeles the following day. Perhaps it was because it offered an admittedly perverted relief from the interminable doldrums that had taken over my life. The riot had been going on for several days and I was curious as to what was happening. I parked near Bertha's house and walked towards the Thrifty's drugstore at Figueroa and Vernon. The governor had called out the National Guard. Soldiers and the police were everywhere. I was standing on the corner of Vermont and Vernon when a large military truck came to a stop not far from me. It was filled with solemn soldiers who stood their rifles ominously in front of them. So this was martial law. What began in my stomach as an uncomfortable swirl of humiliation became an uncontrollable whirlwind of hostile indignation. I wanted to pick up a machine gun and shoot them all. How dare they trespass on my freedom and degrade my dignity? This was not Hungary. This was not Czechoslovakia. This is America. We were the one's being brutalized, imprisoned and oppressed by the police. We were the one's whose rights were being trampled on, and denied. Send out the guard on the police not on us.

The truck went past me, its occupants unaware of my writhing inner rage. At that moment *I became* an oppressed Black Woman. I stood silently and embraced who I had become for the very first time. I was an oppressed Black Woman; my white children were taken by uniformed police from these same streets where soldiers now stood with guns at hand. Yes, my boyfriend was Black, but up until this moment I saw myself as non-racial. I had regarded myself more as a chameleon of sort; who adapted and blended in with whatever environment I happened to be in. No longer did I need to empathize with *stories* of slavery and racism. No. This was not white sheets and burning crosses. But this was real. This was not a story; my children were sent away just like on the "Masta's Plantation." I was a woman of color who had dared to love and protect my white children, in a Black community. I was the woman of color who had failed know my place. A burning rage would now besiege the city and injustice perpetuated publicly upon infants would have to be answered for. I was standing in South Central Los Angeles, a part of America where freedom denied was being enforced by martial law. If the guard had started shooting at that moment, I too would have most likely been counted amongst the silenced and the dead.

# CHAPTER TWELVE

# A Stable Home

I could no longer afford the ram shackled abode that had been home to me and the children. Angie permitted me and my belongings to stay in her storage room until I could move. Maintaining my bond with the children was still uppermost in my mind. No matter what circumstances I found myself in, there was the ever nagging concern that if I did not constantly press my interest in the children, their emotional well being would be permanently scarred.

I called Mrs. Ackerman and asked for a meeting with her and her supervisor. The meeting was arranged for a few days later.

"I'm Mrs. Bissett. I'm here to see Mrs. Ackerman and Mrs. Julius." I said to the receptionist.

"They're expecting you. This way, please." She motioned me to follow her. She ushered me into an office where the wispy officious Mrs. Ackerman introduced me to her thin, darker complexioned supervisor, Mrs. Julius. I was offered a chair across from Mrs. Julius' desk while Mrs. Ackerman sat near the window to my right.

"How may we help you?" Mrs. Julius began.

"First, Mrs. Ackerman will not interview any of the witnesses that I send her to." I began determinedly. "I cannot help it if all my witnesses had moved before she began her investigation. But I did run across a friend who knows all about Mr. Bissett and she won't interview her. All she keeps telling me is that the case is closed. So I'd like you to change my probation officer. I can't get justice from Mrs. Ackerman no matter what I do. Second, I want to know specifically what conditions I have to meet to get my children back."

"I cannot remove Mrs. Ackerman from the case, Mrs. Bissett." Mrs. Julius said cordially. "And she's right. The case is over. As far as the conditions you have to meet are concerned, you must provide a stable home, hold a job for one year, and satisfy us that you are mentally stable."

"That's not so bad. I can do that." I insisted even though I was wary of what she meant by "mentally stable".

"No. You can't do that." Mrs. Ackerman blurted out.

"Why not?" I asked contentiously.

"Because, Mr. Bissett is going to get the children as soon as his finances improve."

Mrs. Julius and I exchanged looks of disbelief. Obviously she had read the file, but was unaware of Mrs. Ackerman's hidden motive.

"I don't give a damn about Mr. Bissett." I spouted angrily to Mrs. Julius. "I'm talking about me, about what I have to do. You see what I mean? She will not investigate any of my witnesses because she wants Mr. Bissett to get the children. Don't you see?" I concluded as I looked at Mrs. Julius pointedly.

"Do you have the name and address of Mrs. Bissett's witness?" Mrs. Julius asked Mrs. Ackerman.

"Yes, but the case is over." Mrs. Ackerman answered insistently.

"Give Mrs. Bissett the courtesy of interviewing her witness even if the case if over." Mrs. Julius ordered and then turned to me.

"The only way your probation officer can be changed is if you move to another district." She offered with a sly wink. "Perhaps you might consider that."

I started to tell her that I was looking for a place, but thought better of it. But I did resolve to move out of the district. "I'll call you in a few days and see what you found out from my witness." I told Mrs. Ackerman.

"Thank you for your time." I said as I left.

In Culver City, we lived in a four unit apartment building, where Chuck's violent outbursts had been well witnessed by all of the other tenants. But the upstairs occupants had moved somewhere in the Valley. My neighbor across from me had been beaten so badly beaten by her husband that her doctor gave her a year to live. When last I heard, her husband's mother had arrived from Tennessee with gun in hand to keep her son away from his wife and children until she finally died.

Meredith Porter lived in a nearby apartment building and had become my best pal. She was a single mother with two sons. An undiagnosed illness worried her to no end. Sick, lonely, and desperately in need of a friend, Meredith spent more time in my apartment than she did her own. She was breakfasting with us on that Christmas morning when Chuck flew into a rage and began choking Rodrick. I encountered her in the grocery store in Santa Monica and told her about my problems with Mrs. Ackerman. She gave me her address and phone number and readily agreed to help me anyway she could. I then called Mrs. Ackerman to tell her about Meredith. She firmly informed me that the case was closed. Insistent, she reluctantly took the information. But the future of my children was at stake. I was not about to yield an inch to accommodate the convenience of a self serving bureaucracy. I was careful not to be rude to Mrs. Ackerman. But I was emphatic. She relented and promised to call Meredith.

Three days after the meeting, I called the probation office and spoke to Mrs. Ackerman.

"Did you get in touch with my witness?" I asked anxiously.

"Yes, I saw your witness." She answered.

"Well, what did she say?"

"She told me some weird story about Mr. Bissett choking his son because of some orange juice?" She asked in disbelief. "He seems like such a nice man. I don't understand why he'd do something like that over some orange juice. Do you know why?"

"You really don't know Mr. Bissett." I offered plaintively. "His own mother doesn't know about that side of him."

"Did Mr. Bissett really do that?" She asked again in disbelief.

"Yes, he really did do that. That's why I divorced him" I replied.

"Maybe I made a mistake." Mrs. Ackerman responded contritely. "But you have to realize the position I'm in. When your file hit my desk, my job was to find you guilty. After what your mother said, I couldn't find you anything but guilty."

"You're telling me that you see me as a file—a guilty file and not even as a person." I said angrily. "So you came in here determined to portray me as a prostitute in front of my own children in order to prove me guilty of something. I know because you were pumping my daughter Victoria about my sexual activities when I was at work. She's a five year old child. Why would you ask her something like that? How come you never asked the older children? You would use a five year old to betray her own family; to speak of things she knows nothing about! When you couldn't prove anything, you twisted everything I said. How come you never asked me the circumstances of my divorce, or looked at the previous court history? How come you never asked my children about their father's abuse? Didn't I keep telling you he's a child beater? Why didn't you ask them why they kept screaming for their father to tell the truth? Why didn't you ask them while you and the police were taking them away, taking them from their mother. The children screamed for me over and over, and for their father to tell the truth? Why hasn't anyone heard anything my family has been telling you? Now you dehumanize what has occurred because I'm just a guilty file!"

There was a long uneasy silence. I waited determinedly.

"Maybe your case is that one in a thousand who's not guilty," she said after emitting a sigh of resignation. "Perhaps I made a wrong decision, but I really thought Mr. Bissett was right."

"No, Mrs. Ackerman. You mean he was White. And I was a woman of color, a Black woman running around with a Black man so I had to be wild and crazy."

"That's not true." Mrs. Ackerman stated defensively. "I though he was such a nice man and really cared about his kids. When your mom said what she said, I concluded that you were dangerous."

"Did you ever stop to consider that my mom wanted me to stay with Chuck no matter what he did to the kids just because he is White?"

"No, I didn't." She answered.

"But you never saw fit to ask me about Chuck, or my mom, or Dr. Walters. Did you? You just listened to Mr. Bissett, assumed that I was guilty and then contrived the evidence to prove me guilty. And that's what you presented to the court, and that's why they took my children!"

"I don't know what to say to you except that I was doing my job." She stated before pausing again. "We've had a nice talk, but I've got to go now. Hope things go better for you." She said and then rang off.

A short time later I moved into a partly furnished apartment near the University of Southern California that placed me outside of the jurisdiction of Mrs. Ackerman.

My workday started at about dawn when I opened the nursery school. By three or four in the afternoon, reflections upon my children would drive me to tears. I took a hot bath to relax my nerves and then ate dinner at a nearby restaurant. The gravity of my frustrations would drive me to cry myself to sleep.

One afternoon after one of my crying jags, I ran a tub of hot water. I became so relaxed in the water that I fell asleep. I don't know how long I slept but the bath water had turned cold and the soap had caked on my skin. As I got out of the tub and reran the water, the anemic light in the bathroom reminded me that I needed to replace the sixty with at least a hundred watt bulb. The re-bath brought only the gloomy realization that all of my bonds of belonging had been severed. Dad was gone and most likely dead. Mom's betrayal remained as incomprehensible to me as it would always remain unforgivable.

My sister, Gracie distanced herself from me as she could ill afford to take on my pain when she could barely endure her own. Chuck was a child beater and had to go. The lives of my children have now been consigned to the auspices of the state where my expressions of concern and love must be filtered through bureaucratic sieves. I felt as though my sense of being was floating hopelessly in a netherworld devoid of purpose or aim. Gradually, I slid myself deeper into the bath water to soften the hardened soap. It occurred to me that all I needed to do was to submerge my face below the water and hold it there long enough for me to transition into the promised realm of tranquility. The life confronting me no longer held any meaning for me. Why not suicide?

My life, such as it was, resided in my children and they were alive. It may have been vanity on my part, but I had to believe that they needed me. Hope was all that I had left. Reason intervened and offered that it was my children who were imprisoned with people who they neither knew nor liked, but making the best of it. I was free. Yes the reality of my children being locked behind a barbed wired facility, institutionalized and alone in their fragile lives had crushed my very being. How arrogant it was of me to indulge my self pity without factoring in their fears for the future. Suicide would be cowardice on my part. It would only confirm to them that life had no value. I could not leave my children a heritage like that. I would not leave my children. I vowed that I would succeed or fail on my own, but would concede to nothing that would cause them harm. Even if I could do nothing for my children, I became determined at least they would always know that I loved them and cared, I cared enough to stay and face whatever would come. They *would* know me, ..... someday.

I realized that I needed a stabilizing force in my life or run the risk of unwittingly yielding to another errant whim of self destruction. On Sunday, I began frequenting St. Marks Lutheran Church. It was a very large church with so small of a congregation that it appeared empty. Its minister was a stocky man of Japanese descent whose sermons mainly revolved around the issue of racial equality. Despite the cavernous environment of the church, the sermons inspired me with the will to keep going.

I received a letter informing me of my new probation officer. Her name was Ms. Hale. I called her on the telephone and asked if she planned to see my daughters before Christmas. When she said she would, I told her that I was having car trouble and asked if I could go with her. I was elated when she promised to call me to arrange the trip.

Christmas was approaching and I would be all alone. I had heard nothing from Ms. Hale and had no money to visit the children at the various foster homes. Wilbur had made plans to celebrate the holiday with Christine and his kids. Christmas Eve found me wandering inexplicably into the church.

"I've come to ask of you an act of faith." I said humbly and tearfully to Reverend Yamasuki. "I have six children who won't be with me this Christmas. All I have now is the Lord. I don't expect you to fully understand and I can't explain it to you. But could you let me have a branch off the bottom of your tree?"

He said nothing as he reached in a drawer and pulled out a hacksaw. He left his office and returned with a branch.

"May God keep you in your anguish." He said in a soft, reassuring voice. "It's perfectly all right."

"Thank you. And may God bless you for your kindness."

At midnight I tendered an act of faith to God and commended myself to His divine wisdom. I placed the branch on the living room coffee table and a saucer on top of it. In its center I stood a small lighted candle. Tears, warm and consoling, rolled down my face as I watched the candle burn itself into a puddle of wax. And then I went to sleep. Most of that Christmas was spent alternating between crying and sleeping. But I trusted in the budding knowledge in my soul that God would somehow work out a solution that would provide all of us a life.

During that Christmas week, I composed a three-page letter to the judge apprising him of my circumstances and informing him that I had been stood up by the probation officer. I also complained that the foster parents in Manhattan Beach would not permit me to visit on Sundays. They spent the entire day in church and did not want their routine disrupted. They also had a wild, red-haired monkey; name Rufuss who had the run of the house, a danger to my small children. He was agile, very powerful and jumped on everything and anyone whenever the mood struck him. During my visits, it would climb all over me and pull my hair. The girl's foster mother would eventually coax it onto the dining room table where she would gently rub its belly and genitals to their mutual delight. The now quieted monkey would go inside his huge cage that hung from the ceiling in the middle of the living room. But in a short while it would rock the cage violently while rendering the air with piercing screams. And now I was forced to sit and watch as my small sweet children are held in this dangerous place, as the observer who could not have any say. I feared all visitations would cease if I dare step out of line.

I mailed the letter and hoped for the best.

My job at the Jack and Jill Nursery School afforded me the opportunity to bestow upon the children of others, the love that I yearned to give my own. About twenty rambunctious kids were placed in the charge of myself and Margot, a very affable and capable French woman. When I left the school five months later, I could lay claim to bringing about remarkable transformations in two of the school's most difficult children.

I catalogued him in my mind as Little Bully Boy. He had fiery red hair and the temperament to match. He refused to wait his turn for anything and would start a fight at the slightest disagreement. At least once a day, he would challenge some unsuspecting kid over a toy that he wanted to play with or for reasons known only to himself. I would "bench" him for his infractions. He would gnash his teeth and leap form the bench to try to get past me while I watched the other children play. Each time that he stood up, I would clutch him by the shoulder with just enough pressure to show him that I was the stronger of the two. And then I would stare straight in his eyes and sternly say: "You will sit here until your time out is up and not before." My tone would convey to him that I had both the determination and authority to insure that he served his time on the bench. Sometimes he would try to fight me. As much as I wanted to slap the hell out of the little cretin, I knew that we were engaged in a test of wills and that I could win only by overcoming his. When his time was up, I would not allow him to rejoin the other kids until he apologized for his actions and received their permission to rejoin them. They would always allow him back, but the air would be tenuous at best. For about three months, Little Bully Boy and I engaged in our ritual of confrontation on almost a daily basis. And then came the moment of truth.

It was a rainy day. The children had to play with their toys indoors. Little Bully Boy had not been benched yet, but the day was still young. He was on all fours playing with the other boys when he spotted one of the girls take one of his favorite toys from a bench. He eyed her with concern from the corner of his eye while continuing to play.

"Hey, that's mine." He shouted threateningly to the girl as she started to walk away with the toy.

The hapless little girl was torn between her desire to play with a toy car that belonged to a fiercely violent boy who was determined to have it no way but his own or to return the toy to the bench.

"I'm sorry." She said with a sigh of resignation. "I'll put it back."

Little Bully boy did not see me as I moved closer to the scene to prevent the little girl from getting hurt and yet not influence his reaction to her obvious breach of his rights as owner of the toy. His usual response to such breaches was to snatch the toy from the offender's hand, push him or her to the floor and close out the issue with flailing fists. So the fact that he paused long enough to consider another option was, for me, an indication that I was making progress. To my surprise, his expression softened.

"You can play with it, but don't forget to give it back." He said sternly and then returned to play with the boys. I never had to bench him after that. He also began to realize the rewards for fostering an atmosphere of harmony far exceeded what he had derived from generating discord and ill will. Whatever victory that may have been claimed was not mine alone. I had only helped a five year old kid tap into that area of his gestalt from which he can explore the possibilities of his own humanity. It was a victory for him and all who will encounter him through life.

The other was a pretty girl whose mother dressed her in frilly lace dresses and adorned her with Shirley Temple curls and ribbons. She was only five but well into establishing a reputation as a tease and coquette. Her mother doted on her to the extent that she seemed destined for life as an object for exhibition. She obstinately refused to participate in any activity where there existed the least possibility of her getting dirty. To me, she was Little Miss Prissy Tease.

One of the routines that I initiated was to allow one of the children to dry the plastic dishes after lunch. It was against the rules for me to do this, but it provided me a practical opportunity to teach multiplication. What I had not anticipated was that the children saw it as a chance for informal therapy sessions. They unburdened themselves of everything to me regarding their worst fears and loftiest hopes. I learned how they felt about their siblings and parents as well as what they wanted for Christmas. I never asked or coaxed them to tell me anything. They trusted me because they sensed that I respected them as kids rather than expected them to behave as pint sized adults. My dish drying project must have been more effective than I thought, because the last person that I expected to volunteer, one day proved my most enthusiastic advocate.

I was astounded when Little Miss Prissy Tease nudged her way to my side and offered to help. Since I had promised the job to one of the other kids, I assured her that she could help the next day. As fate would have it, the owner of the school showed up while we were doing the dishes. I could only watch aghast as the owner yanked Little Miss Prissy Tease out of the kitchen.

"Let go of me. I wanna do the dishes. Let go of me." Miss Tease screamed.

"No you're not. You're going to sit on the bench," the owner said in a domineering manner while yanking the writhing screaming child all the way to a bench in the next room.

"But it's my turn to do the dishes," Miss Tease yelled as she punched the woman with her small fists and kicked her ankles. "I want to do the dishes."

It was the first time that Little Miss Tease cared nothing about her frilly clothes and Shirley Temple curls. She was forthright and direct about what she wanted instead of portraying the role of a seductress. And she was willing to fight tooth and nail for it. I was proud of her.

I felt sorry for her though. But there was nothing I could do. I told the owner that I had let her help me with the dishes primarily because the kids enjoyed the one-on-one camaraderie. The owner informed me that if an inspector had come by, she would have lost her license. She could not allow me to do that again. This was a side of the owner that I had not seen. She had one of those super sweet smiles that reminded me of guess who—Mr. Bissett. She had been a teacher at a boy's military school and commanded total obedience at once. She could very easily have told the child why she couldn't help with the dishes and calmed her down without yanking her like she did. She could have offered her an alternative activity. Her handling of Little Miss Prissy Tease was precisely what I meant about the difference between respecting kids as kids rather than treating them as pint sized adults. I knew that it was time for me to begin looking for another job.

I had been able to apply my understanding of the philosophy of gestalt in children in an environment where I could be objective about my subjects. I began to peer beyond their well scrubbed faces and differentiate between the personal that had been sculpted to conform to the image of others and the quintessential beauty of the gestalt that often lay dormant within them. I felt proud that they were comfortable enough to confide in a total stranger those vital inner thoughts and feelings that they could not express to those charged with the responsibility of raising them. I came to believe that what we in our self serving, self righteous, vanity driven society regard as discipline is little more than child abuse. In our efforts to develop our concept of the perfect child, we inadvertently destroy the essence of that child's purpose for being.

Raising children is almost akin to managing a flask of nitroglycerine. When we seek to impose our will upon them and allow abstinence and ignorance to control our actions, they react by becoming volatile, unstable, and unpredictable. And we have no one to blame but ourselves for the consequences. When well-intending parents attempt to assault the hell out of their children, they run the very real risk of driving the spirit of Christ from them. The gestalt of child transcends the wishes of parents and even the perceived necessities of the society. It is a part of that which is eternal and universal. It is an endowment from God and should be nurtured as such. It is an incontrovertible truth: if we do right by our children, they will do right by that which God has bestowed upon them. Ultimately, that will be a blessing for us all.

Mr. Bissett called me at work with the urgent message that my mother has suffered a heart attack, and had been rushed to St. Joseph's Hospital in Burbank. I was quite apprehensive about seeing mom after the things she had said. After work, I located Wilbur on his trash route and asked him to meet me at Howard's house that evening.

"My mom's had a heart attack and I can't bring myself to go see her." I told him as I sat on a vanity bench while he sat at the edge of the bed across from me. "She said all those mean things to the court. I feel as if I go to see her, it'll be like betraying my own children."

"You mean that sweet old lady had a heart attack?" He asked with genuine affection and concern. I had not told him that she regarded him as a Black devil and that he had been a major issue in my losing the children. He only knew that she treated him with respect when we visited her house for breakfast.

"You don't understand how I feel. I could have forgiven her anything except those things she said. But this is too serious to let go of." I insisted.

"No sweetie. You don't understand." Wilbur said firmly. "She's your mother. She gave you life. She could have smothered you or buried you somewhere and had nothing more to do with you. But she didn't. No matter how hard it was for her, she raised you. She don't owe you a Goddamn thing. You owe her your life. You're supposed to be a good daughter and be at her side in her sickness." He concluded and then got up and went to the bathroom. When he returned, I clung to him tightly as I cried.

"Come on sweetie, you know what you gotta do." Wilbur said compassionately. "She's your mom."

"I don't now if I can do this."

"You're a big girl now. You know how to get on the freeway and go see her."

"Please stay with me a little while until I get myself together." I asked plaintively.

I listened to Wilbur pensively as he reiterated his feelings about my mother. His forthrightness and caring manner instilled the courage in me to commit myself to make the drive to see her. I felt that since God had forgiven me and inspired in me a will to press forward, how could I be so arrogant as to not forgive my mother in her worst hours? It was about ten when I overcame my fear of driving the freeway at night and began the trip to Burbank.

I took an elevator to the intensive care unit. The room was dim except for the night light over her bed. A nurse led me to her. I took her hand in mine as I fought back the tears.

"Hi mom, it's me Miki."

Slowly she turned her head and I kissed her on the forehead. I love you mom. I want you to get well." I whispered softly.

"Oh Miki. I now know why there is so much hate in our family." She lamented wearily.

"Mom, forget about all that. I'm okay and so are the kids. Don't worry about anything. I want you to just get well."

"Miki, I know what I did wrong." She stated, fighting for whatever strength she could muster.

"It's not important now. Everything is going to be alright. You just take it easy and get well." I said while patting her hand to reassure her.

The hall nurse was alerted by the monitor that Mom was over-exerting herself. She ordered me to leave. I stopped off at the chapel and sat for awhile in quiet meditation. I felt as though my act of faith was revealing itself. Through mom, God had reaffirmed that He was honoring my cause. I felt a renewed courage not to equivocate in my contentions with the court. To the depths of my soul, I now knew that God had deemed that I had been right all along. I was no longer afraid or no longer cared what the probation officers thought or did.

Three days later, I visited Mom again. She had been transferred to a semi-private room. The blue light that streamed in from the outside of the building was the only light in the room. I woke her with a greeting and a kiss. She opened her eyes and looked about me excitedly.

"What's that you got?" She asked excitedly.

"Nothing mom, just my purse."

"No. I don't want your money." She said pushing me away irritably.

"I don't have any money."

"Yes you do, and I don't want your money." She insisted as she forced herself to sit up to see if I had anything in my hand. "Get away. Take your money with you. I don't want it"

A nurse hurried into the room. As she tried to settle Mom down, she asked me to leave. Mom's behavior gave rise to thoughts of Judas and his returning the silver to the priests before hanging himself. At the chapel I told God that I had done the best I could, but I would no longer visit mom at the hospital. It was not my intention to hurt her, and my visits were not having the effect that I thought they would. I asked God to forgive her lack of understanding and to take care of her.

She had two more heart attacks. She then ordered the doctors to take her off all of the intravenous tubes so that she could fast before meeting her Maker. My stepfather would not countermand her orders. Three weeks later Arcelio came by the house to tell me that mom had died. He had sold the house and furniture and received the insurance money. He was returning to his native Puerto Rico to live and thought that I just might want to see where my mother was buried. I kneeled beside her plaque and glided my hand across her name. And then the tears began to flow. "No matter what happened, Mom. I love you."

# CHAPTER THIRTEEN

# Just Another File

It was about eleven in the evening and I was asleep when I heard an insistent knock at the door. In this neighborhood, any disturbance at that time of night was cause for alarm. If I did not answer, an intruder would think that no one was home and break in. If I answered, he would reason that only a woman was home and focus his intent on more than just a mere burglary. I left the chain on the door engaged while I opened the door enough to see a young white man wearing what appeared to be some sort of military cap.

"Western Union," the young man responded to the face peering at him through the crack. "I have a telegram for Mrs. Elizabeth Bissett."

Fearing the worst for my children, I flung open the door and hurriedly signed for the letter. It was from the probation office, instructing me to call them to set up an appointment. The next morning we arranged to meet the afternoon of the next day.

The probation office was located near the intersection of Vermont and Washington. It was a maze of cubicles with no doors, except for the supervisor's office where I was ushered in by Mrs. Yudkoff.

"Please have a seat, Mrs. Bissett. Ms. Hale is still busy with a client. She will join us shortly." She said as she directed me to a chair next to her desk as she sat behind it. "In the meantime, I'd like to say that the reports have come back on your children. And you have some very wonderful children," She said enthusiastically.

"Thank you," I responded graciously. Her platitudes did not impress me one bit. I was suppressing my anger until I had Ms. Hale in my sights. She greeted me impassively when she joined us. I sensed that she knew that I was vexed with her and sat away from me as Mrs. Yudkoff proceeded to make her point.

"I read your file and compared it to the reports on the children. I had to reread your file twice and still could not believe that anyone could be the mother in this file and have the kind of children in the reports."

"What the hell do you care about my children or me?" I roared as I leaned toward her. "We're just a Goddamn file to you! But they're my children to me and I don't give a good Goddamn about your files or reports."

The force of my anger caught her totally by surprise. She tried not to show fear as she leaned back in her chair to increase the distance between us.

"Where the hell do you get the nerve to tell me about my children? And yet you leave me sitting when I ask for help to visit them. What the hell do you care if my children are worrying if their mother has disappeared off the face of the earth! What the hell kind of people are you anyway?" I was still seething to the point where I practically came out of my chair. I had been nice to Mrs. Ackerman. What had that gotten me? No longer did I care what these people thought about me.

"You've got to understand," Mrs. Yudkoff pleaded. "Ms. Hale has been in the hospital with pneumonia and has been back to work only a few days. Her caseload has been on hold."

"You mean to tell me that you have all those P.O.'s out there and you couldn't split her caseload so each of them could send out postcards telling us that she was ill? I even see a mimeograph out there. How much trouble could it be to run off a bunch of notices and mail them out? If I were on a job and couldn't think of something as simple as that, I'd be fired."

The dam gates had been opened and I was raving in torrents. The ladies stared at me in shock.

"And I'm the one who's crazy!" I ranted. "Remember?" Isn't that what the file says? That I'm possessed by demons and out of control?"

"You're absolutely right. We should have done something as simple as that. Sometimes we get so involved with our work that we don't see the pain we create for others. You are marvelous, Mrs. Bissett. I can now see why you have such wonderful children. Let's see where we go from here. Ms. Hale went out to Manhattan Beach. It's no place for your children to be. They have no control over that wild animal, the monkey called Rufusss. It tore her stockings to shreds and almost bit her. But we have to re maneuver the children over time. We're going to see if there's an opening at the Episcopal Children's Home and move Julie over there when school's over to be with her brothers. We'll have to try to locate another home willing to take three children. We'll try not to split them up too much. In the meantime, I can assure you that the next time Ms. Hale goes to visit your kids, she'll let you know and you can go with her."

Ms. Hale nodded in confirmation as Mrs. Yudkoff tried to assure me that everything was on track.

"We'll try to do the best we can under the circumstances. Someone made a mistake in your case. We'll have to work this out over time."

"Well, why don't you just write that in your file that the state made a mistake and give me back my children? I asked testily. "That seems simple enough to me."

"That is not possible right now. You'll have to show that you can provide certain stability for these children," Mrs. Yudkoff concluded sounding every bit the Goddamn bureaucrat.

"The state makes a mistake, but I have to bear the burden of proof. Is that your drift?" She looked at me compassionately, but offered no answer. I didn't need an answer. The state never admits to its mistakes.

"And another thing," I began emphatically. "Don't you think for one minute that I'm going to another psychiatrist in order to get my children back. I don't trust them any more than I trust you."

"I understand, Mrs. Bissett. Don't worry about that. We don't see you as needing therapy," Ms. Hale stated assuredly.

At least I could find consolation in feeling that I might have a damn sight better relationship with Ms. Hale and Mrs. Yudkoff than I had with Mrs. Ackerman. On that basis, I shook hands with the ladies and then left.

Some time later, I learned that some of my complaints resulted in changes in department policy. Information regarding the visitation policies at Mc Claren Hall were distributed to all parents. And parents were notified when their probation officers were to be away for any extended period of time.

Ms. Hale and I spent a few hours visiting Julie, Victoria, and Anita in Manhattan Beach. The monkey remained noisily and restlessly in his cage. I suspected that Ms. Hale wanted a first hand look at the interaction between me and the kids. It was a very pleasant visit.

For me, the meeting at the probation office was another affirmation of my act of the faith. I was not alone in my quest to bring my family together. With all the swearing that I did, they never responded. It also occurred to me that St. Mark's church did not go unrewarded for its part in helping me with my act of faith. Within two months after the minister gave me the branch from its Christmas tree he had assembled a choir and a large enough congregation to fill his cavernous hall. The church, with its gothic style that I much more preferred, was torn down and replaced by a structure of contemporary design that was part of the nearby Hoover Project.

I began dropping by the Neighborhood Adult Participation Program or NAPP to check for job possibilities. One day the director informed me that he was recruiting for a new government program that was being launched to prepare preschool aged children for the education process. It was called Project Head Start. Since I had preschool work experience and had taken child psychology courses in junior college, he referred me to one of the projects that was slated to commence in a few weeks.

I looked forward with joy to working in Project Head Start. My employer was the Federation of Nursery Schools and Settlements. I was assigned to the site at the Unitarian Church located at 8ᵗʰ and Vermont. There were two classrooms to accommodate twenty-four kids. Each class had a head teacher, an assistant teacher and a teacher's aide. As a teacher's aide, I was also considered a community aid which meant that I divided my time between soliciting materials so that the children would have things to do, and recruiting children for the program. Soliciting was vital because the government has not released money for supplies, food for the kids or wages. In the mornings we tended our classes. Many of our afternoons were spent listening to pep talks from various officials who extolled the noble purpose of our mission.

All of us were broke and desperate while waiting for the government to release the funds. We took up collections for gasoline so that we could carpool. We kidded each other as to which of the nearby prostitution strolls offered the best financial remedy for our situation. Even though I felt guilty about it, I had little choice but to make the rounds of my co-workers to get a meal. Libby Smith, the assistant teacher of my group, took pity on me and virtually adopted me as one of her family. Most of Libby's friends were inordinately class conscious to the point that she was always pressed to defend her friendship with me.

I thought it was for purposes of morale that the Head Start administrators took us to the theatre to see a film "A Thousand Clowns." But on the same bill was a promotional film for the Head Start Project. About halfway through the film, I heard myself yell out into the crowded theatre.

"There I am!"

There I was, making my silver screen debut standing in the doorway of my Santa Monica house with Sarrah cuddled tightly in my arms, and the kids running around me. I wasn't on very long, but it buoyed my sagging spirits considerably. Mrs. Rose had been a friend to the limit of what she could do. Had she been there I would have hugged her.

I did not see much of Wilbur after I left the trash company. He took a job with another company after Lloyd's disappearance and his wife closed down the business. From time to time I visited him on his route in the mornings before I went into work. It had been a very rough time for me. But a bit of diversion would have made the time easier. I would not see him for weeks and sometimes even months at a time. When I did, we usually spent the evening playing cards with Howard and Alfred or went bar hopping in Watts. It was always about what he wanted to do. We never went to the movies or spent intimate time doing nothing but enjoying each other's company. Given the fact that he was committed to two families and undoubtedly had other relationships blooming, I more or less had to wait my turn. It was a Saturday night about eleven not long after I had started working for Head Start when he made one of his unannounced visits.

"Come on sweetie. Get dressed and let's run the streets," He commanded playfully, completely ignoring the fact that I had been fast asleep.

"Wilbur," I said solemnly as he followed me into my bedroom. "I get the feeling that I'm just a puppet that you play with whenever you feel like it and then throw me in the corner until the next time."

"Well, if you don't like the corner, then get out of the corner," he stated saltily.

"I have to go out to see the children tomorrow so I can't run the street tonight," I said wearily. It wasn't true, but Wilbur had pricked my feelings to the core. I wasn't about to go anywhere with him. "I see," I said knowingly to myself and went back to sleep.

As unsettled as I was by Wilbur's presumption that I was available to him on demand, it was my ex-husband's proposal to regain control of the kids that so agitated me that I dared not trust myself in the classroom. As desperately as I wanted my children back, I was left horrified when he called to inform me that he planned to steal them from the state. Chuck allowed his therapist, of all people, to implant this absurd notion in his mind and then he expected me to help him carry it out. I had to put a stop to this foolishness. Chuck would most likely dismiss my anger as the ranting of a madwoman and pursue this lunacy for the sheer spite of it. Fortunately, I had the telephone number of his therapist who I only knew as Mr. Porter. I was hardly in the mood for formalities when he answered.

"Chuck is talking some weird shit about kidnapping the children," I fumed. "Are you aware of that?"

"Well, he feels that the state is not taking care of the children right and he wants to do something about it," Mr. Porter began somewhat defensively. I imagined that he resented my calling him. "So I told him what I had to do to get my daughter. If you care about your children, you'll do whatever it takes to get them back."

"I don't get what you mean, Mr. Porter. What are you getting at?"

"It's very simple, Mrs. Bissett. If you don't like what's happening, then only you can do something about it," he stated emphatically.

"What do you mean by 'something'?"

"If you don't do something, the state won't think you're serious."

"Are you saying that if I don't like what the state is doing, then I should kidnap my kids and they'll give them back to me because I'm serious? Is that the advice you're giving Chuck?"

"If that's what it takes, "He responded matter-of-factly.

"They already think that I'm crazy. Now you want them to tag us both as nuts. Do you really think that they will give either of us the kids after a stunt like that! It's a good thing I talked him out of it."

"Why did you do that?"

"Because he'll go to jail when he gets caught," I stated emphatically. "I won't be a party to this and I told him so," I slammed down the phone.

Unlike Chuck, I understood the differences between Mr. Porter's circumstances and mine. He could confidently defend his actions through lawyers and his status of being a white professional male.

Whereas, I was an Indo-Rican Woman of color. I had only my hopes and faith to sustain me. And even they came at a premium.

Libby was seated in the room with me and heard my side of the conversation with Mr. Porter. She now realized what I was up against. She had degrees in computer science, library science, teaching, and was studying for anther degree in abnormal psychology. But what she heard between me and Mr. Porter astonished her. Whatever reservations she might have had were quelled.

"I don't know where Chuck finds therapists that are crazier than he is. They all have licenses to fuck up people's lives with a lot of self righteous, self serving presumptions about the human condition," I spouted angrily. The unsettled look on Libby's face calmed me down and I spoke to her somberly. "You know, Libby, Chuck is a sick man and can't help himself, but he was my husband and I have no interest in hurting him. This jerk will get Chuck thrown in jail and it'll be Chuck who'll lose his security clearance and really ruin his life. I know it sounds strange after all he's done. But all I want is my freedom from him. But he's vulnerable to any suggestion from any person in authority."

Libby nodded as though she understood. But her mind was still reeling from my conversation with Mr. Porter. In the rarified atmosphere of intellectual privilege and status that she retreated to after work, situations such as mine were discreetly swallowed by its rigidly managed system and then regurgitated and spat out beyond the China Wall that protected their ordered lives from those irritants that induced desperation and expletives. What I appreciated most about Libby was her willingness to place tolerance before judgment.

My other dear friend at Head Start was Maxine Waters. She was an assistant teacher in the other class. Tough, resilient and deeply concerned about the fate of her community, I was very happy for her when she was eventually elected to Congress. Like Libby, she spent some time with my kids and quickly noticed how down-to-earth and unpretentious they were. She shook her head in disbelief that the state had taken the children from me. Her friendship and ongoing support towards me and my children was without reservation; and I was grateful for her vote of confidence.

Two conflicting philosophies regarding the management of the children began to take form in our class. On one side of the issue, there were those including the primary teacher, who believed that socialization was the most important objective for these "deprived" children to achieve. Others, including Libby and me believed that learning through play should be the primary emphasis. I had thought that learning was what Head Start was all about. Some of the teachers seemed content to put out the toys and games each day and then monitor the kid's activities from what they seemingly deemed a sacred part of the room. From there they could avoid having any personal contact with the children while insuring maximum exposure for condescending, supercilious smiles that I became convinced were government issued.

Having now worked with children who were both, privileged and deprived, black and white, I was now convinced that there were virtually no essential differences between them. Children of the privileged who were deprived of love and attention responded no differently than their economically deprived counterparts. The children responded exceedingly well to me and Libby simply because we respected their humanity and made them feel comfortable about simply being kids. We would have no more force fed their minds than we would force fed their bodied. But everything they did was accompanied by an opportunity to learn something new. In order to avoid confrontations with the head teacher, we repetitiously taught them counting, colors and shapes during trips to the bathroom. It was not uncommon for me to hear a kid counting his steps out loud as he made his way to the bathroom or to pick out a toy and then watch him beam from ear to ear when he realized that he could count. Our teacher would put out a lump of clay on a table for the children to play with. To the children, the lump of clay was a pile of feces that they would have nothing to do with. I quietly began making things like cars, railroad tracks, bicycles out of the clay and then made up stories about the things. The children loved it. Some of them began making up their own stories about the houses, trees and animals that were formed out of clay and their own budding imaginations without the slightest urging from me. By the end of the semester, the children were setting up tables and chairs without being told; dolls were being serenaded with lullabies instead of being spanked and pummeled for imagined offenses; and paint or paper began to reveal studied efforts toward creativity rather than disjointed streaks and splotches of rage and frustration. A group of federal administrators from Washington visited our site and were very impressed with our class, as were the parents of the children whose works were placed on exhibition in the class. For me, teaching by gestalt was the key to education.

To those addicted to authority and control, teaching by gestalt was an intolerable anathema. The idea that three and four year old children should have a voice in the learning process was beyond the comprehension of many of the teachers. Since Libby had education degrees, she was immune to their backroom machinations. I wasn't. At first, a campaign quietly began to have me dismissed. And then it became more vocal as they sought the termination of all assistants and aides without certification.

The dawning of my fate with Head Start occurred during one of our mass pep talks. A black man who unashamedly exuded the aura of that class and academic relics that I had begun to hold in contempt approached the podium and launched into a speech that lavished the certificated teachers with praise and his unflinching support while accusing those of us without certificates of incompetence and ignorance in matters pertaining to child development. I was not sure as to whether it was his arrogance, my anger, or the passion for justice instilled in me by my father that drove me to my feet. It was most certainly not the desire to keep my job.

"Are you trying to tell all of us black women here, that we don't know how to raise children?" I fumed. The women about me squirmed in their chairs and grumbled uncomfortably. Evidently, the conflict between certificated and un-certificated staff had become widespread and the administrators needed to nip it in the bud by trotting out a token black man to put us women of color in our place.

"These people are professionals and you need to learn from them and follow their direction," he responded defensively.

"You sir, are an Uncle Tom," I stated fearlessly. "Instead of the head teachers coming to us, at the grassroots, to determine what we think is important to teach these kids, you try to treat us like we don't have a brain in our head just because we don't have degrees. We want these kids to learn and not just play."

From behind me, I heard both words of support and encouragement along with utterances of reprove and admonishment about my retaining my job. But I had come too far to back away. Someone needed to speak the truth.

"You sir, need to go home and mind your business," I declared and sat down. Realizing that he had tapped into a spring of hostility, the man yielded to a more congenial speaker.

As a result of Project Head Start, many colleges began developing early childhood development curricula in order to provide degrees and certificates for those seeking employment in child care programs. I enrolled in one such class with the intent of gaining certification. Its course of study was totally opposite of what I advocated. It emphasized order and structure and virtually ignored providing the freedom that children needed to grow properly. We were being taught to warehouse children just as the conventional education system did. I was not about to abandon my belief in teaching by gestalt to accommodate a program that treated children as though they were some exotic life form that needed to be herded through each activity like goats. The course was far from difficult. In fact, it seemed childishly easy, but it turned me off. On the finals day of class, the teacher was staring directly at me when she explained to the class that there was perhaps one person in a million who could succeed in a program that allowed freedom without limits. What she did not tell the class was that I was that one person in a million who had somehow managed to fail her course.

I took the failure pretty much in stride, chalking it up as the consequence of my subconscious revolt against a system that seemed blissfully intent on emaciating the soul of its children. I could take heart in the belief that, instead of being a failure in the area of child development, I was simply a martyr. A few months later, I was also out of a job, owing my unemployment to a conveniently contrived cutback in staff by the feds.

My hopes for Head Start and the agenda of the government were diametrically opposed. I realized that it was presumptuous of me to indulge in such a conclusion. But it was the hope of the community that if the program got off the ground, it would be expanded to include more and more children. In any endeavor, good intentions have to be backed by money and the government had the money. Ultimately, it is a matter of commitment and priorities. A nation can quite easily succumb to the demands of power, greed and racism to the detriment of its very own future. To the community, Head Start could provide stable jobs and pride that could yield dividends in the elusive quest for peace and harmony.

The poor had neither jobs nor money. Those few blacks or Latinos who somehow manage to break through the racial barrier gather their well earned resources and plunge headlong into the mainstream, leaving in their wake those pseudo-intellectual pontifications that serve the interest of none but themselves and white America. Programs that valued the input and participation of those regarded as social discards were essential to the growth and self esteem of the community. The system seems to expect its social outcasts to find happiness and contentment working for substandard wages and living under abominable conditions. And when their legitimate rage explodes in rioting and looting, they are reviled as criminals and malcontents.

Head Start had confirmed itself to me as yet another project of seduction. The head teachers were mostly white and middle class; their authority bestowed upon them by virtue of degrees that insured that they knew absolutely nothing about the victims of deprivation and oppression, and that they will toil in constant terror that their ignorance will eventually be exposed by those who did. Because we were browbeaten into believing that the government cared about our needs and future, the community's aspirations would be sublimely sabotaged for the sake of hanging onto jobs.

It was inconceivable to me that such a vital program could be cut back after only four months. No manner of protest by the community changed anything. Like much of America's attempt to validate its own creeds, Head Start was only a token pinprick in the plight of the poor.

Activism without money was out of the question. Nor could I afford crucifixion at a time when the children needed me and whatever energy I could offer them. I located a job as an employment solicitor in my predominately black community. There were very few jobs available for them, and therefore no commissions for me. I left. There was one consolation, however. Mrs. Yudkoff proved true to her word. When school ended for the summer, Julie was moved to ECH with her two older brothers.

# CHAPTER FOURTEEN

# *In My Heart*

It became readily apparent to me that it was to my best advantage to establish priorities in managing the various crises rather than lug them around on my back, accomplishing nothing more than a meaningless test of strength. There was nothing more I could do about my children. At least they were no longer sharing a house with an unpredictable simian monkey. Rodrick, Nathan and Julie were at ECH. Victoria and Anita had settled in with a family in Long Beach while the baby, Sarrah, still remained with the family in Baldwin Park. They were hardly where I wanted them to be, but that was the best that could be done for the moment. Through my faith, I believed that everything will turn out alright, which was not to say that things will turn out the way I hope. At least they were being fed, clothed, and cared for. They were the loves of my life, but I could no longer permit myself to be absorbed with their welfare at the expense of my own. I came to a heart wrenching decision. I called Ms. Hale to ask if we could go out to ECH so that I could talk to the kids. W agreed to meet the following afternoon.

"What's the matter?" Ms. Hale asked, her face reflecting genuine concern as we settled into her office.

"You know that I'm unemployed," I began fighting to control both my tears and despair. "I can't pull myself together like this—trying to find a job and then running all over the county to visit with my kids. I have no money. And then when something comes up, everyone looks to me to deal with it. I'm trapped in a state of affairs that for the moment seems hopeless. I've got to pull it together. But you're all asking too much from me and I just don't have it to give. I need to be left alone. I am tired."

"Oh, I see. How can I help you?"

"I need to tell the kids that I won't be able to visit them for awhile. I don't have the courage to face them alone. So I wonder if you'll go with me."

"I understand. Of course, let's go."

Rodrick and Nathan listened solemnly and sat very still and quiet as their eyes bewilderedly rummaged about me in a hopeless search for understanding. Julie screamed and stomped about the room hysterically. I knew that there was no way that I could inform the children of my decision without them feeling betrayed. My passionate promises to have them with me after I found a job, was a ray of hope too dim for them to perceive in the uncertain darkness that I had cast over them. We were all sullen and depressed when I left. I had spent months crying and alternating between fits of rage and desperation. But the realities of the moment would not yield to what I most desired in the entire world. I would have to find content within myself; nestling them firmly in my heart as I callously drove them out of my head.

The Neighborhood Adult Participation Program found me a job that provided me my first foray into the allegedly rough and tumble world of politics. I was hired as a typist, phone canvasser, and office gofer for a candidate for the California State Assembly. Unfortunately, he was a Republican in a district that was so overwhelmingly Democratic that I seriously doubted that he could garner more than a handful of votes outside of his immediate family. He was an elderly, cordial gentleman who had remained doggedly loyal to the party that had freed the slaves while their descendents had hitched their hopes to the party of the New Deal. The Republican Party contributed to his campaign which was dull and uninspiring from beginning to end. His lone platform for election was to rid his district of the prostitution that plagued the neighborhood of an insurance company that was his primary supporter. Had he accomplished the feats of getting elected and banishing prostitution, he may well have so astonished the Republican Party as to find himself on the fast track to Congress. At the close of business on Election Day, I was once again out of a job.

I was hoping that the probation office would not contact me until after I had steady work. To my dismay, it was about a week into my job at the campaign headquarters that a telegram arrived at my apartment instructing me to call Mrs. Yudkoff as soon as possible.

"Miki, Julie ran away from ECH." She informed me straight away. "We found her on the railroad tracks headed for Los Angeles. Miki, if you don't come and get her, we'll have to leave her permanently in Juvenile Hall. Julie is so intelligent and such a wonderful child. It'll ruin her life. Please, why don't you come and get her?" Mrs. Yudkoff concluded plaintively.

"But I can't afford to keep her." I offered despairingly. "I'm only making forty dollars a week. And that's only until Election Day. I can hardly take care of myself."

"Well, I'll ask Mr. Bissett to give you child support for her. Do the best you can."

"Okay. I'll pick her up," I relented wearily. Mrs. Yudkoff had tugged on my heartstring and I fell for what Wilbur referred to as the "oaky-doak". Chuck's child support payments would amount to only $12.50 a week, which placed me in worse circumstances than before. Without Julie, I could suffer through a job search even to the point of missing meals or sleeping at a downtown mission. But the issue was not moot. I had little choice but to go get my baby.

It wasn't until I arrived at Juvenile Hall that I learned that I was required to undergo psychiatric evaluation before I could get Julie. I was furious after all we had endured, that a shrink stood between me and my daughter. It just seemed to me that the state was intent on drowning me with a torrential downpour of misery. Within the first half hour of my session, I was on the verge of lunging at his throat.

He was a large imposing man who infused his job with an imperious demeanor. It did not seem to matter to him that I was distraught and desperate when I walked into his office. He had a file on Julie on front of him, but knew absolutely nothing about me. So it never dawned on him that my truculence and irritability stemmed from my having to diagnose my own illness and seemingly prescribe my own remedy. I had nothing to say to this man. He had nothing of substance to ask me. What he did ask me did not seem pertinent to my circumstances, but I answered him as best I could. I suppose that my stress infected responses impeded his ability to determine my mental condition.

"I speak and understand English perfectly." He stated so belligerently that I was intimidated into silence. I didn't know whether riling me was some ploy of his profession or he was by nature an insensitive brute. "Why do you keep asking me do I understand? Do you think that I'm some kind of an idiot that I don't understand? Or do you have some idiotic need to ask people if they understand? I don't appreciate you keep asking me to I understand? Do you understand?

His face flushed red with anger. He was taking my responses personally as though I were mounting a vendetta against him. I was mad at the world. It had produced a man who brutalized his children. It had taken my children from me and won't give them back. It was not enough for the state to deem me as crazy on paper, it now seemed determined to drive me crazy in truth. And now the fate of my daughter lay in the hands of a nauseating behemoth who presumably had been trained to be an impartial observer of the human psyche without being its nemesis. As badly as I wanted to dispatch a verbal barrage from both barrels, everything depended upon my maintaining my composure.

"Well, people don't always understand me. So if I asked if they do, what's so idiotic about that?" I retorted seething as I tried rein in my mounting anger.

"Don't ask me anymore if I understand," He concluded.

"Now that we understand each other, can I leave?" I asked testily.

I could sense that we both realized that our session could only continue to our mutual detriment. He gruffly terminated the session and angrily slammed closed Julie's file.

I had nothing to lose. There was very little chance that the shrink would recommend me taking Julie home. I called Ms. Hale from the lobby. The emotional barrels that I could not empty into the shrink; were dispatched point blank into her.

"Why didn't you tell me that I was going to have to see a shrink? Didn't I tell you that there was no way I was going to see a shrink? He was a total asshole. All we did was argue. He got so mad at me that I know he's going to write a bad report. Why the hell should I have to see a shrink anyway? I didn't run away."

"Calm down Mrs. Bissett." Ms. Hale said sympathetically into the phone. "Forget about it. It's required procedure. We're not paying any attention to his report. I'm sorry you had to go through this. Just go and pick up Julie. I'll call and tell them to release her."

I could not have imagined a more joyous eleven year old than Julie when she arrived at the waiting area of Juvenile Hall. She embraced me with all her strength and pelted my face with kisses of relief and elation. She was no longer an animate object housed in a warehouse of systems and numbers. Throughout our bus ride home, she huddled close to me, her hazel eyes sparkling. Now I could see, under the protection of her mother she began to feel secure.

For Julie, it was a time of adjustment and rediscovery. That which other children took for granted, were for Julie gloriously wonderful experiences to be savored and cherished. The hug that greeted her when I returned home from work meant so much to her. Our evening walks to the restaurant on the corner for hamburgers and milk shakes were the high points of her day. The word "Mother" rolled off of her tongue as though she had happily mastered a melodious word from another language. She so delighted in the meager offerings that I extended to her that it never occurred to her to ask for anything more. She became the center of my existence. My most urgent and desperate concerns were for her happiness and well being.

The political campaign came to an end and I once again found myself impaled on the horns of a monumental dilemma. The $12.50 a week child support from Chuck was my total income. Fortunately, I had signed Julie up for the free lunch program at school and we sustained ourselves mostly on cheap hamburgers and milk shakes. Since Julie was still regarded as a ward of the court, I could not apply for welfare without the state picking her up and returning her to Juvenile Hall. Nor was I eligible to draw unemployment insurance.

I make no apologies. It was my desperation, my contempt, my loathing for society and systems and perhaps my shortcomings in landing and keeping a job. Ultimately, it was my problem and I could only deploy the resources at hand in resolving it. There may be that point in time, when I, during moments of reflection, will be able to rattle off available options with the skill of a chef reciting the ingredients for a favorite recipe. But this was not that time. Before me, loomed the harrowing specter of roaming the streets with an eleven year old child in tow, begging for food and sleeping where we fell from exhaustion. I needed to provide for this one child God had seen willing to give to my care, and I would do whatever it took for them not to take her again. I had no concerns for the imperious and self righteous judgments of my fellow beings, but only the hope of forgiveness from a compassionate God, and twenty bucks for services rendered to a perfect stranger.

Perhaps it was because of my quaking fear and trepidation that the faces of the men at the bars took the form of leering predatory animals. I smiled graciously in hopes of masking my anguish. I carefully, but serendipitously, studied the faces of likely prospects. I had only my feelings and instincts to inform me as to who would pay to play or who would be a violent, brutal psycho. At issue, on this my first Saturday night as a neophyte in the world's oldest profession, was whether or not me and Julie would have provisions to sustain us, and a place to sleep.

I did better on subsequent Saturday nights as my fears waned. But they soon gave way to ever mounting feeling of self loathing that I began to find intolerable.

Julie had made friends with the three children of a struggling singer who lived down that hall from us. The girl and her twin boy and girl were much younger than Julie, but there were no kids her age in the building for her to play with. Ty, their mother and I became friends. One night she came by to invite me and Julie to dinner. I opened the door to her and then collapsed to the floor. An ambulance responded quickly to Ty's call and rushed me to County General Hospital. The doctor diagnosed my illness as a sexually transmitted disease. Since I was allergic to all antibiotics, care had to be taken as to how I was treated. I was advised that if the inflammation of my ovaries did not subside, a hysterectomy would have to be performed after New Years. Since my release date had not been determined, I had to call Mrs. Yudkoff to make arrangements for Julie's care.

"Mrs. Yudkoff, this is Mrs. Bissett."

"What can I do for you?"

"I'm in County General Hospital and I don't know when they'll release me. And they're talking about a hysterectomy after New Years."

"Oh. I'm sorry to hear that," Mrs. Yudkoff stated with genuine concern.

"Julie's home alone, you're going to have to come and get her."

"Miki, do you have any friends she can stay with until you get out. Please try Miki. If I pick her up and return her to Juvie Hall, we'll be back at square one and another whole problem. See what you can do and then call me back."

I called Libby and explained my situation to her. Libby passed along my problem to Mary Brown, the supervising teacher from the Urban League Head Start Project, who agreed to take Julie home to stay with her. Fortunately, Mary lived nearby so Julie did not have to change schools. Mrs. Yudkoff was delighted.

Because of the possibility of surgery, the hospital had me sign up for Aid to Families with Dependent children, a welfare program that I sought from the beginning. I spent a week in the hospital and was instructed to attend a class on hysterectomy that was scheduled to start in January. Two days after I returned home form the hospital, Ms. Hale dropped by with yet another jolt from the state's seemingly inexhaustible supply.

"Mrs. Bissett, all of the foster parents want a vacation from the kids for Christmas," she stated solemnly. "So we'd appreciate it if you would come and take yours for the holiday week between Christmas and New Years."

I stared at her incredulously before reminding her of the circumstances of which she was very much aware. "But Ms. Hale, I just got out of the hospital and I'm supposed to return on January 4th. I don't have any money or anything to celebrate Christmas with. I can't even take care of them for the week. You're asking the impossible!"

"If you can't take them, then we'll have to send them to Juvie for Christmas. That's the only alternative. Do you want that?"

I expended a sigh of despair. Ms. Hale knew the only answer I could give. She only needed to hear it.

"Olay, but I'm a sick person. I wouldn't say so if I weren't."

Once again the logic of the state has managed to elude me. It knew that I would not receive my first check until after New Years. If I had no money before I entered the hospital, by what magical process did they expect me to become solvent just before it happened to have been Christmas? When I was well and working, I was considered a pariah to my children. Now that I'm sick and broke, they dump six children on me at a moment's notice. Once again the issue was moot. I had no choice but to call Chuck and ask him to pick up the children and drop them off.

I put in another call for help to Libby. She contacted some churches that were handing out food baskets. Julie an I took a bus and collected two of them. Libby gave me five dollars and the address of a nursery school in East Los Angeles where I could buy toys for the kids for a quarter or less. Mary Brown got me a hundred dollar check from the Good Shepherd Episcopal Church. I decided not to cash the check until it was absolutely necessary.

The kids were ecstatic about being together. They laughed and played until they were exhausted—then rested and laughed and played some more. Only Sarrah gave me cause for great concern. There was nothing we could do for her that would not cause her to cry and scream. None of us could figure it out. If I tried to feed her, bathe her or change her, she would scream at the top of her lungs. The other children tried to play with her with the same result. I had no idea what to make of it something was wrong and I vowed to force the State to find out what.

At about eleven o'clock on Christmas Eve I heard a tapping at the door of my apartment. When I opened the door, I saw a man walking quickly down the hallway. He was a marshal, and he had done his job by taking on a three day eviction notice. Inside, I was very much distressed. But I had to ignore the notice so as not to mar Christmas with my kids. The day after Christmas, I had to beg the landlord to allow me to stay through New Years. Despite Sarrah's curious affliction, possibility of surgery and the threat of eviction, Christmas went very well.

The children were returned to the proper places the day after New Years, leaving Julie and me to get on with fashioning an existence that seemed tenuous at best. Having the children with me over the holidays inspired me to heighten my efforts to get them back. I used $80.00 of the check from the church to rent a two bedroom apartment a block away. A visit to the hospital revealed that my ovaries were okay and that surgery was not needed. I made an appointment with Mrs. Yudkoff and Ms. Hale to insist that they find out what was wrong with Sarrah. They greeted me with the sort of ebullience that usually concluded with champagne and laughter.

"We just wanted to let you know how pleased we both are at how you handled what must have been a difficult situation for you." Mrs. Yudkoff gushed glowingly. "We could have done things differently, but we had to find out if you were the Mother we thought you were. You passed with flying colors. We have no more questions about your capabilities. We're totally satisfied."

And then there was a long pause, as I waited for her to give me one reason why I should give a damn about passing her test. I had resolved not to argue with these people anymore. Their logic and methods of operation were hopelessly beyond my ability to comprehend. I decided to do whatever I had to do, with or without their help. I had more pressing problems on my mind.

"I came here because I want Sarrah moved immediately," I stated stiffly. "She cried and screamed about everything, even eating, and I don't know why. I want her moved right now. Something's wrong in that foster home and you folks are not seeing it.

My first visit to that house was deplorable. I watched this woman wipe my infants rear with the same rag she then proceeded to use to wipe her face." I will not have her there.

The two now deflated ladies stared at each other in askance and concern. I realized that they were often conflicted with their own personal perception of my situation and the dictates of the system that employed them. But, nonetheless, they were my children and irregardless of how the bureaucracy conducted their affairs, I would ultimately be held accountable for the outcome.

"Well, why don't we move Victoria in with you and put Anita and Sarrah together in a new foster home?" Mrs. Yudkoff offered. I was grateful that she took my complaint without question or doubt. "So we'll plan for those changes to go into effect as soon as school is over."

"You just don't understand, do you?" I asked wearily. "You claim that I have to provide certain stability for these children. Isn't the onus on me to stabilize my situation and pull life together? How can I do that? I'm unemployed. I don't have the wherewith all to do this right. All that is going to happen is that I'm going to wind up back here again."

"Then we'll have to try to find another foster home that'll take three children. That's very difficult," Mrs. Yudkoff stated.

"I can't help how hard it is. I just can't do it. This is your responsibility. You handle it. But I want Sarrah moved as soon as you can do it."

Part of me could understand why they put me through a test. Now that I had passed it, they were convinced that I was a competent Mother and that my concerns were, in their minds, no longer the ramblings of a madwoman. They had overridden what had been inserted in my file and yet remained tethered to its official conclusion that the children remain as charged, and wards of the state.

I departed the probation office with a hopeful feeling. At least I figured that they would keep a careful eye out for the children. A few days later, I received a letter form Public Services requesting that I come by for a job interview. My interviewer referred me to Occidental Insurance for work as a clerk typist. I was assigned to a huge bay of desks and typewriters where actuaries diligently pored over insurance applications that were either transformed into policies or rejected. Since my typing skills from high school had diminished only slightly, I was assigned the task of typing letters of response to client queries. It was a pleasant job and I had hoped to keep it. But my supervisor maintained a rigid intolerance toward tardiness. If the bus that I needed to take to work stopped to pick me up, I would easily be at my typewriter on time. If it was too crowded and passed me up, I would be late. A week and a half after I started the job, I was once again unemployed.

I accepted employment as on order clerk at a family owned paint store. It's Greek owners were a blissfully contentious lot whose love of confrontation with one another was only exceeded in their fascination with the assorted complications of romance and survival that darted continuously in and out of my life during the two years that I was there.

The foster family in Long Beach was so pleased with the comportment of Victoria and Anita, they gladly took in baby Sarrah. Considering the horror stories that I have seen and heard regarding foster homes, I was very fortunate and relieved that the kids were placed in a home where they were treated with love and respect. Their guardians were an elderly white couple who lived in a predominantly black neighborhood in Long Beach. Like me, they were avidly against corporeal punishment. On weekends, when Chuck picked up Julie, I would take the bus to ECH to see the boys. Rodrick and Nathan were glad to see me come, but grew more sullen and morose as the time for me to leave approached.

Living with Julie was wonderful. She had a cheerful, sprite disposition and never complained about our meager lifestyle. She had been placed in an enrichment class for gifted children. The primary issue of contention between us was over her struggle to learn long division.

One evening, she finally confessed to me that she was failing math and there was a final the next day that she had no chance of passing. I firmly ordered that after dinner we would sit down and not stop until she had learned division.

"I hate stupid division!" she retorted. "Why do I have to learn that anyway!" she then ran into the bedroom, slammed the door behind her and threw a full blown tantrum.

Calmly I filled a pitcher with water from the kitchen and quietly went into her room. She had thrown the blanket, pillows and mattress on the floor and was sitting on them pouting. I flung the pitcher of water on her. She looked like a drowned rat. I could not contain my laughter. When she realized how she must have looked, she too was seized by laughter. The next day Julie did so well on her math test that the teacher accused her of cheating. When Julie vehemently denied it, she was ordered to the blackboard to do five additional math problems. She completed the problems perfectly. The A that Julie received in math made her a straight A student for that semester. I was every bit as proud of her achievement as I was for the commendation she received from the city council for a health poster that she submitted in a city-wide competition. But the problems that plagued Julie most in school could not be solved on the blackboard nor objectively graded.

The Watts Riot was still very much a sensitive issue with the school administration. It therefore was no small wonder why it caused no end of consternation and concern when the sole white student arrived at school wearing a black button pinned on her coat with the words: "Burn, baby burn" inscribed in the bold white letters. I bought the button when we attended a stage play in Watts of that title. It did not occur to me that Julie would wear it to school. The button created no small degree of anxiety among the teachers, many of whom became genuinely afraid that it would incite the kids to burn down the school. I received a letter imploring me not to permit Julie to wear the button again.

Julie's perceived alliance with her fellow students against racism did not immunize her from their verbal and physical abuse. She endured and suffered the humiliation in silence. I did not learn of it until one day I noticed the bruises on her. From first hand experience, I knew how cruel and insensitive children could be. At the same age, I was the object of their scorn because I was "smart". My daughter suffered because she was white. Leaving the problem in the hands of the school administration would most likely make matters worse. I had no idea as to what to do about race abuse at the hands of children, but something had to be done. I decided to visit her class so that her classmates would see that her Mother was not white; that indeed her Mother was of color. After four such visits Julie proudly informed me that when one of the girls tried to pick a fight with her, the other girls rallied around her and cautioned her tormentor that Julie's Mother was "Black" and Julie was considered "one of us".

With the racial problems between her schoolmates under control, Julie's next confrontation was with the adults. The school had hired a middle aged black man to serve as cafeteria monitor primarily to handle the rowdy boys. For reasons that escaped me, he took issue with Julie for drinking peach juice from a cup instead of spooning it. He ordered her to the "punishment bench", where five or six boys had preceded her for far greater infractions. When the cafeteria was empty he began scolding the boys. By the time he reached Julie, he had worked himself into a frenzy that he unleashed upon her. Julie responded with a burst of temper that sent chairs flying, tables flipping, and the man fending off a withering volley of invectives and curses.

I received a notice that Julie had been expelled from school. It was the possibility of a promising mind being shelved for heaven knows how long that launched me into a state of panic. I realized that if the probation office got wind of it, Julie would be returned to Juvenile Hall and my chances of getting my children would be nil.

It was obvious to me that I could not deal with Mrs. Emerson, the principal as I did with Mrs. Yudkoff and Ms. Hale. She had more discretion in handling Julie's expulsion. I needed to be cool and rational. But I was determined not to leave this woman's office until my daughter had been reinstated. She was a white, middle aged woman who seemed both pleasant and capable.

"Julie is a bright and personable child," she offered as she directed me into her office and to a chair. "She seems more like an eighteen year old than eleven. We never would expect her to behave the way she did. I had to expel her. We have to set some limits of discipline or this place would be a jungle."

"Considering the circumstances that brought on Julie's expulsion, would you expect that another child of Julie's age would have reacted the same way?" I asked.

"Yes. I believe so."

"But Julie's not eighteen is she? She's eleven. And from what you're telling me, her reaction was perfectly normal. So why should she be expelled because you expect her to act like she's eighteen?"

"Touché", Mrs. Bissett."

She reflected, while I waited.

"Well. We'll have to give her a vacation for one week," she insisted. "I can't have her in the cafeteria until this whole thing settles down. And then I'll reinstate her.

And then it was my turn to retreat into a pensive silence. Her offer was not acceptable. Although I could trust Julie to stay at home alone for a week while I worked, I didn't want to take that risk. And then there was the possibility of the probation officer dropping by the apartment unannounced during school hours. Of course I couldn't tell that the Mrs. Emerson.

"She'll lose one whole week of school because she reacted like a normal child would?" I queried. "Do you have a dictionary, Mrs. Emerson?"

She looked at me in askance.

"I think the dictionary will show quite a difference between a vacation and an expulsion. I don't want Julie expelled. It wasn't her back in class. If you want to give her a "vacation" from the cafeteria, I don't care. But I want her back in class."

"Okay, I'll cancel the expulsion. But she'll have to eat lunch in the nurse's office for one week."

"Thank you, Mrs. Emerson. And may I suggest that you look into your cafeteria monitor. This should never have happened."

Julie was delighted. Some of her classmates feigned stomach aches and headaches to keep her company. They would all gather in the nurse's office for lunch, make a rowdy mess, and then rush to clean it up before the nurse returned from her lunch. Julie was also proud of the way I stuck up for her.

At the end of the school year, I received a call asking me to go pick up Victoria and bring her home. Happily, I made the trip to Long Beach. Two children home. Four to go.

# CHAPTER FIFTEEN

# *Spiritual Heritage*

Victoria was a spirited, willful child with intense dark eyes. Settling into the regime that Julie and I had established was difficult for her. Julie had more or less appointed herself more as Victoria's boss rather than my assistant in raising her. Victoria's rejection of Julie's presumption of authority caused confrontations between them. At the time, they did not seem serious enough for drastic intervention on my part. I assumed that this would pass as they appeared to grow close, albeit begrudgingly. It wasn't until the landlord called me up to her apartment, that I learned that their confrontations often degenerated into physical violence when I was not at home. I decided to place them in after school care and pick them up after work. The racism that they experienced at school remained for me a constant and persistent concern. Since my job at the paint store seemed stable enough, I was able to seriously consider moving to an area where the administration exercised better control over the kids. In the meantime, I accepted an invitation from Mrs. Yudkoff to participate in group therapy session for parents of delinquent children.

Mrs. Yudkoff had hoped that my input in the sessions would help these parents to better understand the needs of their children. To my surprise and dismay, many of the parents resented my being there.

One lady was especially vocal in her disdain for me. She was a middle aged white woman who had an especially bitter relationship with her husband. It was obvious to all but her that the rebelliousness of her daughter was a direct consequence of a malfunctioning marriage that neither of her parents would extend themselves to repair.

"What are you doing here?" she asked in an imperious contentious voice that I found offensive. "They told us that your children are not criminals. Who are you to tell us what it's like to have bad children?"

I realized that it would do none of us any good to indulge in personality combat. We were all hurting for our children. It was merely a matter of degrees. But this woman was an irritant to me. I had to let her know that regardless of what she thought of me, I was not the source of her problem.

I stared her squarely in the eyes as I responded. "My children are wards of the court just like yours. I have one son who every time I let him out of the house, I fear that he'll burn down a damn building or something and the police will come to arrest him for arson. He's been doing that since he was six years old. It seems like he's finally changing, but he's thirteen now. I don't know what effect having grown up in institutions will ultimately have on my children. What your children are going through now may be the fate that awaits mine later. I have no idea. What I hope will come out of these sessions is that we will be able to provide an exchange of ideas that will be helpful to us all."

I had no further problems with any of the women. What she did do was to keep me mindful of the fact that, in comparison, my problems were nowhere near as serious as hers and the other five women in the group. But none of them had as many as six children with which to contend. Maybe it was because I had so many kids that I found it somewhat perplexing that these women with no more than three could allow their control over their offspring to deteriorate so badly. As the sessions passed, I began to realize that oftentimes incomprehensible, inconceivable, and improbable circumstances invade our lives rendering solutions and resources worlds apart. As one lady stated it: "Shit happens and there ain't a damn thing you can do about it until it hits the fan."

Towards the end of the session, I tried as best I could to offer what I felt was the essential denominator to these women's complaints that I had heard.

"I was twenty-seven when I lost faith in my mother," I began thoughtfully. "Your children are eight, ten and twelve and have already lost faith in you. All you have done here is run your kids into the ground. How do you expect them to be good kids and obey your rules when you don't like them?"

The women were insulted and glared at me indignantly. They glance at each other in askance before returning to me with eyes that demanded an explanation.

"It was my Mother's testimony that did most to cause me to lose my kids. I would never have believed that my mother could have said what she said. But she did say it and I hated her for it. I never wanted to see or speak to her again. But I had to go visit her in the hospital just before she died and find it within myself to forgive her. She made choices that deprived me of a better chance at life. She allowed things to happen in our home that caused me pain. She was from another culture, so she raised me from her heart. She may not have done all that was right in my eyes, but she never deprived me of my humanity. That's why, as a child, I never lost my respect for her and always had faith in her authority. Do any of you understand what I'm trying to tell you?" I asked pressingly. "How can you as mother condemn your children as bad and incorrigible and, at the same time, expect them to respect you as "Mother" and have faith in your authority? You guys don't like your kids and they know it."

The room fell silent.

Them women stared pensively, ashamedly into space until one who seemed most affected broke the heavy silence.

"Is what she's saying true?" She inquired of the probation officers.

"It's in my file," I responded emphatically.

Mrs. Yudkoff and Ms. Hale nodded affirmatively.

I can't be sure what effect my story had on the group, but in the final session one of the black women whose son had been arrested for stealing defiantly demanded that her son be returned.

"You're going to have to fight for him if you really want him," I stated when she began to waver in her demand because she thought it might be too late to get him back.

"Then that's what I'm going to do. I don't care if I have to tie him down to keep him from stealing. I want my son home! I love him and I miss him and I want him home."

"Oh no, it's not too late. Come by the office tomorrow and we'll get the process started to get your kid home," Mrs. Yudkoff offered reassuringly with Ms Hale nodding in agreement.

Instead of moving away from the racism as I had hoped, I found a small house located even deeper into the ghetto. After having more than second thoughts, I concluded that it was too good a bargain to pass up. It would have to do until my finances improved. Julie had been adjusting very well to being around blacks. She had begun cultivating what I construed to be a "black attitude". Within two weeks after starting her new school, she had her first major confrontation with another girl. When the other children realized that Julie would neither back down nor be intimidated, she had no more problems; and neither did Victoria. Nonetheless, I detested the fact that violence, rather than reason, was the choice of resolution even for children in elementary school.

Just as I was preparing to move into the house, I got a call from Mrs. Yudkoff requesting me to meet with her in her office. There was a hint of urgency in her voice. Anxiously, I made my way to her office.

"Miki, you've got to come and get the boys," Mrs. Yudkoff pleaded as we closed into her office. "It has been our experience that after about three years, an institution mentality begins to set in. Once that happens, your boys may spend the rest of their lives in and out of institutions. That would be a shame. They're really good boys."

She knew, of course, that I would not let pass a chance to get my children if they were in danger. I was hardly jumping for joy, though. To this point, every resource was another goal yet to overcome. I had been strained to the limit just caring for Julie and Victoria. At least I could be thankful that I did not let the inner city location dissuade me from buying the house. About a month later, Rodrick and Daaniel were dropped off at my door. And now there were four kids home; two to go.

Everything was far from blissful. My belief in raising children by tapping into their gestalt had not diminished. The problem I was confronted with was that of teaching them to re-learn and experience the goodness of their gestalt, while working to feed and clothe them. Rodrick would allow no offense to pass without retaliation. At fifteen, he was obstinate, aggressive and listened to no one. Nathan, now thirteen, was less aggressive but had retreated into a world of his creation and slammed the gate behind him. I soon realized that any hope that I had of maintaining a household required my establishing my authority. It was Rodrick who provided me with my first make-or-break challenge.

It was one of many nights when food was sparse and had to be doled out carefully so that everyone got one ample serving. Angry words were exchanged between Rodrick and Victoria. Victoria was still holding her plate and hadn't started eating yet. I could see the anger rising in Rodrick's face.

"Don't hit her!" I yelled to Rodrick.

He stuck her anyway, causing her to drop her plate of hamburger, rice and beans to the floor. There was no food left to replace it. She was going to have to go to bed hungry.

"I told you not to hit her," I stated angrily. "Since you made her drop her plate, you will clean this mess up off the floor."

"No I'm not," he retorted defiantly. "She shouldn't have been snotty at me."

"I don't give a damn what she shouldn't have done. I said clean this up!"

"I'm not cleaning anything. I don't like it here anyway. You got favoritism toward Victoria and I want to go back to ECH."

"I'm not going to take you to ECH. But you are going to clean this up," I said, my anger rising almost beyond my control.

"Then I'll call the police and tell them to pick me up and take me to ECH," He stated as he picked up the phone and dialed the police. He told them what he wanted and how I had shown favoritism towards his sister. I grabbed the phone out of his hand and spoke resolutely.

"I don't care who you are, but don't you come out here. If he can't respect me now, how the hell do you expect him to respect you later. When you have to pick him up off the street, you're going to be the first one who's going to ask: "Where's his Mother been?"

A thin female voice, controlled and resolute came on the line. "You didn't hear what I told him. I told him to 'shut up and put up'. I'm not sending anybody out there. You're right. He's got to learn respect somewhere and he better learn it with you than with us."

"Thank you." I hung up the phone. I then turned to Rodrick.

"Are you going to clean this up?"

"No, I'm not."

His insolence could in no way go unchallenged. I abandoned all hopes of maintaining my self control. I pulled a leather belt from the closet and began furiously whacking at him. He ran into the kitchen with me in pursuit, still whacking him with the belt. The other children had taken refuge on the small porch behind the bathroom. Rodrick ran into the bedroom and slid under the bunk bed. With a surge of rage-induced strength, I yanked the bed away and whacked him again. He moved clear of the belt and cocked back an angry fist to strike me.

"Rodrick, if you land that fist, you better be sure you knock me out real good," I said with the belt poised to whack him. "Because when I get up off the floor, there won't be a hole in hell that you can hide in that I won't find you."

We glared defiantly at each other until Rodrick realized that I was in dead earnest. He lowered his fist. I stopped hitting him.

"So you want to go back to ECH?" I stated in breathless anger. "Go then". Then like a whirlwind, I grabbed all of his clothes and threw them in the front yard. "Walk to ECH for all I care. But you will not come back into this house until you clean that up off the floor."

I slammed the door behind him and then went to console my other children. It was about two in the morning when I heard a gentle knock on the door. Rodrick stood before me with his head bowed.

"I'll clean it up, Mom," he said softly.

For the first time, I had resorted to corporeal punishment to discipline a child. Perhaps, I could have justified it to myself and eased it out of my mind. But that would have meant acquiescing when others justify corporeal punishment as a means to of child control. I was angry with myself. Rodrick had pressed a hot button, but that was no excuse for me to lose control. He had succumbed to the institution mentality in which only violence commanded respect. He was letting me know that I had control over nothing, not even over simple logic. I knew that tolerance and understanding on my part were the roads to improving our relationship, but none of this could be achieved without him recognizing my authority. For the sake of the other children, my authority had to be established and maintained. It was a victory of sorts for me. I was not happy about the manner by which I achieved it. Nor was I about to give it back.

The institutions had created a wider gulf between me and my children than I thought. Each of them had to manipulate his or her gestalt for the sake of their mental and emotional survival. They all had to relearn trust, consideration of others and self esteem. In their minds, I had abandoned them at a time when they needed me most. It mattered not that the State had taken them away from me. All that mattered was that they no longer regarded me as a reliable resource for the security that they desperately craved. I hated the courts and juvenile authorities for what they had done to my children. I hated the smug arrogance by which they quoted codes and regulations as though they were edicts from God. I was totally confident that, on balance, bad parents with a little help were infinitely better than the self righteous contrivances of the state with all of its resources. Even while stumbling within the parameters of their love, bad parents have a far better chance of bringing out the best in their children. Whereas the State in its efforts to salvage the children "by the number" so badly mangle their gestalt to the point where they emerge as little more than savages.

Nathan and Julie graduated from elementary school and joined Rodrick in Junior High. Within a few weeks of the start of school, the environment of the institutions that enabled violence to share the gestalt of my children was played out on the playground of their school. Julie was attacked by anther girl at school. This time I visited the parents of the girl and attempted to solicit their support against intolerance against my children. The girl never bothered Julie again. But, unfortunately, racism continued to plague my children and I was powerless to do much about it.

My struggles continued to be both internal and external. Externally, juggling the needs for food, clothing, and mortgage payments consumed my time and energy. Internally, I despaired over my inability to create a harmony and order within the family that transcended the need to resort to violence. The lingering power of institutionalization struck me full force when Nathan defiantly declared his issue of battle—dishwashing.

It seemed a fairly simple request that I made of Nathan. Rodrick had come down with a case of the flu. I asked Nathan to take his brother's turn in the dishwashing rotation.

"No." He stated adamantly to my request.

My anger soared. I called the job and informed them that I would be late. And then I called Mrs. Yudkoff in the hopes of warding off the impending violent resolution. She was no help. I burst into tears. I could have gotten Julie or Victoria to do the dishes, but then my authority would have eroded in daily baths of tears. When he refused my order again, I grabbed the belt and began lashing at him as hard as I could. Amidst his tears and screams, Nathan ran to do the dishes. For me the urgency of the crisis had not passed. I needed a sense of bearing. I called Ms. Hale and demanded a meeting with Chuck and Nathan for that very afternoon.

My confrontation with Nathan had cost me a half day wages that I sorely needed. When Ms. Hale called me at work to inform me that Chuck and Nathan had arrived at her office, I joined the gathering in a foul mood.

"I'm not going to have any child of mine disrespect me," I said angrily to Chuck and Ms. Hale. "You guys have ruined my life and my children's lives and then you send them back to me like animals. I'm not going to have it. If you don't like how I handle things, you can take them back. Since the "State" presumed to know better than me how to raise them, then you can undo their disrespectful behavior. I'm not going to have it."

Ms. Hale stared for a long time at the welts on Nathan's arms and neck and then sympathetically at me. I sensed that she was in a quandary as to what to say or do. Had she acknowledged the welts, it would have been tantamount to charging me with child abuse. She would have no choice but to herd the children and their distorted gestalts back into their emotional dungeons with little hope of their emerging until they were fully institutionalized adults. I was hoping that she and my ex-husband would instill enough fear in Nathan to provide me some advantage in our future encounters. As she spoke to Nathan, there was a tone of intimidation in her voice that made me hopeful.

"Perhaps you don't like the way your mom has everyone do the dishes, Nathan. Would you rather she rotate the dishwashing chores among you a week at a time or maybe even a month at a time?

"A whole month?" Nathan said as his eyes bucked wide and panic sprang to his face.

"Well, you obviously don't like the arrangements your mother has now. Maybe she should change it."

"No. Mom's way is okay." Nathan answered hastily.

"I'm still not going to have a child in my home who doesn't respect my authority." I interjected firmly.

"So Nathan," Ms. Hale said sternly. "Are you going to do what your mother tells you? Because if you are not, then I'll have to put you in Juvenile Hall."

"Yes, I'll do what she says." Nathan quickly responded. Chuck finally spoke to Nathan. His tone paled badly in comparison to the honest authority of Ms. Hale.

"Nathan, you have to respect your mother. You have to do what your mother says."

Nathan nodded. The meeting ended hopeful.

Despite the fact that order was restored in my household, I still had to concede that managing it proved an insurmountable task. The new job that I had taken at another paint store increased my pay by only fifteen dollars a week. With two children, it would have been difficult, but workable strain. With four growing children, it was virtually impossible. The court had deemed that Chuck's allowance was more than generous, so there was no use in my pressing for an increase in child support. One night in desperation, I returned to the streets hoping to turn enough tricks to buy a pair of shoes for Victoria or a dress for Julie. But the feeling of self-contempt so overwhelmed me that I aborted the effort and never tried it again. I had not asked for the children to be dropped on me when they were. I needed more time to pull together the resource that they required to at least have a tolerable existence.

I had no choice but to return to Mrs. Yudkoff and prevailed upon her to take the children back until I could do better. She referred me to Aid to Families with Dependent Children. There I was confronted with the curious anomaly of being offered the option of keeping my job and receiving no aid, or of quitting my job and receiving child support that amounted to much less than I needed. Their father had learned of my distress. Since he had formed a relationship with a woman who agreed to be his housekeeper, all six of the children were placed in his custody. This time I was sullen but didn't cry. My turn at nurturing the children had now come and passed. I had failed badly and had no choice but to concede that I could not provide the stability they desperately needed.

Having been raised as a woman of tradition, facing life without children and a husband, cast me adrift in an expanse of time and space devoid of reason or purpose. Fate had rendered its decision. Slowly and begrudgingly, I reconciled myself to live with it.

I should have known that the essence of my heritage would eventually take over my life. My Grandmother had been what I could only deduce as a "Witch Doctor" in an Achee village in Indonesia. According to my father, she had been vested with powers even beyond those of its fabled warriors. My father's culture did not raise ornate edifices to dazzle the eyes of God. Nor did it worship in halls rescued from abandoned stores where God could be both praised and assailed with cacophonous blends of joyful noises. There were only huts of mud and reeds mounted upon bamboo stilts. It was there that the tribal denizens sought relief from a sudden siege by some malevolent force or a surge of hope that some eminent enterprise will be favorably resolved. Perhaps they understood better than we that vigilance against the pillagers of one's hope for eternal salvation was a constant one that could best be undertaken from a watchtower maintained in the center of one's soul. Both my Mother, and her Mother before her had been unalterably convinced that adherence to the eternal will of God would reap an infinitely superior bounty than investing one's soul in the self serving connivances of mankind. From my Mother's culture I learned that since it was virtually impossible to escape the evils of this world, one's sole duty in life was to accommodate them as little as possible. My spiritual heritage compelled me to believe without reservation that the sullen drudge that my life had become would be overcome by a simple act of faith. What I did not expect was that the hollow place within me created by the departure of the kids would be filled to almost overflowing from a deluge of spiritual revelations that would lend substance to my faith.

I was returning from shopping at Sears when, to my horror, I noticed a large pair of dark brown eyes staring down at me from out of the evening sky. The eyes remained fixed upon me for a few minutes as I gradually regained my composure. I reasoned that the eyes were peering at me from eternity. Why me and for what purpose, I could not begin to understand without the help of someone whom I regarded as a kindred soul.

Three years had passed since I had visited Mother Mary for a spiritual consultation. When I went to see her, I was informed that she had moved away. There was no shortage of spiritualists in Los Angeles. Finding one who could help me connect with the spiritual force that had imposed itself upon me was the problem at hand.

From a newspaper advertisement, I settled on a Bishop Rogers who dispensed his consultations out of his comfortably appointed home in the midtown section of Los Angeles. I was ushered into a waiting room by his wife, a cordial black woman of about middle age. There were about fifteen people in the large, sparsely furnished room waiting to see the bishop. My attention was drawn to a very attractive woman with dark sultry eyes and provocative features. Like the others, she sat in pensive silence, pondering the desperate plights that drove her to seek out the services of Bishop Rogers. She greeted me with a friendly, inviting smile as I approached. Assuming that she was a Latina, I asked in Spanish how long we would have to wait. She understood what I said but responded in English. She invited me to sit down next to her. She was about my age and introduced herself as Laurie. She was originally from Puerto Rico and now lived in Hollywood. Her refusal to speak Spanish, was part of her effort to pass for Anglo. She confided in me that she was married to one man, but in love with another. The other man rode with a biker gang and in Laurie's mind that was his first and maybe only love. I told her about my relationship with Wilbur. We then proceeded to both lament and curse our dismal fortunes with men until she was called to visit with Bishop Rogers. We exchanged telephone numbers and promised to keep in touch.

Bishop Rogers was an elderly, compassionate man. He listened with patience and interest as I told him how eyes that looked like mine stared at me from out of the sky. He could not tell me what the vision meant, but concluded that I had spiritual capabilities that God wanted me to nurture. He suggested that I come by whenever I had bouts of anxiety and depression. I returned to him often primarily because he was sympathetic and receptive and I was so totally alone. He provided me no answers to my problems or predictions about the future. We prayed together and then I would leave with a candle and his assurances that things will work out in my favor. I began to realize that Providence had offered Bishop Rogers to me as the ideal catalyst during my spiritual development. There was the harrowing vision of a giant wrecking ball crashing into my house in the middle of the night that woke me up. A few days later, I saw two hands clasped in prayer against the clear blue sky. One of the strong hands extended itself towards me as though offering me something. Streams of unintelligible voices assailed my ears, leaving me startled and confused. As with the loss of my children, I was once again overwhelmed by forces that were beyond my control.

# CHAPTER SIXTEEN

# Go And Live

The almost incessant thrusts of dreams, visions, and apparitions began to create within me a sense of transformation. I had no idea of what I was becoming. I only knew that I was no longer the same. Bishop Rogers was always available to counsel me at his home even though he had contracted a severe case of emphysema that was sapping away his life. At night I would light the small candles that he gave me and prayed for strength and guidance through these spiritual trials and ordeals.

One morning I got up to go to work only to discover, to my shock, that my left thigh had become hard as a rock. I felt no pain and there were no restrictions in my movement. Normally, such an occurrence would have sent me scurrying to the nearest doctor in a state of distress. But the course of my life suggested that there were spiritual implications to consider. After three days of ceaseless anxiety, I concluded that it was either time for the spiritual forces to affect a cure or I would have to go to a doctor.

As best I could determine, I contrived the exorcism of the demon affliction to my thigh on the spur of the moment. On a table I mounted a photo of a painting entitled "The Sacred Heart of Jesus" that I had purchased some time before. In front of the photo of the kind, compassionate face and his exposed and illuminated heart, I placed a lighted tall white candle and a cup of olive oil. A prayer asking for deliverance from this affliction flowed solemnly past my lips and towards the picture. I rubbed the olive oil on the thigh and then took a hot bath. Nothing happened. I resolved that a visit to a doctor the next day would be the only sensible course, even at the risk of him diagnosing my affliction as psychosomatic and me as psychotic.

That night, my calm and peaceful sleep waned into a dream that I will never forget. I was escorted into a great dining hall where men, like my guards, were dressed in the black uniforms of the Gestapo. They were harsh, cold men with fierce sadistic eyes. A man more intimidating than any I had ever seen sat at the head of the very long banquet table. Slowly, he raised a black wooden ball where his right hand should have been. Extending from it was a wooden middle finger. With a stern menacing glare he motioned that I be taken from the room. For whatever purpose he had in mind, I had been rejected. I was taken outside and placed upon a cross of thick, heavy, wooden beams that lay on the ground. I struggled in vain against an invisible force that pinned me down on the cross. From above, an axe head descended onto my leg, slashing it crosswise through the bone from toe to groin.

"Oh God!" I screamed in agony, even though I felt no pain. "Must I go through this?"

As the axe continued to make the deep incisions through my leg, something began choking me. I let my head go limp as if I were dead. The invisible hands loosened their grip.

"Lord help me!" I heard myself scream as I popped out of the dream and sat upright.

Beads of sweat had formed on my brow while my heart palpitated wildly. I looked about me and saw nothing but the darkness of the room. Realizing what had happened, I returned to sleep, confident that God would see me through. The next morning, my leg was back to normal.

Bishop Rogers listened patiently while I related my spiritual experience to him. He reassured me that I had nothing to fear—that God had enlisted me as an agent for His divine works. Bishop Rogers had grown frail from the emphysema and tired easily. A fleeting glint in his eye suggested to me that he was impressed by my spiritual calling. Although he might have perceived me as a spiritual flower that was blossoming before his eyes, my now tottering world of critical thinking began to assert itself, demanding to know how I could presume to abandon it for an excursion into a realm that seemed so well beyond its reach or understanding. The dreams and visions were agonizing plaques that rendered my temporal concerns to insignificance. In the mirror, I saw a face clouded by self loathing as questions of my worthiness plied incessantly on my mind. I began to feel as though I were about to embark upon the life of a foundling who, in the dead of night, had been abandoned on the doorstep of God.

A few nights after my visit with Bishop Rogers, I bought three candles to symbolize the Holy Trinity and placed them upon my makeshift altar in my bedroom. I stood in front of the altar and offered a solemn proposition to God.

"God, I thought that I was an intelligent person. But now I don't think I'm so smart. Every time I think I'm taking one step forward, I end up taking two steps backward. So I must not be very smart at all. I know of nothing else to do to stop me from spinning around in the same circle. So I have come to submit my life to your will and not mine. I ask only one favor. Take care of my children and give them life." The tears began to stream uncontrollably down my face. "I don't know what you want from me. Had you asked me sooner, I would have done it. I will endeavor to do Thy work, whatever it is. If all that it takes to live on is bread and water, then so be it. If I must make this journey alone, then give me the courage and lead me on. In the name of Jesus, let thine will be done."

It felt as though an angry fist had knocked the wind out of my stomach. I doubled over as my knees collapsed to the floor.

"I'm sorry. I'm so sorry," I repeated as I struggled to regain my breath. But I didn't know what I was sorry for.

In my mind's eye, I could clearly see the image of the old man on the throne who had commanded me to "go and live". He was now seated in front of the candles watching me with hopeful interest. He displayed to me the palm of his right hand. It was a hideous sight made up of living particles, scampering and scurrying about in aimless desperation, creating ever changing patterns of red and black. Although the face remained impassive, the fingers curled as though suffering pain even greater than mine. Slowly I began to realize that the living particles were sinful humans who were like ravenous cancer cells intent on consuming the hand. If the cancer did not somehow enter a state of remission, the old man would have no other choice than to amputate the hand. He sat painfully and yet compassionately hoping that the particles would eventually realize that they cannot consume the hand without ultimately destroying themselves.

"I'm sorry. I'm so very sorry," I offered in heartfelt earnest. "I didn't know."

The apparition departed but the intense feeling of contrition remained. My knees were stuck to the floor and remained there for about an hour as I sought to firmly grasp what had been revealed to me by the Holy Spirit.

From the depths of my understanding, it came to me that those who are chosen must endure the trials of change until they submit. If one is unable to forfeit that which is most dear, one cannot become a good and dutiful servant. My life from now on will be under constant threat from those forces opposed to my submission to God. There will be certain powers bestowed upon me by the Holy Spirit that the forces of darkness will seek to subvert. My vanity and ego must also yield to the will of God. I need to trust only in God and pass judgment upon no one. When in doubt as to what to do, I must be still and know that God will respond in due course.

As I sat on the edge of the bed rubbing the soreness out of my knees, I wondered what submission really meant and what God expected me to do. I felt little difference except that I now had a contriteness of heart. In the bathroom mirror, I saw that the cloud of self contempt had drifted from my face. I knew that my face was the same, but I had changed.

Sleep came slowly to me that night. As I shifted about restlessly in my bed, the essence of my gestalt emerged revealing to me its heretofore latent arrogance and vanities. In my heart, I forgave Chuck; thereby freeing myself of the all consuming bitterness that had concealed itself even among my hopes for salvation. It was after I realized that humility was not the same as passivity that I drifted off to sleep praising God for his generosity of spirit.

A few days later, I experienced my first flat tire. It was while I was returning home from work. The rush hour traffic crept past with little concern for the large car blocking a lane in a no parking zone and the woman in obvious distress. Having no money to call for road service, I reasoned that changing a flat tire was as much a part of the life of a woman who had declared her independence as changing a blown light bulb or fixing a leaky faucet. An inordinately sadistic turn of mind challenged me to change the tire even if it took all night. The moment I began attempting to assemble the jack, I chalked up the task as hopeless. I did manage an assembly that struck me as feasible, but could determine no relationship between what I had assembled and hoisting the car. Mercifully, a car pulled up behind me and a short, stocky built black man approached me with an offer to help. I etched on my brain his every move as he re-assembled the jack and made short work of changing the tire. Never again would I be intimidated by a flat tire.

My distress had been alleviated by a man who introduced himself as Samuel. He was a transplant from the mountains of Tennessee. He worked as a caretaker and maintenance man specializing in seasonal mountain properties. Physically, I did not find him appealing, but I was grateful for his help and his refusal to take payment. Reluctantly, I gave him my telephone number but made no commitment to go out with him. Within the week, Samuel called. He invited me to spend the weekend with him at a cabin in the San Bernardino Mountains. Since I was in midst of a period of fasting, sex was out of the question. When I stated as much, Samuel assured me that he only wanted some company while he performed maintenance on a cabin and that he would respect my religious beliefs. I realized that I would be taking an awful chance, but something inside me compelled me to accept his offer.

Officially, my two day period of fasting ended at sundown on the Saturday that Samuel picked me up. The long ride was pleasant enough until after we stopped off at a grocery store in Palm Springs. From there it was a harrowing ascent on narrow every spiraling roads until we arrived at a cabin that bore not the slightest resemblance of what I imagined to have been Lincoln's birthplace. It was not a cabin of logs, but of mostly stucco and wood paneling. Inside, the cabin was rustic only to the extent that its interior designer could insert the theme into the more practical ends of easy living. While Samuel put away the provisions and prepared dinner, I napped on a sofa that was so soft and comfortable that it seemed to have been manufactured out of clouds.

I awakened to a tantalizing aroma that flowed from the kitchen. Samuel called me to the dining table where he served up a bowl of what was far beyond the best vegetable soup that I had ever tasted. As I partook of this marvelous soup, I was struck by a severe and violent headache centered behind my eyes that drove from the table and back to the sofa.

"Please! Get me a very hot towel and some aspirin," I asked of the distressed Samuel. I placed the steaming towel over my eyes. He could find no aspirin so he left to buy some at a shop in the village. In the meantime, I drifted off into a trance. I could not determine as to whether what faded into my mind's eye was a rerun of a scene from an old Sherlock Holmes movie that I had seen on television or some subtle spiritual intervention through the redoubtable Mr. Holmes and Dr. Watson. It was an eerie scene in which they and a contingent of bodies broke down a door of a Victorian mansion, and pursued what appeared to be a male vampire running up a staircase. The vampire reached the first landing and then hurled himself through a stained glass window. The scene ended. My headache disappeared. When Samuel returned with the aspirin, I took one out of courtesy and then returned with relish, to the soup.

I stared out of the window with swelling elation at the ferns glistening from the morning dew and the gentle sway of the pine trees. The awe inspiring glory of God awakened my soul to a higher sense of His reality. Samuel prepared a wonderful breakfast of barbeque broiled lobster and eggs. He then finished his work on the cabin and we returned to town. I never saw nor heard form Samuel again.

Our shared heritage drew Laurie and me closer in friendship after our meeting at Bishop Roger's house. As with me, it was man trouble that had driven her to seek out guidance from the spiritualist. I knew that there was little hope of me and Wilbur building a life together. Nonetheless, I still loved him and very much needed to figure out what to do. Laurie's circumstances were considerably more complicated and intricately woven than mine. Joey, her former husband, lived in the adjoining apartment with their two children. After divorcing Joey, she met and fell in love with Marty. She had hopes that once Marty moved in with her, the motorcycle club to which he was devoted would be relegated to a distant second to her affections. Their relationship became stormy and violent. One evening during a fit of temper, she slashed him across the back with a knife. Marty left, vowing never to return. However, he did return. But it was not until after Laurie had married her current husband, Hanley. Mild mannered and tolerant, Hanley was ill prepared to confront the volatile Marty or his willful wife even during the week that Marty moved in with them after claiming that he had no other place to go.

We talked frequently on the telephone and made the rounds of Hollywood clubs. Mostly we exchanged views about men and despaired over our inability to find that magic formula for finding happiness with them. We were two chicks who, in severing the strands of tradition, were free falling in an uncompromising, mystical space, desperately yearning to be rescued by that omniscient, omnipotent force that will set us upon a path of joy and tranquility. One evening Laurie invited me to her apartment for a gathering of friends. I exchanged pleasant greetings as I threaded my way through a crowded living room and took a seat that was offered me. I was there a very short while, everyone began to slowly make their excuses to Laurie and leave until only she and I were left.

"Laurie, did I do something to run off your guests?" I asked in utter dismay.

"Miki, it's not your fault. You just don't see yourself. When you walked into the room, you were surrounded by rays of light. It made everyone feel like tiny ants. So they had to leave."

"I had no idea," I said in disbelief.

"I know Miki. Want some tea?"

"Okay," I responded, reeling from Laurie's revelation.

Since no one else had told me of such a light and I certainly did not see it when I looked in the mirror, I allowed the notion to drift from my mind. It was Bishop Rogers who resurrected the possibility when he concluded one session with a request that rendered me almost speechless.

"Miki, I'm very ill and I could use your help," He began solemnly.

"We are brethren in the spirit," I said. "You need only ask."

"God bless you for your compassion. I could use your help with my work. You'll need to know how to bless the candles. But first I'd like for you to be ordained."

I could not believe what I heard. Nothing that had happened to me suggested my being called to the ministry, and yet it seemed I was. I was more than grateful just to grow beyond my love for Wilbur and into the eternal will of God. The church for me was a means to salvation, not salvation itself. I vividly recalled my Mother's experiences with the church and her disillusionment brought on by its petty concerns and self righteous mean spiritedness. Besides, I had no structured theology and could be comfortably inserted into any denomination, Pentecostal notwithstanding, and had grown contented with the rituals of my own design. Of course, I could say none of this to Bishop Rogers. But my misgivings had to be set aside if I was going to help him.

"I'm not asking for an answer now," Bishop Rogers said with a knowing wisp of a smile. "But I have spoken of you to someone that I would like you to meet."

Bishop Rogers drove me a few miles away to the C.C. Lewis Church of the Apostolic Faith on Central Avenue. The church occupied the floor above a secondhand store and appliance repair shop. A heavy set man wearing the clothing that denoted his status as minister greeted Bishop Rogers effusively. Bishop Rogers introduced the man as Bishop Elliot, the pastor of the church. A wave of apprehension swept through me when Bishop Rogers reminded Bishop Elliot that he had spoken to him to have me ordained. Bishop Elliot looked me over with critical eyes. He was not impressed. In fact he seemed both disappointed and perplexed as to why Bishop Rogers thought so highly of me, when his eyes detected nothing at all. But Bishop Rogers was a brethren of the cloth and was dying. That entitled him to the benefit of the doubt.

"I don't know her. Is she good?" Bishop Elliot asked skeptically. Bishop Rogers nodded feebly. The sheer act of him forsaking his sick-bed to bring me before him softened Bishop Elliot's resistance. "Well, get up in the pulpit and say something," He ordered me in a tone of resignation.

I was not prepared to say anything and had no idea what the bishops expected me to say. My sole interest was to accommodate Bishop Rogers and get out of there as soon as possible. The bishops left the pulpit and became my congregation. I suppressed a riot of nerves and began reciting whatever flowed into my head.

"In Jesus' name, there is none good except the Father. So the devil and I are enemies. He thinks he's smart and slick. But I am here to fight on the side of the Lord. I hate the devil with every ounce of my being. And so I commit myself to doing the Lord's work in fighting the devil and delivering his captives into the hands of our Lord, Jesus Christ."

As I spoke, Bishop Elliot's demeanor changed from determined skepticism to profound interest. At the end, his eyes were aglow and a smile beamed across his face.

"She is good!" He exclaimed to my surprise. He then came and stood in front of me. He adjusted his manner to the austerity of the moment in which we were about to enter. He placed the palm of his right hand on my forehead and spoke in a voice of grave seriousness.

"In the name of the Father, Son, and Holy Ghost, I ordain you a minister in the Apostolic Faith."

He took my hand firmly in his.

"Welcome Sister Bissett to the war against the devil."

Wheezing and coughing badly, Bishop Rogers managed to express his congratulations as I accepted his frail and trembling hand. It wasn't until Bishop Elliot handed me a certificate of ordination that I began to realize what had happened to me. Suddenly, I found myself a minister in the faith my Mother had grown to distrust and I had made every effort to avoid. Whatever benefits my ordination served Bishop Rogers would not be realized. He died about three months later without ever showing me how to bless the candles.

As time passed, I began to treasure my ordination as an act of faith. But for me, joining the church was out of the question. Religion still remained an imposing intruder into my realm of critical thinking, dashing my best hope of offering God a soul unsullied by the seemingly indelible stains of self serving, self righteous doctrines and traditions. I had no intentions of pursuing the adulation and accolades dispensed by pretentious and arrogant men who exerted authority over their churches at the expense of the eternal truth of God. The earth revolves around the sun. The Catholic Church could not convince God otherwise irregardless of the number of heretics it burned at the stake. There were times when I believed that the human experience had degenerated into one unredeemable synergy of blasphemy. I could envision no hope of escape by adhering to the judgments and rituals imposed upon those ordained in the Apostolic or any other faith. After he presided over Bishop Rogers' funeral, I never saw Bishop Elliot again; nor was I contacted by the church. It was about this time that I met Emmett who would be a source of badly needed strength.

Emmett Morris was one of those rare black men with a light complexion, course blonde hair, and green eyes. From our first meeting at a domino game at a nearby playground, I knew that a relationship between us had virtually no chance of blossoming. He was totally self absorbed and very domineering. He was an auto mechanic, but assured me that this line of work was only the entry level of his aspirations. There was an inherent decency about Emmett that drew me towards him even though his arrogance kept me at arms length.

One evening our conversation settled on my children. I explained to Emmett how I had been unable to take care of my children and that the court had turned them over to their father.

"You're going to visit your kids!" Emmett asserted so defiantly that I was startled and bewildered. "You're not going to give them white folks the satisfaction of denying your kids their black Mother. I'll drive you out there. You're going to see your kids."

I found myself caught up in a dilemma. In the church there is a saying: "Take your burden to the Lord and leave it there. Don't pick it back up." Ultimately I believed that the children were in God's care. I wanted to leave them alone. They had a right to make their lives without them being emotionally torn time and time again. But Emmett was also right. I could not let my children drift into feelings of being absolutely abandoned by their Mother.

Despite Emmett's encouragement, I was nervous and apprehensive as we made the drive to the City of San Fernando. I sent Emmett to the door to tell the kids that I was there. Chuck's girlfriend answered the door and refused to let the kids out unless I came to the door. I wanted to go home, but Emmett talked me out of it. The girlfriend opened the door to my timid knocks. She was a large, rawboned woman, with a contentious manner. Her hair was black and stringy. When I asked that the children come out to see me, she insisted that I come inside. The imperious tone of her voice caused me to bristle. She had assumed the role of Mother to my children and there was little that I could do about it, even though she and Chuck had not yet married.

"Could you tell Chuck that I would like to speak to him out here? I didn't come to see you. I came to see them."

We matched glares until she realized that I had no intentions of blinking and then she left in a huff to retrieve Chuck.

When Chuck joined me on the porch, I lashed out at him loud enough for his girlfriend to hear every word.

"Chuck, I've come all this way to see the kids. And I expect to have some privacy in my visits. I will not have them supervised by your girlfriend. Now, you either let the kids out of the house or we go back to court. No court in this land is going to deny me privacy when I want to see my children."

Chuck flung the door open wide. "Kids, your Mother's here to visit. Come on outside," he called.

We all piled into the car and began sharing kisses and hugs. My visit lasted only about half an hour. The children were in good spirits and were getting along quite well. Emmett had been right. The children needed to be reminded that I was still their Mother and that I had not abandoned them. A short while later Emmett crashed my car into a bridge. That was the straw that broke the back of our whirlwind romance. Later he landed a job in some area of naval logistics and I never heard from him again.

Over the years Wilbur continued to dart in and out of my life. We generally made the rounds of clubs for about a month or so before I would come to my senses and break off the relationship. We had both grown to regard each other as necessary diversions: him from the grim realities of his job as a trash hauler and of juggling the needs of two families; me from the loneliness that nudged me ever closer towards the bottomless abyss of depression. But I knew this too had to stop.

It was during one of our on-again periods, that I went out looking for him. I stopped off at his co-worker's place where I was invited inside by his wife, Genella. Only Genella and her friend Doris were there. We exchanged greetings as I sat at the end of the table away from their conversation. I had seen them on a few occasions when I accompanied Wilbur there. They usually gambled with the men and said very little to me. Genella was short, buxom and sullen. Doris was taller, well proportioned, and animated. She turned her attention from Genella and studied me for a long moment before turning her chair to face me.

"You have the power. I know you have the power." Doris insisted. "I know 'cause I'm a hoochie-koochie woman and I can tell you have the power. My Mother was a hoochie-koochie woman and so was my Grandmother. They taught me things to do to make certain things happen, but I try not to use them."

I had not heard the term "hoochie-koochie" since my childhood in Brooklyn. The idea of my attempting to exhort and coerce the earthbound spirits to do my bidding through bones, potions and unintelligible incantations seemed too far fetched to me. Yet my own Grandmother could be called a "hoochie-koochie" woman. I had no desire to demean her faith. Nor did I want to convey the impression of being of a kindred spiritual mind. On the other hand, I was curious as to what she was getting at.

"How can I help you?" I asked tepidly.

"I have a friend. And this friend had an old man that she loved above all else. But he would take her money and beat the hell out of her. And it would hurt me to watch my friend suffer, but she loved him. Then she met another man who cared about her and was good to her. But she didn't love him, nor did she want to give him a chance. So I did something and her old man went out of her life. My friend finally accepted the other man and is with him today. But when her old man went out of her life, the joy in her spirit went out also. And I can't undo it. Doris lamented as the tears began to stream down her face. "I have watched her for years now and the joy has not returned. But you have the power and I need you to help my friend."

"Have you asked God to forgive you?" I asked.

"Yes, many, many times." She answered, her voice reeking with desperation. But Doris' tear drenched face reflected a deep shame that would yield only to remorse and atonement.

"Now, why don't you turn to your friend and ask her for forgiveness," I offered softly to Doris.

She mustered her courage and slowly raised her tear drenched face sheepishly to Genella.

"I am so sorry, please forgive me," Doris whimpered in heartfelt humility.

Genella glared at Doris incredulously when it struck her that she had been the subject of Doris' witchcraft.

"You put some shit on me!" Genella raised fiercely across the table at Doris who had slumped ashamedly into her chair. "You had better get it off of me. And I mean right now," she concluded threateningly.

"Genella," I said gently; "she just said that she can't take it off. Look at her sorrow. Don't you think that if she could have taken it off, she would have done so a long time ago? She's been suffering in silence along time, praying for God to send a deliverer."

"What do you mean you can't take it off of me? I don't care how long she's been waiting," Genella fumed in a maniacal rage directed toward Doris. "All I want is this shit off of me. Do you understand! And I mean I want it off right now!"

Genella's body quaked from anger as her eyes grew wide from rage and astonishment. It was not for me to judge as to whether there had been, in truth, a spell cast upon her by Doris. Nor was it my place to abdicate the role of deliverer that Doris had cast me in. She obviously had seen something in me that had eluded me completely. I felt that I had been called upon to do God's work. There was nothing else I could do but to summon forth my best efforts to help these two people in distress.

"Please Genella," I began sympathetically. "Let us not forget that just because we are not in a church, it does not mean that we are not assembled before the throne of God. Before you, me and God, Doris has bared her soul and confessed her wrongdoing. Don't you see? She was trying to help purely out of her love for you. She was not trying to hurt you. But she did it the wrong way. Think Genella. If she had known this was going to happen, would she have done this to her best friend?"

"I guess not," Genella admitted reluctantly. "Well, let's forget the past. I just want this off of me."

Genella was still upset but had begun to gather her composure. I gauged that with a little more effort on my part she would be ready for what I would have to do.

"Genella," I began solemnly. "Before, you, me and God, Doris recognizes me as the deliverer come in Jesus' name. She's asking me to help you. I can only help you if you want me to help you. I can do nothing against your will."

"Of course I want you to! I don't care who gets it off. I just want it off."

"Then we have to do this my way. Is that okay with you?" I asked.

"Okay."

Genella grew calm and relaxed. Doris was still slouched in her chair gazing sullenly onto the floor.

"Do you accept her apology?" I asked Genella. Doris shifted her eyes penitently and stared hopefully at Genella.

"Yes, yes," Genella answered anxiously.

"Do you believe that I can remove the spell from you?"

"Yes, If she says you have the power then I believe you can do it," she said with conviction.

I turned to Doris. "You already know that you are forgiven. But don't do this anymore. The price is too high."

Doris nodded.

"Genella, get me a large bowl of clean, clear water and a Bible. I'm going to give you a spiritual bath, right now," I said with a comforting smile.

Genella placed a bowl of water on the table. I opened the Bible and the sixth chapter of Isaiah revealed itself to me. I asked God to bless the water. And then I began to gently sprinkle the water upon her as I prayed that Doris's spell be removed. I placed my hand upon her forehead and commanded her deliverance.

"Our Father, I come before you to ask your mercy upon this woman that any spells be washed away by your love and forgiveness. I beseech you, Oh God, to remove the spell right now that was cast by one who meant no offense against your eternal will and purpose but who thought she was doing right to help a friend. I ask this in Jesus' name."

Within me streamed a feeling of well being. I knew that I had been empowered, exalted. But I felt tremendously humble. I had indulged in an act of faith of which God was well pleased. I asked Genella to read a passage from the bible that she selected at random. When she finished, I offered a short prayer of thanks to God and brought the exorcism to an end.

"Doris, how are you feeling?" I asked.

"Much better," she responded as a smile formed on her face. "Kinda nice."

"Can you two be friends again?"

"Yeah. She meant well, but she shouldn't have done it."

Genella went over to Doris and they hugged warmly. She then went to make coffee for us. Ever so softly and sincerely, Doris thanked me.

I did not wait to see if Wilbur would show up. I never saw the ladies again after that night. Later, Wilbur told me that Genella and her husband had bought a house in a very pleasant area north of the city. I was happy for her. Their moving indicated to me that God had given Genella an opportunity at a new and joyful life. I heard nothing about Doris. Now and then, I would wonder how she is doing and say a little prayer for her.

Except for feelings of gratification, my first foray into spiritual exorcism was inauspicious. There were no claps of thunder. The earth did not quake. There were no blasts from the trumpets of angels to herald my foray into the world of spiritual warfare. Yet both ladies believed that they had been released from spiritual captivity. Perhaps for them, that was the extent of their spiritual need.

For me, it became painfully clear that we humans tend to view God more as an instrument of our wants and aspirations, rather than the Orchestrator of an incalculable array of cosmic concerns. We want what we want when we want it with little regard for the consequences until we are confronted by them. We configure and contrive our attitudes, conscience, and system of reasoning to accommodate those dogmas and polemics that promise us security, and power. We reserve for ourselves the right to sit in judgment and condemnation of our fellow man, without affording them the same right to sit in judgment and condemnation over us.

Under the harsh glare of reason, what happened with Doris and Genella may amount to less than a drop of water in the ocean. Doris came to realize that the power of evil cannot be used to do good. Genella had endured being physically abused by her lover and then spiritually abused by her friend. I had done my best to deliver two captive souls; one by forgiveness and the other by prayer.

# CHAPTER SEVENTEEN

# No Mercy

No fixed time or date had been established for me to visit the children. About every few months, the urge to see them would become so overpowering that everything else would be driven from my mind. The accumulated stress of living had created within me an acute phobia that made driving over freeways, bridges and hills virtually impossible. So I would have to find someone to drive me to see them. Wilbur was far too impulsive to be depended upon. His promises were always well intended. Then he would end up leaving me anxiously waiting, well past the agreed upon time, but it would have been at least two weeks before I heard from him again. By then he would have gotten over his guilt and avoided the brunt of my anger.

I had met Kahlil during my ill-fated stint as an employment counselor after my dismissal from Head Start. He was a tall, lanky young man with a very dark complexion. He served time in prison for an offense that he would not discuss. It was while doing his time that he converted to the Muslim faith and endured brutal persecution at the hands of the prison system because of it. He was consumed with such loathing for whites that he sincerely believed that whites had used the word "God" as a mocking perversion of the supreme deity because it was "dog" spelled backwards. He was very gracious and protective towards me. I became tolerant of his very extreme political, religious and social views. I regarded them as part of what for him was a very painful journey of growth and discovery. He introduced himself by sending me a very lovely green dress because he thought that I had been very gracious and considerate towards him during his quest to find a job. Kahlil was capable of extreme and impetuous violence which made our relationship tenuous at best. He was also in love with me, so I treated him delicately when it came to his feelings. He would have taken me to San Fernando for free, but I refused to go until he accepted payment for the trip.

The children ran out of the house and greeted me joyously as Kahlil pulled his van to the curb. But my joy soon turned to shock when I directed my attention to Julie. She had dyed her hair platinum blonde and applied lipstick and rouge heavily on her face. She was twelve years old, but could have easily been mistaken for a twenty year old hooker. I called Chuck out of the house and confronted him furiously about Julie's appearance.

"Chuck, what I've got to say, I'm going to say in front of Julie. Why are you letting Julie dress like a hooker? If I ever come back here and find her looking like this, I will take you to court."

Chuck shifted uncomfortably, but said nothing. I took Julie by the arm and walked her towards the house.

"You will wash all this crap off right now and don't ever let me catch you looking like this again." I scolded angrily and then shoved her forward before returning to the other kids.

I felt badly about scolding Julie. After all, she was only following the peer group at school. But it was beyond me why parents and teachers did not exert more control over the kids. In my mind, the fact that I was absent did not negate my responsibilities as her Mother.

A month or so later I visited the children again. Julie had reverted to her sweet twelve year old self. Victoria and Anita complained about the ill fitting and oversized clothes that Chuck's girlfriend had been buying for them at garage sales. I let it pass. On my next visit, the girls complained bitterly about the food they were served. What galled me most was that while the kids had to contend with liver that they swore tasted like dog food and spaghetti that they described as terrible, Chuck and his girlfriend dined grandly at a nearby steakhouse.

The moment I returned to town, I went to see a Lawyer. He understood my situation and provided me the forms as well as instructions on filling them out and filing them. A few weeks later, a probation officer from the Valley showed up at my door. I could tell by the looks of her that I did not stand a chance. She had blue eyes, shoulder length blond hair and the same supercilious smile worn on the face of the owner of the nursery school. She looked around my tiny house, but said practically nothing to me as she scribbled her impressions on her notepad.

Kahlil agreed to take me to my hearing at the San Fernando courthouse. We sat toward the rear of the courtroom while the probation officer sat across the aisle with Chuck and his girlfriend. When the case was called, the referee asked Chuck how he responded to my charges.

"Your honor," he began uneasily. "I realize there are problems and I have signed up for some therapy. And I am taking steps to correct our food problem."

"I recommend that the children remain in the care and custody of the Father," the probation officer responded officiously to the referee's query.

"Are you sure about that?" The referee asked in dismay.

"Yes."

A reproving scowl appeared on the referee's face as he scanned the papers in front of him. He repeated his query and received the same response. Seeing nothing on the papers to justify overruling his own investigator, he issued his ruling in a voice barely above a whisper.

"I'm sorry, Your Honor. I didn't hear you." I called from the back row of the courtroom.

He lowered his head and issued his ruling into the table. I heard enough to know that I had lost. But I wanted to hear the entire ruling.

I walked up to the bench and asked him point blank for his ruling.

"I am awarding Mr. Bissett the children," the referee stated with his head still lowered.

I stormed out of the courtroom. My heart was breaking. It was all I could do to keep from becoming hysterical. As we were leaving the courtroom, Kahlil flew into a rage. To my astonishment, it was directed at me.

"You fuckin bitch! Why did you bring me out here to watch whitey put the yoke on black people!" He yelled loud enough to draw attention from one end of the corridor to the other. Everyone in the hallway craned their necks and fixed their stares on the source of this outburst.

"They're putting the yoke on me, not on you." I retorted in a voice cracking from pain and embarrassment. "I asked you to drive me, but they're my kids and not yours."

"You goddamn mother fucken bitch! You must get some fucken pleasure out of making me watch the white man fuck over black people." He fumed as we descended from the courthouse steps.

The inexplicable gush of vulgarity lashed at me unmercifully as we walked to the van and drove towards home. I prayed that he would calm down before we reached the freeway. But his frustration surged through him and onto the accelerator. Now he was not only cursing me, but racing at full speed and recklessly darting from one lane to another.

"Kahlil, why are you driving so fast?"

"You mother-fuckin bitch! If you say another goddamn word, I'll throw your goddamn ass out on the freeway!" He screamed.

I took him at his word and settled for silent prayer as my means of protest and anger. By the time we reached his house, Kahlil had calmed down considerably. He tried to apologize and hug me. But his histrionics and insensitivity had transformed me into the human equivalent of ice cold water. There was nothing he could do or say to change that—ever.

With the exception of Laurie, I had no friends in which to confide my anguish and frustration. I had little choice but to distance myself from her because she had sought my help in vanquishing a prospective competitor for Marty's affection by means of a voodoo curse. She had claimed that a girlfriend in New York had taught her the ritual involved in placing the curse, but she did not believe she had the power to make it work.

"I wouldn't do that if I were you," I admonished when she solicited my help in performing a ritual that required her to bury a doll that would be symbolic of her competitor. "You don't know the consequences of what you are doing. I want no part of it."

Laurie performed the voodoo ritual without me. The competitor proved to be merely a party in business transactions involving Marty and her suspicions were a contrivance of her own jealous and possessive nature.

The judgment of the court and the venom that Kahlil had spewed out afterwards left me depressed and distraught. I visited Laurie and lamented my grief to her. She listened attentively, but said nothing of consolation. A few days later, she called me and spent the better part of two hours berating me for what she had concluded were plights of my own doing.

In her mind, Chuck was right. Why should he stand for his white children begin raised in a black ghetto? She offered that if I really wanted my children, I would be trying to pass for white as she was doing, in a white neighborhood. She stated emphatically that no positive end can come from running around with black people. It did not matter to Laurie that I was their Mother and that I was much too dark to pass for white. She carried that discrepancy by insisting that all I needed to do was act white, then they wouldn't take me for being black. It was my second tongue lashing within the week. As in the case of Kahlil, I was bombarded with invectives as though they, not me, had been denied the children. Also, as with Kahlil, Laurie was long on rage, but well short on what I needed most—compassion. I had not expected either of them to offer solutions to my problems with the legal system. But I was hopeful that they would acknowledge the severity of my circumstances and lend me a shoulder to at least deposit some of my grief.

Laurie's mindless rambling began to take a toll on my patience, but I dared not give her the satisfaction of knowing that. My silence eventually conveyed to her that she was bouncing her righteous indignation off of a stone wall.

"There's no sense talking to you. You're either too obstinate or too stupid." She said then slammed down the phone.

I couldn't wait to hang up the phone so I could release the billowing rage within me. Tears flowed uncontrollably onto my bed. Sleep eluded me, as well as resolution. I cried, raged and hated. Oh, cursed racism, why must you raise your evil head! Why must you raise the hate in my being! Oh God, what have I done so bad that I must be condemned and degraded except for the color of my skin! Was I not a Mother first? Am I not a human being? The spirit was right. Those whom I help may well become my enemies. Laurie has the sensitivity of a mindless shark and she had shown me her teeth. I resolved not to bother her again.

About three months later, she called me on the job.

"Miki, Connie's been killed on a motorcycle. Could you come over?" She said desperately.

"Yes, Laurie. I'll be there as soon as possible," I responded without the slightest hesitation.

"After all the bullshit that woman's put you through?" My boss asked incredulously when I asked for the rest of the day off.

"I know. But her daughter Connie's been killed. I am a minister first. I have to put my pride aside for some other time."

Laurie was crying uncontrollably when I arrived at her apartment. I sat beside her on the sofa and put my arms around her. She was relieved to see me. She told me that her nineteen year old daughter was riding on the back of her boyfriend's motorcycle. She was thrown off the motorcycle when it swerved to miss a passing car. Laurie wearily informed me that the doctors worked frantically in a futile attempt to save Connie's life. She had been unable to sleep in over thirty hours. I gently rubbed her hand until she fell asleep. Aside from going to work, I remained with her for three days until the funeral.

A week later I dropped by to see how Laurie was doing. Her eyes were still swollen from mourning for Connie, but her interest and concerns were directed on what had transpired between us.

"I now know how you must feel," she began somberly as we sat together on the sofa. "At least I know that my daughter is at peace with God. But you have a cancer that never heals. Every time you think that it is in remission, it flares up again. I don't know if I could constantly be going through that. Even though I grieve for a long time, I have the knowledge that she is with God. I don't have to worry about who is mistreating my child and then being slapped down by courts. I didn't understand it before. But I understand it now. How you must suffer."

Laurie's tears of compassion drew tears of gratitude from my eyes. But it disheartened me that it took a tragedy in her own life to realize that a Mother's love knows no color and that the yearnings in her heart cannot be subjugated to social and economic conventions. Several years later she called me. She was still grieving over the death of her daughter.

The time had come for me to end my obsession with Wilbur. Somehow, I had to get him to accept the fact that my life had taken a different course and he had to let me go. I was hoping that I could get him to agree to an amicable termination of our relationship that he would honor. It was with this purpose in mind that I sought him out on his route. I caught up to his truck at about noon, only to be informed by his co-worker that Wilbur had passed out and was rushed to the hospital.

I had to see Wilbur. But I didn't want to go during regular visiting hours and risk a confrontation with either of his families. An understanding nurse allowed me to see him.

"Hi sweetie. What's new pussycat?" I said as I leaned over and kissed him on the forehead. He opened his eyes from his snoozing.

"Hi, sweetie."

"Whatever happened to you?" I asked.

"They think I caught something while I was rabbit hunting up near Bakersfield. But they don't know what."

"Well that's what they said. So they're keeping me here under observation."

"Honey, can I give you a spiritual bath right here and now. Maybe you don't believe in what I do, but if I can help other people, why not you? It can't hurt."

"Do you really think it'll help?"

"I don't know, but it can't hurt."

"Okay, sweetie. Give it your best shot."

I took the pitcher of drinking water from his nightstand and blessed it. I then sprinkled him from head to foot and prayed.

"I'm going to go now. You get as much sleep as you can, okay."

The next day an ebullient Wilbur informed me that the doctors could find nothing wrong and would be sending him home. To what extent the spiritual bath effected Wilbur's recover, I dared not speculate. For me it remained an expression of hope rather than a cure. What had stricken him remained undetermined. My concerns for his health placed our relationship on hold. But about a week later, a strange and disturbing dream intruded upon an otherwise deep and restful sleep.

I saw myself descending steps into a medieval dungeon-dank and dim. I took a key dangling from a hook on a column and walked quietly passed a sleeping guard. I opened the door to one of the cells. Wilbur stood before me wearing briefs so perfectly white that seemed illumine scent against his dark skin. His head and face were bound with strips of leather that criss-crossed, forming a mask. I motioned for him to remain silent as I carefully removed it. The impressions from the leather strips left his face hideously bloated in checkered puffs. I led him out of the dungeon to a sparsely furnished chamber. A man with a thick beard and kindly manner assisted me in seating Wilbur in what appeared to be a barber's chair.

"He can't leave until we drain his face so he'll look normal." The man said placidly.

"But we have to leave." I insisted.

"No, we must do this first," He retorted. "If you want to leave, you can. But he has to stay. We'll take care of him."

I looked about and could see Georgia, Wilbur's second wife cleaning up and hanging curtains in the turret of the castle. A thick beam of blue light streamed through a large window. I concluded that she was preparing the place for Wilbur's return. Outside of the chamber, the drawbridge was being slowly raised. Standing on the draw chain at the end of the bridge was my Mother, dressed in a loose-fitting black dress with white buttons down the front. She was yelling to me.

"Jump, Miki, jump."

I realized that if I stayed with Wilbur in the chamber, I would never be able to leave. I started running as fast as I could across the slowly raising drawbridge.

"Miki, Jump." Mother yelled frantically as I approached the end of the bridge. I leaped off the drawbridge at the last possible moment. I had no idea of what my fate would be, but I had to trust my Mother. To my surprise instead of dropping like a rock, I floated towards the moat below like a feather. From nowhere, a small raft with a white sail billowing from its shaft floated beneath me and caught my fall. I remained on all fours as the suddenly rushing waters carried me away from the castle and to a place where bright, yet gentle, sunlight glistened against the unblemished beach. In the distance, I could see the castle being enshrouded in black, ominous clouds.

The wake of the dream remained a prominent part of my consciousness over the next few days. I thought long and deep about its spiritual significance. I concluded that I took a big chance going into the dungeon to get Wilbur out. But I was accountable only for my own actions and not of those whom I delivered from captivity. The white briefs Wilbur wore conveyed forgiveness and certainly not a purity of spirit. Georgia was waiting to receive him. The black clouds would eventually pass. Wilbur and Georgia needed only to endure and persevere. But it was only a dream. Wilbur and I were not yet free of each other. I was well aware that because of the plate in his head, my severing our relationship could cause a violent reaction.

It was about a month after the dream that I met Billy. A gloriously handsome, virile man, Billy Hammond reminded me very much of Wilbur. Like Wilbur, he was capable of sudden shifts from deep sensitivity to incomprehensible, insufferable rage and arrogance. We met at a restaurant that I frequented. He had been hurt on a construction job and was awaiting a settlement. A few weeks after we began dating, he moved in. To avoid a confrontation, I had to seek out Wilbur to get my house key and to bring our affairs to a close. It was about five in the morning when I pulled up behind his car and flashed him to the curb with my headlights. I was nervous and apprehensive as we met on the street as I searched within myself for the right words and the right tone of voice.

"Wilbur. I have met another man." I began deliberately. "And I think I can find some happiness with him. So I've come to get my key and to ask you to leave me alone."

He said nothing as he slowly retrieved the key from his wallet and gave it to me.

"I bet you thought I was going to get ignorant. Didn't you, sweetie? Fooled you, didn't I?" He said with a soft giggle. And then he looked at me with sincere, solemn eyes. "If there's only one person on this earth who deserves some happiness, it is you, sweetie," he paused and expended a sigh of resignation. "I am a strong man, but you are much stronger. I couldn't have gone through what you have without going ape. I will have to wait for another time and place to love you. You no longer belong to a man. You belong to mankind. You belong to God. But if you think another man can give you the happiness you deserve, then I won't stand in your way. I left one set of kids. I won't leave another. They're innocent in all of this. Someone has to be responsible for them. So I will let you go."

I kissed him tenderly on the cheek. He returned to his car and drove off to work. Wilbur had become transformed from a man of reckless emotions to one of moderate reasoning. My heart and soul had invested six years of hope and anguish in a relationship that was virtually doomed from the start. But I had done some good for the man I loved. I felt both pain and joy over my loss and his inner growth. I cried all the way home and long after I got there. Billy was both upset and dismayed that I would carry on like this over a man that I didn't love anymore.

Wilbur did not try to contact me. But he did express his desire to resume our relationship in the form of lodging his paycheck stub in the crack of my door. Billy would become furious and accuse me of secretly continuing my affair with Wilbur. One Saturday, Bill became so enraged when he found a paycheck stub in the door that he threatened to leave me if he found another one. He then stormed out of the house. I bought a half pint of Southern Comfort from the liquor store and drained it. Under the throes of my booze induced boldness, I telephoned Georgia.

"Georgia, this is Miki."

"Miki, I don't know no Miki. Who are you?"

"Don't give me that bullshit. I've been in your life for six years. And you don't know me! Now you just shut up and listen to what I've got to say. You want him, you got him. Just tell him to leave my high yella ass alone. I'm not bothering him and I don't want him bothering me. You tell him to leave me alone. Cause he sure don't want me to come over there."

"You better not come over here. I'll blow your mother fucken brains out," Georgia said defiantly.

"You and what goddamn army? You better tell him what I said," I threatened and then slammed down the phone.

I didn't like talking to Georgia as I did, but I had to make her understand in the only way she would that I was deadly serious. I had no doubt that I had unleashed a major plague into Wilbur's life and she would remain one until he mended his philandering ways. I did not see or hear from Wilbur for nine years. I encountered him one evening when I stopped at a restaurant on my way home from seeing a client in Long Beach. His appearance and charming manner had not changed. He and Georgia were still together and he had advanced to route foreman on the job. I had never known him to go to church except for funerals. Now he was an elder. The dream had been realized. God had taken care of my concern and I was well gratified.

Billy and I spent about a year together. His jealousy and paranoia became more and more intolerable even as he lauded me for bringing peace and stability into his turbulent life. A deeply troubled woman was referred to me for spiritual guidance. She called almost every other day promising to commit suicide because of a marriage that was terminating after twenty years. I would spend hours with her at her house attempting to pull her from the edge. Billy could not bear having to share me with an act of mercy even in my own living room. I asked him to leave when he accused me of passing messages to other men through my client. Much later, I learned that he had won a large sum of money at the racetrack and was killed not long afterwards under mysterious circumstances. I guided the woman through the suicidal phase of her marital crisis. I promised her that the problem would be resolved in her favor within five years. But she wanted him back immediately and deemed any resolution to the contrary as a failure. Five years later she called me to announce, to her surprise, that her former husband wanted reconciliation. She turned him away.

The spiritual visions and, of course, the dreams usually intruded upon my sleep. At the paint store I was grateful that I could manage the accounts payables and receivables without spiritual distractions. But one day I became so emotionally and mentally absorbed by what was unreeled inside my head, that all efforts to work ceased.

My Mother was looking as she did when she summoned me to jump off the drawbridge. This time she was hovering above the middle of a busy freeway as the traffic flowed beneath her feet. There was a look of stern resolve on her face as she frantically appeared to be directing the traffic onto six different routes. Approaching her was a car containing my six children. Since the course of the traffic did not respond to her direction, I concluded that she was imparting guidance to the children.

Not long afterwards, I learned that while moving the family to their new home, the trailer that Chuck used to haul their belongings almost jack-knifed on a two lane winding road. With considerable effort, Chuck was able to avert going over the side of the road. On my next visit, all of the children confessed to me that they had become involved in religion with no prompting from their Father. To me, the vision confirmed that God had granted my petition by sending Mom in the spirit to take care of my children. And for them to have life, they would have to come to believe in God.

A few months later, I received a phone call from Julie informing me that she and Victoria had run away from home and were about to board a Greyhound from Oxnard to downtown Los Angeles. Hurriedly, I drove to the bus station and then waited impatiently for them to arrive. I was glad to see them, but very much concerned about what they had done.

"Julie, Victoria," I said solemnly after we loaded into my car. "I have to report this to the police or your Dad might accuse me of kidnapping. I have not choice. I have to let him know that you're with me. And whichever way it goes, we have to take it."

We went directly to the Southwest police station. A policeman placed a call to Chuck.

"Your two daughters are standing her before me. They've run away to be with their Mother. They're okay."

The policeman scowled as he listened to Chuck.

"Don't send the Sheriff down here," the policeman stated firmly. "We will not turn the girls over to them. They have a guardian and they came voluntarily. That's our primary concern. That they're not on the streets alone."

He listened impatiently as Chuck was undoubtedly stating his case for the return of the girls.

"We're not going to get into the middle of a custody battle," the policeman protested loudly and emphatically. "If you disturb Mrs. Bissett, we'll have to arrest you. I'm telling you right now. Don't send the Sheriff either, because we will not recognize their authority in this matter. Why don't you let the girls stay for Christmas and then all of you can decide what to do after New Years? Don't you think that's a good idea?

He listened patiently as Chuck responded and then brought their conversation to an end.

"I'll tell her, Mr. Bissett. And you have a nice holiday," the policeman said and then rang off. He then turned his attention to me.

"Go home and have a nice Christmas. I don't think he'll bother you for now. He'll call you and arrange to meet you after New Years. But for now, go home in peace."

The moment we reached the house, I sat my daughters down and demanded that they tell me what happened.

"Mom, I had a dream," Julie began. "I was wrapped in this quilt that was so light that I felt weightless. It was so peaceful. When I woke up, I just knew that I had to leave Dad's house. I just knew it. Mom, I was so unhappy. Dad's wife gave me the chore of ironing for ten people every day. I started getting loaded to keep from thinking about ironing. But I don't like being loaded. I want to stop. But I don't know what to do about being so unhappy. Only you can help me, Mom. I need you. I wanted to bring everybody, but I knew I couldn't. I picked Victoria. She looked like such a helpless kitten. I couldn't leave her behind.

"Well, how did you do this?"

"We climbed out of our bedroom window and hid at a girlfriend's house. She called a boy who had a car. He came and took us to the bus station. We didn't have any money for bus fare so we started panhandling. Some Sailors came into the depot and we hit on them. I told them that my Dad wouldn't let us go to visit my Mom for Christmas.

And we had no bus fare to go to LA to see her. They took up a collection and gave us enough for bus fare and something to eat. I called from the bus depot. And here we are." Julie concluded spritely.

My heart was aching. My beautiful baby had become a drug addict and she could not turn to her father for help. I embraced her tightly and then stroked her golden blonde hair. I wanted so desperately to convey that I was there for her and always will be.

"It's okay, Julie. I love you. But where do you get all these drugs?"

"I can get them at school when I have money. But the Stepmother has all kinds of pills in the bathroom cabinet," she then began to rattle off the names of the drugs.

"And these people think that they are better than me," I murmured to myself.

I began to think about Julie's dream and how it figured in the order of things. Part of what she said was a dimension of the spiritual and the rest was a misunderstanding that only maturity and time could correct. Within the quilt, she experienced the ecstatic spiritual peace. But what she did not understand was that such a level of peace can only be attained when a harmonious balance of forces such as love, faith and futility, and hate are maintained within the crucible of one's life. The drugs were an unfortunate catalyst that enabled Julie to deaden the deep and lingering inner pain that is an inevitable consequence when a thirteen year old must endure the crush and grind of this life's inequalities upon her gestalt, alone. Perhaps the ultimate benefit of the quest for a spiritual center is the rejection of the temptation to sit in judgment of Julie's addiction. It would be so much easier for me to take the socially acceptable scenic route of self righteousness, blame and retribution. But my daughter was crying out for help from the very depths of her soul and that was where I would have to go to save her.

And if I could not reach it, then I would have to trust that God would.

# CHAPTER EIGHTEEN

# Back To Court Again

It was a happy time for Julie and Victoria given the sparse accommodations that I provided. They brought with them only the clothes on their backs and I had no money to buy them any. They wore my nighties and robes and made fun of each other while romping on my bed like carefree puppies. Since I used no hard drugs and the children had no money, Julie had to resign herself to the fact that the pills that she filched from her stepmother were no longer available. Fortunately, she was not yet addicted to drugs and suffered no ill effects from her deprivation.

One night during this Christmas season, I was visited by yet another dream. In it, I was escorted past a door by a tall, thin woman with light brown hair wearing a white long sleeved blouse and a black floor length skirt and a face of serene devotion to her purpose. We entered what I could only presume to be a room in the firmament. The room was devoid of floor, walls, and ceiling. She directed me towards a dark wooden cradle that was the sole object in the room. Inside the cradle, seemingly in peaceful sleep, was the face of what I had come to regard as God. From her waistband she took a key and inserted it into the side of the cradle, turned it on and then silently walked away. Slowly, the eyes opened and He stared up at me. The strands of his dark gray beard began to unfurl and then curl as though they had minds and, perhaps, even souls of their own. To the left of me appeared a holograph depicting the Virgin Mary seated on a rock with Jesus lying next to her with his head resting on her lap. The holograph disappeared, but the face of Jesus, calm and peaceful as in a gentle death, appeared in the cradle next to that of God. Slowly his face began to merge with God's. His eyes opened and he gazed at me with tender compassion. With love and reverence, I began to stroke his face. Then the cradle began to fill with water. My eyes were transfixed on the superimposed faces of Jesus and God's shimmering under the water. Suddenly a bright white light filled the cradle. I was consumed by the ecstatic beauty of the moment. It compelled me to climb into the cradle. As I lifted my leg to climb into the cradle, my escort came rushing towards me.

"No, no. It's not your time," she scolded, backing me away from the cradle. "You have to go back."

She turned off the cradle and walked away. In the doorway, the Virgin Mary appeared cradling a baby in her left arm. The baby was smiling and grinning. It reminded me so much of my baby Sarrah. I asked the Virgin Mary about my future. But it was the baby who conveyed to me a telepathic message.

"Everything is peace and love. Isn't it beautiful? Enjoy it. Why are you worrying about things like that?"

"Things have been going too badly for me," I implored. "I just want to know. Please tell me"

The baby rested his head on the Virgin Mary's shoulder and looked at me shyly before responding to my query.

"Seven years."

"Julie, Julie." I yelled as I jolted from the dream, trembling from the joy of the experience. Julie hurried into my bedside. Her voice responded with alarm and concern.

"What's wrong Mommy? Are you alright?"

"Oh, yes." I stated, gushing with elation. "I was with God. It was so wonderful. I cannot describe it, Julie. It was so wonderful that I almost didn't come back."

"That's nice Mom." Julie said noncommittally, and then she left the room somewhat disappointed that her prompt response to my urgent call did not yield a crisis worthy of her concern.

The fulfillment of the dream could not have begun more discouragingly. New Years found me once again out of a job. The incident that led to me quitting the paint store seemed so trivial that my boss' outburst caught me as much by surprise as my intentions to throw a metal calculator at his head if his harangue persisted. From some inexplicable reason, he resented the painting contractors coming up to my second floor office to drop off money to me as a Christmas present. The more he tried to stop them from climbing the stairs to my office, the more they insisted on doing so. When I took a quarter out of the cash register to buy tissues, he verbally lashed out at me to a point of accusing me of stealing. I returned the quarter and quit.

After New Years, I met with Chuck and Mrs. Yudkoff to confer on the placement of Julie and Victoria. The girls were adamant in their desire to stay with me. Chuck had little choice but to defer to his daughters' wishes. There was then the matter of support until I could find another job. Since verbal abuse by an employer was not considered an appropriate reason for leaving a job, unemployment payments were denied me. Aid for Dependent Children would not honor my request for help until an application for custody made its way through the system nor would they allow me even food stamps. Chuck was not required to make payments and didn't. From time to time clients were referred to me for spiritual counseling, and I made myself available to taxi those neighbors who were without transportation. Despite the rough times, the girls took it all in stride and rarely complained.

Julie had made friends with Jerry Haynes, one of the young men who hung out in the neighborhood. He was older than Julie and very thin. What impressed me most about Jerry was an exuberance that seemed boundless even in this depressing and often hostile environment. The first time he visited Julie was during one of my spiritual readings. He sat quietly while I administered a spiritual bath and prayed over the lady's plight. She was married to a man who got paid, got drunk and then got abusive towards her. She had come to me hoping that I would somehow intervene on her behalf to God to "make Willie good." After a solemn prayer, I turned to her.

"You have the power of the Holy Spirit to make Willie good," I stated assuredly. "Now when are you going to pick up a pot of boiling water or something to let Willie know that he's not to beat you?"

"Oh, I can't do that. I love Willie." The woman said aghast that I, presumably a woman of God, would suggest violence as means of solving her problem. "I can't hurt Willie. I love him."

"Then Willie is going to keep beating you until you use the power God has given you to stop him. Is that what you want? For Willie to keep beating you? I'll be damned if I won't do something if my man was beating me."

Jerry broke into a fit of hysterical laughter. I explained that it was not God's purpose to resolve that which only requires a bit of common sense. I was well aware that Jerry was not accustomed to hearing a preacher dispense a resolution drawn straight from the manual of the streets. He was more accustomed to preachers advising their troubled parishioners to pray to God and do nothing until He responds. Since the woman loved Willie too much to leave him, the only rational course was for her to understand that love does not require her to be his punching bag.

A few weeks later, the lady returned to apprise me of what transpired.

"I ran into one of those guys who sells clothes out of the trunk of his car. He had these three fine dresses for thirty dollars. I tried to talk him down to twenty. Since we were in a restaurant parking lot, I invited him in for a cup of coffee to talk about it. Just when we were about to cut a deal, that damn Willie showed up talking wild and crazy. The man got scared and left. I got so made that I grabbed a fork and jabbed Willie in the arm as hard as I could. He jumped back and stared at me like I was some kind of crazy woman. I told him he better stop acting a fool about my money or I'd do it again. Now, every time he takes a notion to hit me, I grab a fork and he heads out the door. He better not hit me no more. And he better not mess with my money. I'm serious as a heart attack!" She concluded with conviction.

Not long afterwards, Willie himself showed up at his wife's insistence for spiritual counseling. He had been arrested for burglary and was facing forty five years in prison. Despite the fact that he was drunk, we talked and prayed for a long time. Julie intervened to explain to Willie how the cops knew that he was lying. A look of amazement appeared on Willie's face when he realized that the jig was up. We convinced him that it would go better for him if he told the truth. He promised to do so. He struck me as a descent man with a good heart. The judge must have seen that in Willie. He served two years on weekends while working his way up to foreman of a building maintenance crew.

Jerry told his friends about this "cool preacher lady" and then brought about eight of them to meet me. For awhile, my house became the neighborhood hangout for Jerry and his friends. I had only one record of a religious nature. It was "Oh Happy Day". Its upbeat tempo and simplistic message of joyous anticipation, made the record an instant favorite with them. For me it was both gratifying and amusing to watch as many as ten young men doing their "Holy Ghost Dance" to this one record for two or three hours at a stretch. When they wore out my record, they bought another and wore that one out too.

Like his friends, the nature of Jerry's life, in itself, was a plea for help. Gradually, he began to realize that I was someone that he could trust with his pain. Whenever we were away from the others, he would convey to me his anguish over his Father's abandonment of the family and the contentious relationship he had with his Mother. I understood from my own experiences that Jerry's Mother was struggling as best she could to manage under circumstances that were virtually impossible and he did nothing to lighten her burden. But Jerry needed to find a focus for his own life and could not do so in a place where he could not find peace. Despite my own grave circumstances, I allowed him to move in with us.

Not long afterwards, Julie showed up with yet another young man struggling to find himself and his way. Franklin Taylor was tall, lanky, with a jovial and carefree disposition. Julie met him through a mutual friend after one of his many escapes from Juvenile Hall. Franklin was a gifted pianist who became addicted to drugs. After exploring all avenues at their disposal to rehabilitate him, his parents left him in charge of the juvenile authorities. Yielding to Julie's urging, I took Franklin in and then called his probation officer. He warned me that Franklin's escapes from Juvenile Hall were legendary and that he never remained in one place very long. I decided to take the chance. The probation officer then recommended that I commence the process of becoming a licensed foster parent. After I laid down a strict set of rules, the five of us settled into a life of both desperation and faith.

It turned out to be the busiest period of my life. Just about every day, someone came by in need of transport to the market or to keep an appointment. In addition, I was getting more referrals for spiritual counseling. Nonetheless, we were squeaking by on a day to day basis. I was surprised at how quickly my motley family grew in the spirit of mutual respect. They were tolerant of each other's space and idiosyncrasies. Good natured kidding and laughter usually accompanied the meager fare that I served at mealtimes. Jerry's friends usually came by in the evening and all the cares of the world were then rendered to insignificance by the frenetic rhythms of "Oh Happy Day" and the unbridled physical exertions that was "Holy Ghost Dancing". By taking Jerry in, I derived another benefit that I had not considered.

I assumed that Julie would be attending nearby Washington High in the fall, but Jerry was adamant that I send her to school where whites would be in the majority.

"Ain't no white chick going to make it at Washington High," Jerry stated assertively. "Around here everybody looks out for Julie and

Victoria, because they know you're good people. But we can't protect her there. The racism is too deep."

I was both flattered and grateful that Jerry and his friends had taken such interest in my daughters and me. I took Jerry's advice and enrolled her at Westchester High. It was a long ride on the bus for her, but I felt much better knowing that she could learn in an environment not so heavily charged with racism.

One evening at dinner Jerry confessed to Julie that he would get loaded on "reds" and then ravage his mother's house.

"She's always on my case about something." He responded despairingly to Julie's query as to why. "Even when she knows that I didn't do it, she gets on my case like I did. Sometimes I just can't deal with it. So I get loaded and trash the crib."

"You know Jerry," I said with the utmost patience. "Your Mother's a saint. You think that I'm a good Mother, but I'm not. If you did to me what you say you done to her, you would have been in a coffin six feet under a long time ago."

Jerry began to giggle, but I could tell that he got the point.

"You should be kissing your Mother's feet and doing everything she asks of you," I scolded. "I'm telling you, Jerry, you have a wonderful Mother to tolerate the things you've done. Don't you know that she loves you, man? Love or no love, my son would not do this to me because he'd know that home is the refuge against the world. And if he got loaded like that, he would have to stay in the streets until he got unloaded. So you see Jerry, your Mother's a saint and you should respect her better than you do."

Jerry nodded knowingly. A few days later, he moved back with his Mother. The relationship improved, but Jerry succumbed to the lures of the street and slowly drifted out of our lives.

The probation officer was ecstatic because Franklin had spent three months at my house without running away. He told me that whenever Franklin was returned to Juvie Hall from one of his escapes, he would be gone again by the time they came to change the sheets on his bed.

I understood, probably more so than his parents, that Franklin needed to find a place within himself from which to express himself. But there were forces within him warring for his soul and forces without fighting for control of Franklin. All that he needed was a sense of peace where he could sort out his own gestalt. I asked only of him that he respect my home and refrain from using drugs. For the opportunity to seek inner tranquility, Franklin gladly did as I asked.

One day in early March, a sedan with a state government seal on the door pulled up to the curb in front of the house. My stomach churned as all manner of possibilities passed through my mind. A young man moved hurriedly towards my door. I braced myself for what I concluded as yet another bureaucratic bombshell as I opened the door.

"I'm from the Unemployment Office. I'm looking for Elizabeth Bissett," the young man said.

"I am she." I admitted bewilderedly. "Come on in."

"I've got a job that you might be interest in. They will teach you how to use the PBX and you'll be proofing the accounts payable for the data processing department. But this is the last day for interviews. You've got to be there by three o'clock."

Since I was unaware that the state sent out people to personally delivery job referrals, I chalked it up as a small miracle and hurriedly made the drive to the address that I was given. It was a sofa manufacturing plant. I got the job. About two weeks later both the AFDC and the foster checks came. Franklin wanted to go to a place in Oregon where he felt he could get a handle on himself. Since he was only about three months shy of his eighteenth birthday and emancipation from the juvenile system, I gave him some money and bade him Godspeed. A week later, Franklin was sitting on my bed when I got home from work.

He was depressed and sullen as he told me that he had traveled along the coast only as far as Malibu when he stopped off to visit friends. With them he indulged in drugs and partied. During one of his drug "trips", he claimed he couldn't see himself in the mirror. His friend began to appear to him in all manner of demonic forms. He became frightened and left. He then realized that "tripping" was no longer the fun he thought it was. He had begun to realize that there raged within him a battle for control of his soul. Since he had spent all of the money I gave him, he concluded that he was not yet ready to go to Oregon. But he did believe that he was ready for a spiritual counseling. From there Franklin commenced in quiet, but determined effort to study the scripture to fortify his resolve against what he recognized as the darker forces of his nature.

I went by to visit with Franklin's probation officer and to inform him of Franklin's status. He not only knew all about his aborted trip to Oregon, but he greeted me with enthusiastic praise. He was elated that someone had finally made a breakthrough with Franklin. He called me "a miracle worker".

Although Franklin's ears were wide open to whatever spiritual counseling I had to offer, he was in total shutdown when it came to obeying one of my major house rules. I was beginning to believe that it was some sort of generic aversion that caused men to rebel against doing dishes. When I was unemployed, I did the dishes rather than to attempt to manage a system of rotating the chore. But now I was in no mood to put in eight hours on the job, cook dinner and then do dishes. Whenever Franklin's turn came to do the dishes, he would flatly refuse to do them. Any concessions on my part towards him drew vehement protests from Julie and Victoria. The issue reached a point to where I had no choice but to call his probation officer.

A woman came by from the probation office to return Franklin to Juvie Hall. Since he was so close to his eighteenth birthday and had done nothing criminal, she gave him the option of going anywhere he chose as long as it was not my house. He pleaded with me to allow him to stay. But I feared that both he and my daughters would dismiss my authority as little more than a joke. Besides, since Franklin would soon be entering the real world, now was as good a time as any for him to learn that there were consequences to his obstinate behavior. He left with the probation officer. About a year later, Franklin wrote me from a Christian commune in Oregon. He was doing well and thanked me for showing him the way to Jesus. He and his wife once came by to visit but I was not home. I never heard from him again.

About a month after I started at the furniture plant, I was promoted to controller. Handling accounts payable and receivables at paint stores hardly qualified me for the position. But the company was in dire straits. The company had to move to a temporary location until a permanent one could be found. The fiscal year was about to come to a close which meant that a certified audit had to be prepared. Its books were a mess. When the company could find no accountant to take on the task, I was promoted to take it on. After devoting a month and a half of eighteen hour days to reviewing bank reconciliations, analyzing errors, and researching omissions, the company owners waited in desperate anticipation. In the end, Julie, Victoria and I dined most grandly when the CPA and his wife invited us to one of the finest restaurants as a reward for a job well done.

I never considered myself psychic, primarily because I never regarded myself as endowed with the gift of prophesy or the ability to read the spiritual aura of others. For me, spiritual counseling meant tapping into a source within myself that seemed well versed in the problems of my clients. But I never felt fully confident in the advice that I gave, primarily because there were no substantive assurances that what I offered was in truth valid. Such was not the case with my daughter, Julie. Whereas I had to open my mouth and hoped that whatever flowed from it struck the nail on the head, Julie needed only to stare at my photo of the 'Sacred Heart of Jesus' that I kept on my altar, and somehow draw from it a fact or two that applied precisely to someone in the room. She would then turn to that person and explain exactly what she saw. The person then would stare at her in wordless amazement. We were delighted with her power to see events and names in the picture until the night a lady brought her boyfriend to me for spiritual counseling. Julie began reading the picture and then looked at the boyfriend accusingly.

"You just lost a lot of money gambling," she said.

"No, I didn't," He replied.

Julie looked at the picture again.

"Yes, you did," she said pressingly.

"No I didn't," the boyfriend retorted almost belligerently.

"I see cards being dealt in front of you and your money disappearing off the table," Julie stated decisively after referring again to the picture.

The girlfriend turned to her perplexed and annoyed companion. "Why don't you tell her the truth? We just lost $160."

She was at a loss as to why he would not own up to his losses. Julie too was in dismay and was determined to press the matter when I intervened.

"Julie, cut it off," I stated firmly. "If he says he didn't, then he didn't."

Julie looked at me in askance as I aborted the spiritual counseling session. When my clients left, I turned to Julie. I was not angry at her. But I had to make her understand that her powers were a blessing and that when people do not respond, she must proceed with great care.

"Julie, you were right. But when people deny it so hard, they have something to hide and are afraid the Spirit might reveal it. They might have robbed or killed somebody and we might be hurt if they think we know. So we won't do this anymore. It's too chancy."

Perhaps had I not made Julie promise not to use her special gift she would not have latched on to Ben Travis. I knew little about him except that he had been introduced to Julie by Franklin and that he was from Westchester, one of the older middle class communities of Los Angeles located near the airport. He had curly blonde hair, brown eyes, powerful build and seldom traveled without Dylan, a German Shepherd, who was extremely protective of him. He was always courteous and respectful towards me. I was unaware of the depth of their relationship until one night I came home form work and, to my horror, found my scantily clad daughter in my bed beside a very drunk Ben Travis.

"Ben. Get up and get out of here," I ordered angrily, "and I mean right now."

"No, I can't," He mumbled through his drunken stupor. "I can't go nowhere. I ain't got no place to go."

"I don't care if you sleep in an alley. Just get out."

"I'm not leaving. And if I leave, I'm taking Julie with me," Ben stated as he and Julie cuddled closer.

I started towards them, but was halted by a menacing growl from Dylan who was poised to attack me had I grabbed hold of Ben as I intended. I stormed from the house, called the Sheriff, and then waited outside for them to arrive.

Two squad cars pulled up at my house. I told them about the dog. They drew four pump guns from their cars and aimed them at the door. I was then told to order Ben from the house. Ben got dressed and came out with Dylan behind him. Having no cause to detain him, the police let him go.

"Don't come back or I'll charge you with statutory rape." I yelled at him.

"Oh no your not"; Julie stated defiantly as she grabbed me by the shoulder from behind. "You're not going to do that Mom."

I turned and grabbed Julie by the front of her shirt and pinned her hard against the side of the house.

"We're not animals. Do you understand me? There are rules that we have to live by," I screamed. "Don't you ever in your life grab me like that again. If you want to become an animal, I can become an animal too. Don't you try me. I'll hurt you! So help me God! I will hurt you! Now get in the house before I hurt you."

My rage had been so sudden and intense that the Sheriff deputies stared in shock with their rifles trained on me. A pastor from the neighborhood left his Cadillac in the middle of the street and sprinted onto the scene. Not even he would approach me until my fury had run its course.

"If that bum comes around here again," I screamed, "I'll have him thrown in jail. Do you hear me!" I yelled into the house after her.

Ben was Julie's first love. Despite the fact that he had no positive life prospects and was an abusive bully, she was obsessed with him. I needed only to consult the course of my own life to understand what Julie was going through. She was sixteen and her budding feelings of approaching womanhood were no different than those of any other normal sixteen year old girl who had ever walked the earth. I knew that my job was to make her understand that she had responsibilities, choices, and time over which only she could exert control. But words were no match for the overpowering yearnings that were readily accommodated by the sexual mores of the time.

A sculptor who lived around the corner and was studying for a master degree in primitive art began tutoring Julie in his art. He even took her along to assist him when he dissected cadavers at one of his classes at Long Beach State. Julie's interest and talent benefited immeasurably from the instructions from the sculptor. But what accentuated her enthusiasm for art was that she was able to meet Ben Travis at her tutor's house. She began skipping school to be with him. My hopes now lay with time and maturity as the agents to turn her away from Ben and onto a path of true self realization.

As I expected, Julie's behavior gradually became a mode for that of her sister Victoria who was entering junior high. She had begun engaging friends who were more interested in boys and gossip than in school work. Both she and Julie respected the sanctity of my home. But unfortunately, home could not accompany them to school or chaperone every aspect of their social lives. Eventually, I suspected that both became involved with drugs. Ben most likely provided them for Julie. With Victoria, I was never sure. I suspected that her drug usage was minimal at best, held in check by the funerals that she attended for her friends who overdosed. I continued to hope and pray.

The furniture manufacturer filed for bankruptcy and was on the verge of liquidation when a buyer was found. The buyer consolidated the operations of my plant with his. Once again I was out of a job. But the CPA for the furniture manufacturer referred me to a dress manufacturer with such a glowing recommendation, that I was hired as its bookkeeper right on the spot. My self esteem soared. I felt empowered. I had value in the workplace. Never again would I have to take any job that came to hand at whatever salary that was shoved in front of my face. My staunch adherence to critical thinking had not paid me the dividends that I had hoped. But it enabled me to become one fine bookkeeper and provided me some foundation to build a future upon.

Each time that I visited the kids in Camarillo, Anita and Sarrah urged me to take them home with me. Quietly, I rejoiced that the girls regarded being with me as being "home". My eldest son, Rodrick had "escaped" by joining the Army. Nathan was approaching eighteen and wanted to decide for himself where he wanted to be. Since the issue of custody for Julie and Victoria had not been resolved in the courts, I decided to pursue custody of the four girls.

Despite the fact that the girls were now old enough to articulate their own wishes, Chuck was determined to make a fight of it. When we appeared in the Superior court of Ventura County, the judge ordered me, Julie, and Victoria to meet privately with him in chambers.

"Where do you live?" He asked me no sooner than we settled in our comfortable chairs.

I knew in my heart, that Chuck and his attorney were plopping the race card defiantly on the table.

"I live between Watts and Inglewood," I responded calmly. "That's all I can afford, Your Honor. But it doesn't mean that I don't love my children and that they do not want to be with me. I lost them because I was a dependency case; not because I was a bad Mother. I am no longer dependent. For all of these years, I felt like a cymbal in an empty forest. No matter how loud I clang, no one hears me. You don't know what it feels like to be burdened with so many expectations and so little help from those who claim to serve the best interest of the children." I did not want to weep. But I could not help myself.

"You don't know what my Dad and Stepmother are like," Julie

interjected emphatically. "Anything we complain about, they just say "we understand", but they never hear what we have to say. He says that he can't help it if he's a bigot. But he doesn't want us to live with our Mother. No matter what color she is, this is my Mother. And my little sisters have a right to be with their Mother sometime in their life."

The judge's demeanor softened noticeably as he hung his head in despair. He patted me sympathetically on the hand as he spoke.

"I'll do the best I can, but their Father can opt for a trial. If he does, I'll have to leave everyone where they are rather than disturb the children until the matter is resolved."

He then called in Chuck, his attorney, Anita and Sarrah for their private session. I later learned that Anita and Sarrah were too frightened to speak for fear of retribution from their Father. The judge then returned to the bench to issue his ruling.

"If both parties agree, I can render a decision now. If not, you are entitled to a trial and I can render an interim decision. But what I have heard thus far disgusts me as much as anything I've heard before. It galls me that such a case should be placed before the court."

Chuck opted for the trail. It was scheduled for a month later. I felt that the judge had betrayed me with his reprimand. Although it was not directed to anyone in particular, Chuck had to conclude that the judge would award me the children had he not elected to go to trial. But the judge's solid demeanor at the outset of the hearing, I felt certain that he was inclined to award custody of the children to Chuck. But his meeting with Julie, Victoria and me in chambers had tapped into his sense of shame. Having found no fault in me as a Mother, he felt outraged at having to be placed in the position of having to rule on the case of Mother vs. Racism.

I was provided a Lawyer from Ventura County Legal Aid. He took my money, took my case and at the trial gave away my children. Many of the obvious points of issue that he should have introduced and pursued were totally ignored despite my urgings. But the end of the trial, I was all but certain that he and Chuck's attorney were in collusion.

I was overwhelmed with anecdotal situations and false innuendos that created a totally distorted picture of my control over Julie and Victoria. Chuck's attorney belabored the impression that it was I who was teaching the children to hate their Father because he was white. Unfortunately, Jerry and Franklin were black and therefore, inherently became an issue. With the exception of the Holy Ghost Dance, no acts that could be construed as unsavory were attributed to them. It was their mere presence in the household that created a tidal wave of concern in the mind of the court. Fortunately, Ben Travis was white and created little more than a ripple of concern even though I caught him in bed with my daughter and drunk. All of the children were awarded to Chuck with the exception of Julie who the judge deemed old enough to make her own decision. I left the courtroom disheartened and disgusted.

One morning, soon afterwards Julie imparted to me at breakfast a reason to once again hope that all would be well.

"Mom, Grandma came to see me last night," she began solemnly. "She said that it was the best she could do for us now. She tried but she was sorry that she couldn't do better."

"It's okay, Julie. We just have to continue to have faith. If you talk to Grandma again, tell her 'thank you' from me."

About that time, I had a vision of my own. A tall white candle sat on my altar. It's flickering light was suddenly extinguished and its smoke became a great grey tornado swirling into the heavens. From its wake came the voice that I had heard many times before.

"Do this no more. Jesus is the light of the world and needs no candles."

A few weeks later Laurie called me. She had come across a house in a very respectable black neighborhood that she described as a "steal". Since none of her friends were interested in living in that part of town, she thought of me. She informed me that the seller required no down payment and was willing to accept rent towards the option to buy at a very reasonable fixed sales price. After Laurie described the house to me, I told her that I would take it sight unseen.

The house was much more that I had imagined and Laurie had described. It was located on a quiet, well kept street. It had a living room, family room, large dining room and kitchen, two bedrooms with an unfinished third, a guest house, a two car garage, and a view. When school closed for summer, Julie and I moved in. That August, my son Nathan called to inform me that the Holy Spirit had told him to come live with me on his eighteenth birthday. On September 20th, his birthday, he moved in.

# CHAPTER NINETEEN

# *Fate Of A Child*

Once again a deep and restful sleep was intruded upon by a dream that was strange and disturbing. The white haired Superior Court judge who had refused to adjudicate my case was seated in his chambers with me and a young attorney. He turned from the attorney and addressed me in a stern paternal voice.

"I'm assigning you an attorney and he will question you before we go into the courtroom."

He then got up and left me and my new attorney alone.

"Tell me about 'the man'," the lawyer said, leaning on the door-knob after he closed the door behind the Judge.

I found myself chatting uncontrollably and unintelligibly to the attorney, who nodded knowingly.

"Oh, that's too bad. I would have liked to have married you my-self," he said with a sigh of regret as he opened the door and we left for the courtroom.

The courtroom was not arranged as I had expected it to be. Chuck was seated in a witness stand to the right of the judge, and I was seated to his left. Our respective attorneys were seated in front of us. Between the two attorneys sat what appeared to be a witness who was a compos-ite of my sons, Charles and Nathan.

The judge listened intently to the testimony of this witness. His words were garbled and unintelligible to me. But the judge heard them clearly and became enraged. The intensity of his feelings caused a pain to surge up my right arm. "He's got it!" I thought to myself.

"Take your children and get out," he said to me seething, "and don't come back."

The dream ended, but I remained in a quandary long afterwards. As far as I was concerned the case was over and I had lost. The last thing I needed was a cosmic rerun that accomplished nothing more than to rub salt in my wounds. But just as I was about to dismiss it as some manner of mental aberration, I was once again compelled to return to court and endure yet another tortuous round with Chuck over the custody of the kids.

About three weeks after the dream, I received a telegram from Ventura Juvenile Hall informing me that Victoria had been placed there. I boarded a Greyhound to Ventura, anguishing over possible reasons for her re-institutionalization.

"Victoria, what happened?" I asked anxiously as we embraced in the visiting area of Juvenile Hall.

"We were having physical ed., and I came down with a stomach ache. I asked the teacher if I could leave. She wouldn't let me. So I left anyway. When I got back, she sent me to the principal's office and she called the stepmother, who called Dad. He had me placed here. But I don't care, Mom. I had a dream. I dreamed that I was in Juvenile Hall. And I'd rather be here than with dad and that stepmother. You know Mom, Dad tried to use a Karate chop on me once he got home. I sidestepped the blow and he broke his pinky on the edge of the bar. I don't even care if they put me in a foster home, Mom. I'm not going back there."

At first I did not know what to make of the fact that Victoria and I had our dreams at about the same time. But later I learned that the white haired judge who had tried my previous case in Superior Court had recently passed away. I concluded that he had been dispatched to me in the spirit to complete some unfinished mortal business.

Victoria spent two days in Juvenile Hall waiting her appearance in Juvenile Court. She considered it more a vacation than a punishment. Judging by the charges that Chuck brought against her, I could understand how she felt. She was accused of being incorrigible and out of control. She was also accused of having sex with a boy in a nearby park. I was not surprised that he would impose such a moral burden upon his fourteen year old daughter without as much as a shred of proof. Victoria was livid when she read the charges and denied them vehemently. She was assigned a public defender. I appeared in pro per. Chuck appeared with his attorney confident that his sordid interest would be well served. He seemed not a bit affected by the fact that he was seeking to sacrifice the emotional well being of his own daughter merely to save his own wounded ego. Were it not for the emotional harm that he was inflicting upon Victoria, I would pity his mindless mean-spiritedness. But because of it, I hated him more than ever.

Prior to the judge making his appearance, the public defender spoke to Victoria.

"Victoria, do you want to go home with your Mother?" He asked.

"Yes, but I'm not guilty," Victoria responded defiantly. "I've never had sex in the park, or anywhere else."

"Listen, saying that you're guilty means that you can't get along with your dad. It has nothing to do with sex. If you don't say you're guilty, you won't get to go home with your mom. Victoria, please, say you're guilty. Victoria, please," the attorney pleaded.

The judge arrived at his bench and brought the session to order. After we all identified ourselves, he looked to Victoria and asked how she pleaded to the charges that had been read.

"Guilty—to a point," she responded grudgingly.

The judge then looked to me. He agreed to allow me to speak and that he would try to protect my rights since I had no attorney. Then Chuck's attorney spoke.

"Your honor. This case was litigated in Superior Court a few months ago and should be sent back there as a continuance of that case. Therefore, we feel that Juvenile Court has no jurisdiction and a change of venue is in order. We also feel that Your Honor is not acquainted with the complexity of this case and move that is be adjudicated in Superior Court."

I could not readily grasp the basis for the attorney's recommendation. But it did not take me long to deduce that by returning the case to Superior Court, Chuck and his attorney would, in effect, force a verdict to maintain the status quo. To me it was reprehensible and unconscionable that Victoria would either be returned to an environment that she regarded as hellish or confined to the custody of the state for the next four years. Either way, the matter would be beyond my control. There would be no way that the Superior Court would reverse itself and award me custody of Victoria. It had not only deemed me the guardian of last resort, but of no resort. In the eyes of the Superior Court, I was completely out of the running for custody of my daughter.

The judge's secretary interrupted the proceedings to inform him that he had an important phone call. Hastening from the bench, he promised a ruling upon his return. A faint smile of smug self confidence appeared on the face of Chuck's attorney. I glared at him with stark disdain, while inside I had transcended hate, fear, and anguish and settled on a numb acknowledgement of a hopeless situation.

The judge returned and quickly rendered his ruling without offering a trace of emotion.

"First, I will contact Superior Court and determine who has jurisdictional authority. Secondly, if I have authority in this matter, I will review this entire file to determine what is so complex about the case to preclude my adjudicating it. In the meantime, Victoria will be placed with her Mother during the thirty day continuance that I now impose.

"Objection," Chuck's attorney challenged emphatically. "We don't think that Victoria should go with her Mother. We prefer that she remain in Juvenile Hall until this case is resolved."

"Why?" The judge asked in astonished disbelief. "Why would

you rather have her stay incarcerated for thirty days than go with her Mother? What's going on here? What is wrong with her staying with her Mother? Is it her house or what?

The attorney motioned to Chuck to respond.

"Oh no, Your Honor." Chuck gushed with an enthusiasm that, in my mind, virtually blew his case. "She has a beautiful house. There is nothing wrong with her house."

"Then what is it?" The judge demanded with soaring exasperation and anger.

The suddenly fierce demeanor of the judge stunned both Chuck and his attorney into stoned silence. I knew that Chuck could say nothing without exposing his bigotry. And his attorney was not acquainted with my present living arrangement. To the judge it seemed a simple enough question and yet neither could summon forth a single syllable to address it.

"Victoria will go home with her Mother," the judge fumed when he realized no answer was forthcoming. "And we will convene here in thirty days."

It was unbelievable. All the time that Victoria, Julie and I made the long ride home, I could not believe our astonishing turn of fortune—at least to this phase of the trial. Victoria had been spared the trying ordeals of Juvenile Hall or of remaining in Chuck's custody for no other reason than two judges interpreted the word "home" differently, and I owed it all to Chuck.

Victoria was taken from me not because of the "house" she lived in, but cause it was the "home" and its environment that Chuck and his attorney had convinced the previous judge was unacceptable. Had Chuck's attorney cited what had been entered in the Superior Court records, I would have been forced to prove, with or without an attorney, that I was no longer a part of that environment. Most likely, that would have meant Victoria going to Juvenile Hall instead of home with me until I could do so. The juvenile court judge had not read the case and was unaware that the "home" setting of the previous case was the unsavory environs of Watts. By inquiring about the "house" instead of the "home", the judge had inadvertently diverted Chuck away from expressing his bigoted perceptions of my home environment.

Victoria was very happy living with me, Julie and Nathan. But the thirty days passed all too quickly and we were all back in court. The judge wasted no time in rendering his decision.

"I have consulted with the Superior Court and I do have jurisdiction in this matter. Change of venue is denied. Now, call Mr. Bissett to the stand."

Chuck walked confidently to the stand and was sworn in.

"Mr. Bissett, are these charges true?" the judge asked, referring to the charge sheet.

"Yes, Your Honor"

"You can get down now."

Chuck looked perturbed as he left the stand. He probably assumed, as I did, that the Judge was going to permit him to ramble on about how incorrigible a child Victoria was. The judge was finished with the plea phase. He then turned his attention to me.

"Mrs. Bissett, I'm assigning you an attorney. Inasmuch as I must protect Victoria's rights, I cannot protect yours. The clerk will give you the name of an attorney." He then paused and leafed through the folder in front of him. "I have read this file from cover to cover. It is my experience that whenever a Mother has to come to court to ask for specific visiting rights, then someone is using the children to play games. I have eight children of my own and I cannot get them out of my house. When kids are happy, they don't want to leave or run away."

He then lifted the folder and pointed to the bottom part of one of the court orders.

"Do you see these last two lines on this order? It says that the members of Mr. Bissett's family are to desist and refrain from denigrating the Mother of these children." He then put the folder down. "That is a shame that a Mother has to come to court to ask for something like that. I couldn't believe it when I read it. But here it is. So this is what I'm going to do.

I will allow another thirty days continuance so that you can come up with a custody agreement that all parties concerned can live with. If you cannot decide on a custody agreement, I will pick up all the children from both homes and place them in permanent foster homes. Then all of the games will be over."

My heart cheered to the heavens. The judge got it. But the case was not over, so I had to maintain my decorum. A few days later, I called the attorney that the clerk had given me.

"Mr. Stone, I'm Mrs. Bissett. I was referred to you by the juvenile court judge."

"Oh yes, Mrs. Bissett, I received your file and I'll try to arrange a meeting with the other attorney."

"Well, we only have another twenty-three days, and I get nervous. I just want to bring this thing to a close."

"Take it easy. Don't worry."

"Mr. Stone, there's a very unusual circumstance, you should know about." I paused to figure out how I was going to tell him.

"Mrs. Bissett, neither the judge nor I are prejudiced. So don't worry. I won't let race become an issue."

"Thank you," I said, and hung up the phone.

I no longer felt that I was a clanging cymbal in an empty forest. Someone had heard me.

Chuck and his attorney were already there when I arrived at Mr. Stone's office. It was two days before the trial. To my disgust and dismay, Chuck had let his attorney convince him not to compromise with me and leave the decision to the Judge.

"Why are you being so hostile?" Mr. Stone asked Chuck's attorney. "You're supposed to help these two reach an agreement."

"No we're not. We're going to leave it to the Judge," the attorney said as he and Chuck got up to leave.

Mr. Stone was obviously not used to such haughtiness. He stared at them, embarrassed and flabbergasted. I was scared. I wondered if Chuck heard the Judge when he told us the he would assign the children to permanent foster homes if an agreement was not reached. Would he really do that just to keep me from getting one child?

By the day of court, all of our nerves had been worn to a frazzle. Julie had arranged for a friend with a van to take us to Ventura. I grew more and more apprehensive as we grew close to the time we would have to leave in order to be at the court on time. While we waited, Julie spoke her inner mind.

"I wish dad had a better conscience than he does. After all, conscience is the first line of communication between man and God. If he had, we would all have some peace."

Julie's insight surprised me. I took it as the Holy Spirit summoning us to prayer. I called everyone together for what I realized was our first family prayer.

"Father, help us this day to find the road to peace. I'm sure this is just as nerve-wracking for Chuck as it is for us. He too is a child of yours just as we are, but he doesn't understand some things. Only you can touch him so that we can find some peace. I'm sure that in his mind, he thinks he's right. And yet you and I know that both he and I are wrong. I have done everything that I thought was morally right and yet I have been deemed legally wrong. I have done everything that seemed legally right, but may well have been morally wrong. I can only ask that you father God forgive us all so that wisdom and justice might prevail. If he doesn't know how to pray, please accept this prayer on his behalf as well that we may all go forth and let thy will be done in Jesus' name. Amen."

The van pulled up outside just as I finished the prayer. I had no ideas as to the probably outcome of the trial, but I felt a sense of humility inside me as we made the drive to Ventura.

Chuck and his attorney were waiting in the lobby of the courthouse for the trial to start when we arrived. My attorney had not yet arrived. Victoria's attorney called Mr. Bissett and his attorney to his office, while I stood at the front door fervently praying that Mr. Stone show up in time for the trial. I was terrified at what they might be cooking up and yet I couldn't let myself go to pieces. About twenty minutes later my attorney showed up. Chuck's attorney had just come out of the public defender's office and was anxious to confer with my attorney. A short while later he emerged and reported to me.

"It seems that they still didn't want to budge on making an agreement. But Victoria's attorney laid it all out for them. He told them that they didn't know this Judge like he does. If they don't come into court with an agreement, Chuck will end up spending thirty days in jail for contempt and all of the children will end up back in foster homes. He told them that he works with this Judge everyday and this Judge doesn't play around. If he says to bring in an agreement, that is exactly what he means. So they propose the same child support as before. You get Julie and Victoria, but Anita and Sarrah stay with him. This should fly for now. Later on you can put in for their custody. I'd take it for now if I were you.

"Okay, I'll go for that for now."

The attorneys got together to hammer out the agreement. I approached Chuck. I felt no bitterness towards him—only pity for one whose humanity could not transcend the need to be autocratic to the extend charity towards his very own children.

"Chuck, thank you," I said softly.

"That's okay, Miki," he responded. "The children have already been through enough foster homes. And I'm not so insensitive to put them through that again."

The Judge accepted the agreement and brought the proceedings to an end. As I left the courtroom, the dream I had flashed through my mind. Although the superior court Judge had died, the juvenile court Judge manifested the same moral indignation as the Judge did in the dream. The child who was the witness in the dream and composite of my children had been the personification of the whole file. Chuck and I were equals as parents. But there existed distortions and confusions that were reflected in the child's testimony. As parents our role is to provide the physical, emotional, and spiritual context that guide our children through the precarious and often pernicious journey through life. Through our contemptuous regard for one another, both Chuck and I may well have destroyed the emotional well being and self image of our children, and gravely imperiled the moral and spiritual focus of their lives. For myself I can only pray that, although I may never receive the blessed assurances that my heart woven efforts to atone for my parental sins will be acceptable to God, my faith would be strong enough for my children to find peace in spite of their Parents. Perhaps Chuck may well have experienced a softening of his own heart now that God had spoken to him in a language he understands. Perhaps it may well have dawned in on him that the price he would have to pay for his recalcitrance might have been the sentence he was willing to have imposed upon his own daughter— exactly the same, thirty days in jail.

Winning in court is hardly the same as winning a foot race. In a race one triumphantly picks up one's trophy and basks in the ecstasy of victory. My winning in court meant only the beginning of the arduous task of stabilizing relationships in a family where siblings must redefine their views of love and themselves even when their futures remain vague and tenuous at best.

CHAPTER TWENTY

# *Self Determination*

I n spite of all that they had been subjected to, the children remained relatively well mannered and respectful. This certainly does not suggest that they were not less willful and obstinate than they had always been. It also did not mean that they were prepared to abandon their primordial survival skills that had been integrated, and imbedded in them from years of living in Institutions. Nathan, Julie and Victoria all attended the predominantly black Crenshaw High. Each had devised a way of coping with racism that kept conflicts to a minimum. Nathan was able to rise above his classmates without appearing to be imperious or judgmental. He was reserved, in obtrusive and very studious. He made no friends and no one could find enough fault in him to mark him as an enemy. Many of Julie's classmates knew her from Junior High and had not forgotten that it was in their best interest to imagine her as being black rather than to press the reality that she was not. Victoria's dark, smoldering eyes and hair-trigger temper conveyed the impression of her as being a hellcat. Since each of the major street gangs at the school assumed that the others were trying to recruit her as a member, they took care not to incur her enmity for fear of driving her into a rival's camp. It was not until she was cornered in the lavatory by a knife wielding girl classmate that she adamantly proclaimed that she had no intentions of joining a street gang. Shaken but unharmed, Victoria left school and never returned. Later, I enrolled her in a private school, but she dropped out after about a year in that school as well.

I did not delude myself into believing my life had taken a turn onto a smooth glassy highway. Given the turmoil and turbulences that had made indelible imprints on their lives, I did not expect the children to make seamless transitions into adulthood. My eldest son, Rodrick had joined the army as soon as he came of age. Although the war in Vietnam was winding to a close, it was not until the troops were brought home that my fears for him were allayed. I had no problems with one fighting in defense of one's country. It is a necessary imperative that comes with maintaining a society of self determination. I could only hope that Rodrick's decision to join the army was not an escape from confronting his own issues of self determination.

I had taken a job as assistant controller for a multicultural Education Grant organization. One of my primary functions was to verify requests for purchases to insure that they conformed to the guidelines of the Grant. It was an often stressful and contentious environment created by the demands of the black and latino factions that vied for control of the Grant. The hours were long and left me little time and energy to attend to the growing problems within my family. I arrived late one night from work to find Julie and Nathan there, but Victoria wasn't. When I asked where Victoria had gone, Nathan unfurled what for me was a story of horror.

"Victoria was making a skirt for herself on the sofa," Nathan began. "I told her to use the floor so I wouldn't get stuck with the pins. But she wouldn't listen to me. When I came back from the kitchen after getting something to eat, I sat on the sofa and got stuck by a pin. I jumped up and punched her in the face. She started to scream and run from the house, I wrestled her to the floor. I tried to stop her from screaming and fighting me but she was like a crazy person. Julie ran in and tried to help me. We both decided to tie her to a chair with a rope and gag her so the police wouldn't come. Somehow, she got loose and ran out of the house. Mr. Brown next door came out and took her home with him. Then the police came. He told them that some boys were horsing around but he ran them off. So the police left."

"Why didn't you sit on the other sofa, Nathan?" I asked him pleadingly. "Why didn't you let her finish the skirt? You didn't have to punch her."

As I listened to Nathan with ever mounting anger, I was unable to fathom what could incite him to such a surge of mindless violence. I was too tired and distraught to think about him. My only concern was for Victoria. I hurried from the house to see the neighbor. He wife had put Victoria to bed and I suggested that she stay there until morning.

The next day, Victoria came home with two black eyes that would keep her out of school for almost two weeks. There was little I could do to Nathan except to prevail upon his sense of reason and conscience. He was enrolled in an alternative school program that provided him an opportunity to take computer classes at the University of Southern California. I did not want to jeopardize what appeared to be a promising future. But as I drove him to his computer class on my way to work, I endeavored to leave no doubt in his mind that violence would not be tolerated in my household.

"Nathan, I don't want to run this incident into the ground," I began, "but I have one final thing to say. You are over eighteen. If you ever do this again, I will have you arrested. And I will not drop the charges. You will go to jail."

Nathan turned to me and responded defensively, "Nathan I understand it already. Do you think I'm some kind of beast?"

"Nathan, I think you need to ask Victoria that. I don't think you'll like the answer."

Nathan never resorted to violence against his sisters again. But that did not quell his need to exert a masculine dominance over the household. He decided to install himself as what I could only describe as "The Lord of the Bathroom". Each morning he would make it his business to be the first on in the bathroom. He would lock himself inside and ignore our protests and implorations derived from urgent necessity. I decided that it was time for me to take matters in hand and seek out some form of family counseling.

The counseling sessions never really got off the ground. Victoria would slam out of the office at the slightest perceived offense and lay out on the lobby floor. Julie was so venomous in expressing her feelings that I would be reduced to crying uncontrollably And Nathan regarded them as entertainment and us as "very interesting". No one was willing to concede anything to anyone. But the violence had ceased, leaving each to seek other means to contend with his or her inner rage.

In addition to my work at the Educational Grant, I began taking on a few bookkeeping clients to help make ends meet. Just when I thought that things were taking a turn for the better, Julie left home one Friday evening without a word to anyone about where she was going. I spent the next week frantic with worry, not knowing whether she was alive or dead. Even as I began to fear the worst, I resisted the compelling urge to call the Police for fear of having to once again contend with the courts. Since it was the week before Easter, I began to fast on that Thursday. Julie showed up Good Friday morning. She refused to tell me where she had been. Later, Victoria informed me that Julie had been with Ben Travis and about two thousand bikers somewhere along the Colorado River. I had two jobs scheduled for the day that I could not cancel.

"I'm not leaving you and Victoria at home alone," I said to Julie. "I will have to baby-sit you on the job. I expect you to behave mannerly, and when we get home tonight, we'll have to talk."

Julie was incensed at having to tag along with me and Victoria from the liquid soap manufacturing plant to the paint store. The first employer looked at me with pity, but said nothing. The second employer had been a co-worker at another paint store as well as a friend.

"I see the prodigal daughter has returned," Randy chided.

"It's none of your goddamn, fucken business," Julie retorted viciously as if she was ready to take him on hand to hand. "You ain't got nothing to say to me. So mind your own goddamn business and stay out of mine."

Both Randy and I were stunned into silence. Finally he shook his head and left the room. It took all of the willpower that I could muster to keep me from slapping the mess out of Julie. I reasoned that because I had been fasting, the devil was trying to tempt me into something that I would regret. This time I was able to restrain myself, but it was obvious that the time was fast approaching when I would lose control. Returning Julie to Juvenile Hall was my only alternative even though it meant possibly involving Chuck and the courts. I called Mrs. Yudkoff to advise her of my decision.

"Oh, Miki. Isn't there anything else you can do?" Mrs. Yudkoff asked with deep concern.

My greatest fear was that I might seriously hurt Julie if her attitude persisted. I tried to impress upon Mrs. Yudkoff that my decision was the only choice I had. Since Julie was only about eight months shy of her eighteenth birthday, Mrs. Yudkoff was not receptive to the idea of returning her to the system

"Miki, before you do that, let me talk to one of our staff psychiatrists and let me get back to you. I'll tell him about your background and that you are involved in spiritual counseling. Maybe he can help you get through this without sending her back to the State."

About an hour later, she called me back.

"He told me to ask you one question and everything depends upon your answer. If a parent came to you with an identical problem, what advice would you give them?"

"If the child was this haughty," I began assuredly, "You bet I'd tell them to put him in Juvenile Hall. I can't just tell them to pray. I've been fasting since yesterday and Julie is worse than I ever expected. We need a break to think about things before we talk."

"Well, he said that whatever advice you would give another Parent is the advice you should take for yourself."

"Eleanor, you must know that I hate doing this. Throwing my own child back into Juvenile, after all I've been through! God knows how I hate this, but what am I to do?" I lamented. "I can't let her get away with this without any consequences."

After work, I drove to the nearest police station.

"I'd like to put my daughter in Juvenile Hall," I said to the desk Sergeant.

Before he could answer, Julie started emptying her purse and pockets on the counter like she had been through this more than a few times before.

"You'll have to see the Juvenile Detectives at the end of the hall." The sergeant stated impassively.

"There's nothing we can do for you." The Juvenile Detective responded after listening patiently to my story. "She's back with you now. We can't do anything because she's not missing and she ain't broke any laws that we know of."

"But you don't understand." I said pleadingly. "I'm fasting and we need a break. If she does this to me again, I may not be responsible for my actions. I'm asking you to help me."

"I understand how you feel, Mrs. Bissett. These kids will tear your heart out. You work to try to provide for their care and then they do whatever they want. You try to set some rules and they act like you're crazy. I know how you feel. They deserve the spanking of their life. But until she runs away again, there's nothing we can do. If she does that again, report it right away. If we pick her up, we'll put her in Juvenile Hall immediately."

"How can you say that there's nothing you can do?" I asked in desperation. "I'm trying to prevent a possible tragedy. Don't you understand? I'm trying to do the right thing before God, and you say there's nothing you can do about it."

My mind blanked out and a surge of pain struck the pit of my stomach. Before another thought entered my mind, I swung my balled up fist as hard as I could and landed a blow on Julie's jaw. She fell against Victoria who fell hard against the file cabinets. I grabbed Julie by the hair and began pounding her head against the counter. She screamed while I snorted like a ferocious animal. More than half a dozen Policemen seemed to come from out of nowhere and pulled me off of her while I fought like a wounded tigress to finish what I had started. I was dragged to a chair and pinned down by four Officers, while a fifth sat on my lap. Even then I was still lunging at Julie. My adrenalin was up, but the Police held me firm in the chair and wouldn't let go.

"Bring her here." The Juvenile Detective ordered as he motioned towards Julie. "I'm putting her in the cage."

"What about her? Aren't you going to arrest her? The Policeman asked about me from my lap.

"Oh no. She can go. I'm arresting the Daughter to protect the Mother."

The Policeman looked perplexed at the detective as he got up, but didn't question the Detective's decision. I figured that the Detective was simply going to let me get in a slap before sending Julie home with me and Victoria. Instead, Julie did spend the weekend in Juvenile Hall just as I had wanted. I spent the entire Easter weekend crying.

I knew that if I did not retrieve Julie quickly, she would be swallowed up by the system. Her future, not my present, was uppermost in my mind. Perhaps I was not brimming with patience but my love for her was boundless. I would never abandon her no matter what. The day after Easter, I was at Juvenile Hall bright and early to pick up my Daughter. We were assigned a probation officer. Julie was ordered to attend school regularly and undergo therapy until she was eighteen. Julie complied without complaint.

She was scheduled for an appointment with her probation officer after school. A premonition swept through me as I drew some money from my purse to give her. I had a feeling that she was somehow moving into harm's way.

"Here's some money to keep your appointment," I said as I handed her the money. "Don't spend this on anything else. I don't want you hitchhiking. You understand?"

When I got home that evening, Ben Travis was sitting in my living room, while Julie paced about the room chattering in shock and pain. She was clutching her right arm. It has been badly scraped down to where the bone of her elbow was visible.

"I spent the money you gave me, and hitchhiked home." Julie said frantically into my look of horror. "When the guy who picked me up drove passed where I asked him to let me off, I told him to stop. He said that if I wanted to get out I'd have to jump because he wasn't stopping. I looked at him and, Mom, it seemed like every demon in hell was in his face. I clutched my purse to my breast, opened the door and jumped out. We were going about thirty five miles per hour. I was in so much pain and shock that all I could do was sit on the grass crying until somebody came by. This man went around and gathered all the stuff that fell out of my purse. I couldn't stop crying, Mom. So I gave him Ben's phone number and he called him to come pick me up."

All that I could do was listen to her tell and retell the story all night long, while comforting her as best I could. But inside I was furious that once again she had ignored my directives. Once she became sexually involved with Ben, she refused to accept that there could be anything more spiritually fulfilling. Not long afterwards she turned eighteen and terminated both therapy and school. About a month later, she announced that she and Ben Travis were going off to Vegas to get married. I was certain that she was about to enter a match made in hell. But I knew there was nothing that I could do about it. On the other hand, I sensed that she was pleading for me to somehow stop her. Rather than to throw the tantrum that would have slammed the door on our relationship, I offered a proposition that was a surprise to me even as I spoke it.

"Julie, Ben. Why don't you both use the third bedroom and try out marriage for size? Ben that'll give you a place to stay while you look for a job. Then if you decide that marriage is what you want, you'll have a better chance at making it a success. And I'll do my best not to interfere."

It took me about five months to become intolerably sick of this arrangement. Ben ate everything in sight. He and Julie would run the streets at night with Ben's biker friends and then stay in bed until four or five in the evening. Ben then would leave to make a half hearted attempt at finding work. When I could take no more of it, I invited them into the living room and issued my ultimatum.

"Ben, you've got two weeks to leave my home. I don't mind helping you, but you obviously have no intentions of helping yourself. Who on this earth goes job hunting at five in the evening? I don't know why you think you're better than God. God worked six days and rested on the seventh. You rest all seven. Well, this sucker has had it. I'm through."

"And you Julie. You should be telling him this instead of me. You should have kicked him out as soon as you realized that he was not looking for a job. Do you really expect to make a life with him? This is nothing but bullshit. And you're going for it? Well, I'm not."

"I did tell him, Mom." Julie protested tearfully.

"Well, he's not listening to you. He's still here and without a job. But he'd damn well better listen to me. Two weeks and not a day longer." I reiterated firmly as they started towards their bedroom.

For two weeks I begrudgingly held my peace. Nothing changed. Ben had no intentions of seriously looking for work or moving out. And Julie refused to exert any pressure on him to do so. I was in a quandary as to what to do without losing my Daughter.

The pressing demands of the Educational Grant were uppermost in my mind when I looked up from my desk. To my surprise, there was Rodrick standing in front of me erect and handsome in his green army uniform. He had visited me twice during the four years he had been in the military. He had grown into a tall, well built man with a light tawny complexion reflecting a hint of his Indonesian and Puerto Rican heritage. His manner was direct, but respectful. He told me that his tour of duty was over and that he was ready to give civilian life a try.

"How are things at home?" He asked.

I told him about my problems with Julie and Ben Travis.

"What do you want, Mom?"

"I want him out."

"Mom, he'll be out by the time you get home." Rodrick stated confidently.

"Rodrick, it's not that easy. I know you're wearing your jump boots and all," I said. "But Ben is used to fighting with bikers. And then there's Dylan. That Dog won't let anyone touch him."

"Don't worry Mom, I'll figure out something." Rodrick said and then left.

But I was worried. I was afraid that Rodrick would do something rash and get himself badly hurt or even worse. After work, I hurried home. Ben was still there, but the house was quiet. I sat down on the sofa in the living room to watch TV. The suddenly Ben bolted out of the bedroom hopping towards the front door while pulling up his pants and putting an arm into the sleeve of his shirt. Dylan was at his heels. Behind him ran Julie crying and screaming. Ben and Dylan ran past me and out the front door without a word or hardly a break in stride. I hurried to block Julie's way.

"You will stay here," I demanded. "You will not leave with him."

Dejectedly, Julie returned to the bedroom. Rodrick and Nathan showed up a short while later. Almost immediately, Julie charged Rodrick with fists flailing. He pinned her against the dining room wall as I wedged myself between them.

"Ben would have kicked your ass," Julie screamed hysterically. "It was me who told him to leave. It was me,I couldn't have him hurting my brother."

Rodrick released Julie. She ran back to the bedroom. Rodrick and Nathan both were elated that their plan had worked. They had phoned the Police from a nearby restaurant. And then they called Ben Travis and warned him that he had ten minutes to be out of the house before they would come and put him out. The Police did arrive, but Ben was long gone. A few days later, Julie moved out to be with him, and there was nothing more I could do. I had gone as far as I could go. Julie was now on her own to fashion a life as best she could.

It lasted about two months. Julie called me one evening to come get her.

"Mom, I can't live like this. A day here, a week there, at the mercy of whoever will feed us or give us a place to sleep. I guess I'm just too middle class for this. Mom, I have to have some security.

I tried to be understanding. After all, had I not been obsessed with a man? She was too young to wile away her life chasing behind a bum. But she had choices to confront and then consequences to face because of them. My responsibility as her Mother was to be there for her when she stumbled and fell then help her to her feet, brush her off and somehow get her back into the fray. Life's punishments were severe enough without my compounding them with self righteous judgments. I welcomed her back home. She took a job as a waitress in a restaurant, but still would not rid herself of Ben Travis. Eventually, he was arrested by the Police on the charge of burglary and sentenced to six months in prison. Julie's world collapsed.

She quit her job and took to her bed, leaving it only to visit the bathroom. I would check in on her when I came in from work. She would be writhing in her own sweat, and the room took on a pungent stench. She ate nothing and hardly spoke. I was very much concerned about her, but there was nothing I could do. I had to have total faith in her as a spiritual being. To the depth of my soul, I believed that she would be offered flashes of revelations that would draw her from the pit of despair and onto a path of self realization. I could not bring myself to scold or berate her for her devotion to Ben Travis. But I could do a lot of praying.

About a week after Ben went to prison, I saw the first sign that Julie was coming out of her depression. She was out of bed and pacing about the house like a caged animal, bemoaning her inability to free herself of her circumstances. And then some of Ben's friends began drifting by, hoping to take up where he left off with her. She was glad to see them. The attention they lavished upon her noticeably bolstered her self confidence, so much in fact that she took a job working as a dancer in a strip club. She was very good at it. The same creative passion she had invested in her sculpting formed the essence of her expression in dance. She was making more money than ever, and winning the weekly dance contests that the club held. I had hoped that Julie would have taken a different path. But the path she did take inspired her with hope greater than I could imagine. When Ben was released from prison, he came by her job with the intention of resuming their relationship. She told him that they were through and this time she made it stick.

Upon graduating from high school, Nathan was awarded a silver medal for academic excellence. He also scored high enough on the S.A.T exam to be awarded a California state scholarship to Loyola Marymount University. He and three of his college classmates rented a house near the school in Westchester. Rodrick then moved in with us and began to immediately comport himself with all the sensitivity of a storm trooper. He issued orders, barked commands, and presumed that all aspects of human existence were either covered by a military manual or should be. We rejected out of hand his suggestion that we all get up at five in the morning to do calisthenics. He was passionate in his belief that virtually every eligible person, including Victoria and Julie should join the military. About a week after he moved in, we were seated at the dining table when Rodrick turned to me and spoke in a voice that was surprisingly sincere.

"Mom, I must hand it to you. Most women might have hung in there for two or three years and then cut us all loose. They wouldn't have hung in there for ten or eleven years like you have Mom. They would have tried to make a life for themselves and said the hell with all of us."

"I thought of doing that, Rodrick," I responded solemnly. "But I wouldn't have been able to face myself. No matter how hard it was, I had no choice but to hang in there."

"Well all I can say is that you're pretty tough."

I was nowhere near as tough as Rodrick thought and it was

beginning to take its toll. The desperation that I had to suppress in order to confront the endless stream of travails seemed now poised to attack me on all fronts. Within a few months fatigue and insomnia began to overwhelm me. I would make breakfast for myself and then stare blankly out of the window and not even seen the tree in the front lawn. At other times, tears would stream down my face without me knowing why. One morning while sitting alone at the dining room table, I felt as though I were falling apart. I winged a prayer heavenward.

"Oh Lord, I need your help. You know that I'm scared of shrinks, but I'm coming apart at the seams. Look at me Lord. I can't take anymore. I don't know what's happening to me. I need a shrink who won't try to change me. And only you can do that. Oh God, I am so scared!"

# CHAPTER TWENTY-ONE

# My Children On Gurneys

I returned to the Southeast Satellite of the County Mental Health system, the site of my aborted effort to help Nathan, Julie and Victoria cope with their suppressed anger. I was assigned a therapist named Stan Jamison. As I made my way down the corridor to his office, I admonished myself not to expect too much from psychologists.

"I've had many years of therapy," I began pointedly as we closed into his cubicle of an office and I accepted the chair he offered me. Mr. Jamison hardly fit the stereotype of the psychologists I had seen. He was a handsome man in about his mid thirties with clear blue eyes and curly blonde hair. "I've resolved my problems with my mother and father. So let's not get too Freudian. I've got problems with my kids. They were made wards of the court and have been shuffled from one foster home to another. They have lived in Institutions, foster home after foster home, and now with a stepmother. Four of them have come back to me, and I don't like the way they are. Heaven only knows what the other two will be like. They're all dysfunctional and I don't know what to do about it. They have no respect or consideration for me. I feel like I'm stuck in a madhouse."

Mr. Jamison smiled knowingly. "I used to think that when women complained about their Husbands they were, in reality expressing their feelings about their Mothers and Fathers. But I have come to learn that they are in fact talking about their Husbands. And so I'm not so quick anymore to be too Freudian. If you say it's about your kids, then it's about your kids."

In my heart, I believed that God had answered my prayer and I was thankful. It was during my third visit that the course of my therapy became firmly set.

"I don't understand why Dr. Walters did not tell the court about the child-beating," I lamented to Mr. Jamison. "Why couldn't he understand why I couldn't submit to the control of my husband? He was asking me and the children to submit to the control of a Madman. God knows I don't understand it."

"He counter-transferred," Mr. Jamison offered. "He lost focus of your problem and allowed his feelings for you to obscure his judgment."

I blurted out a scream as my mind focused on Dr. Walters and the possibility of him seeing me as more than just a Patient. The notion of me losing my kids because my analyst might have had the "hots" for me sprang forth an outrage in my soul that sent me reeling into a tear drenched tantrum that lasted almost a quarter of an hour.

Mr. Jamison slumped forward and stared ashamedly at the floor. He said nothing until I had finished and then spoke to me penitently.

"I feel like I want to give you some part of me so that all of this would not have happened to you. But there is nothing I can do. I feel so helpless to try to help you. I am so sorry that society has done this to you." He leaned back in his chair and looked at me compassionately as he continued.

"You are the most together woman I have ever met," he said. "There is nothing wrong with your psyche. There is nothing I can do for you except to give you a safe place to rage. And you are entitled to rage. Whatever Freudian notions I might have entertained are completely out the window. How you got through twelve years of this crap is so very far beyond me. I must hand it to you. You can call me anytime you think you need me, Miki."

Mr. Jamison touched me deeply with his concern and the simplicity of his caring. To him, I would not be a case study to be shoehorned into some category of theoretical or pop psychology. He simply acknowledged my humanity and understood why I was flapping and gasping on the banks of the mainstream like an out-of-water salmon. At the following session, he offered a prescription that I hardly expected.

"You've got delayed Post Traumatic Stress Syndrome just like a lot of Vietnam Vets. You're also manic depressive and a little schizoid. So I want to apply for social security disability. I don't want you to look for work or to work. You have severe burnout and you need a rest. And for awhile, and it may be hard, I want you to ignore your kids. You're entitled to a life too. I want you to find it. I want you to get something out of life other than just hell."

The man was being magnanimous as well as caring. But now my ego was shattered. I had never seen myself as a person who could not work. I felt distraught and unsettled. I had been trying to put up a brave front. I felt as though I had slammed into a brick wall. Stan was right. I needed time to recuperate and working would have only added to the stress. During my next visit, Mr. Jamison offered me another ingredient in his recipe for saving my life.

"You're too intelligent a woman to let society waste you," he said after we closed into his office. "If it were up to me, I would just award you a degree and make you a member of the Mensa Society and let you do your thing. Right now, the important thing is for you not to allow melancholia to creep up on you and imprison you for life. You need to get back into the swing of things—but at your pace. So I want you to sign up for college. Miki, I believe strongly society owes you that much."

I was full of gratitude and hope as I left his office. This man was actually trying to help me retrieve a part of my life that I thought was gone forever. Stan Jamison brought to mind Mrs. Fletcher, the teacher in high school who tried to fan a spark of possibility that she saw in me by procuring me a scholarship. I signed up for philosophy and a course in religion at a local Los Angeles college. Once again, I was living from hand-to-mouth. My budget allowed me hot cereal in the morning and a hamburger for dinner. But I began to feel very much hopeful and alive.

Julie moved into an apartment with a girlfriend, leaving me, Rodrick and Victoria as the family unit of the moment. I virtually ignored them and plunged into my studies. But they regarded me as a mental aberrant to say the least. Rodrick had enrolled in the same college under his G.I Bill. In his mind, that qualified him as guardian to his Mother who was compelled to sustain her education and survival on small grants. He took it upon himself to tell me when to get up, when to study, when to go to school and when to go to sleep. Gradually, he took on all of the attributes of the monitor from hell.

Victoria was feeling her way through adolescence. Evidently part of the process was to assert her independence. She regarded me as a hostile enemy who had no other purpose for existing than to engage in a constant reconnaissance into her life. Virtually every query that I posed to her brought an accusation of me invading her privacy—whatever the hell that meant.

During one of our sessions, Mr. Jamison was busily scribbling on a pad while I stared blankly at the wall beyond him. A vision began to unfurl before me. I began describing it to him, as I witnessed it...

"I'm having a vision right now, Dr. Jamison. I see all of my children on gurneys in a dimly lit morgue. I'm trying to wake them up but they keep telling me to leave them alone."

"What do you feel about this vision?" Stan asked, leaning towards me with great interest.

"My kids are dead to me. I've got to learn to accept it or it is going drive me crazy. But I know me. For me to accept it, would mean hating life. And it would take all the will I can muster for that hatred not to turn into violence."

Stan looked at me with pity.

"Do you get these visions often?"

"No. Not as often as I used to," I responded. "I'm trying to separate my psychological needs from my spiritual beliefs. And I know how you therapists think. But these are not hallucinations. I have had a lot of dream analysis and I know what power dreams are. These are not power dreams or visions in the usual sense. These come from a different place in my psyche and then into my consciousness. When you go to sleep one night and the following morning you can do things that you couldn't do the previous day, then whatever it is, is not of my power. It must come from a spiritual realm and I have no control over it. And don't get paranoid. None of my spiritual dreams order me to kill anybody, not even the devil. They usually show me rescuing people or giving sermons."

"My girlfriend has a gift like that," Stan stated with a knowing smile. "She'll see a parking space she wants and we'll go around the block and the space will be vacant when we get back. I don't know how she does it, but she does it every time."

"Oh, so you're a believer in spirituality," I offered.

"Not really. I'm Buddhist, but she keeps doing that. I can't believe it. But she keeps doing it." he concluded, shaking his head in disbelief.

"But Buddhists believe in the spirit. So you must be coming to a point of becoming a believer."

"I guess so, but I haven't met many people with spiritual gifts," Stan concluded, as he abruptly changed the subject. "Anyway, I have a client that I want you to meet the next time you come. Perhaps you and he and a few others can start a mental health advocacy group."

I was not enthusiastic about putting any more on my plate than school, family, and pulling together my own life. But I agreed to help Stan anyway that I could.

We were nearing the end of my next session, when there was a knock on the door. A tall thin man with sunken eyes and a gaunt expression entered and lingered indecisively in front of me as Stan asked us to wait while he took a phone call.

"If you got connections with the Man upstairs, put in a good word for me," the man said as he took the empty chair next to me. There was a presumptuous tone in his voice that caused me to bristle and respond sharply.

"If the Lord hadn't been standing right there over you, you'd been gone a long time ago. Believe me, you'd been gone a long time ago. Why don't you put in a word for yourself?"

He sat still and solemn as we waited for Stan to get off the phone.

"Hi Louis," Stan stated jovially. "I want you to meet Miki."

"We've already met," I answered and then repeated to Stan what I said to Louis.

"So what else are you getting?" He asked me with genuine concern.

"I'm having difficulty breathing. I keep on wanting to take deep breaths and let the warmth of the sun go through me. He needs to get up in the morning and appreciate the sunlight and take those breaths and let them go through his body. He needs to thank God every day, first thing in the morning for whatever time he has left. Now I'm getting this rush going through my chest and up and down my arms. I can't turn it off."

Stan watched incredulously for about twenty minutes as I tried frantically to rub away the surges of sensation that swept through my arms and chest. When the feeling finally subsided, I got Louis' phone number and I left. At my next session, Stan informed me that Louis was having death therapy. He was suffering from a lung ailment that had been diagnosed as terminal. It had reached a stage where each of his lungs would collapse. It was only a matter of time before they both collapsed, and that would be the end. Stan also informed me that Louis had confirmed that there had been a problem with his arms, but would offer nothing more than that. Stan's skepticism as to my spirituality diminished considerably after that session.

I called Louis to set up a meeting with him and the other members of our advocacy group. Five of us met at his house and then I wrote up the objectives that we hoped to attain. Later we visited the Norwalk Metropolitan Hospital to observe its operations. The attending psychiatrist explained to us that the primary objective of the hospital was not to cure anyone, but to insure that the inmates, when released, would not be a danger to themselves or to others. His orientation struck me as somewhat heartless and insensitive, and his autocratic attitude generated images of the Gestapo in my mind. But then he took us on a tour to see the inmates. To my dismay and horror, they brought to mind a pack of huge unruly rats. I began to understand the doctor's predicament. These people were beyond rational hope. They seemed to talk to you rationally and then do something so irrational that you felt under constant threat. I certainly would not want to meet them on the street. I concluded that we were not qualified to investigate their claims and advocate any specific reforms. We would have no way of determining for sure who was sane with legitimate complaints and who would be gaming us. The others in the group were enthusiastic about getting the advocacy underway. I wasn't. When Louis died a few months after our visit to the asylum, I drifted away from the advocacy project and allowed it to die on the vine.

About three o'clock on Saturday morning, Julie staggered into the house reeking of alcohol. I ignored her, hoping that she had come by to sleep off her drunk and let me get back to sleep on the sofa. But she sat on the edge of the sofa and placed a hand gently on my shoulder.

"Mom, can I talk to you?" she slurred.

"Of course, Julie," I responded groggily. I hated heart to heart talks where intentions and feelings had to be strained through the effects of alcohol. But I reasoned that any talk was better than none.

"I knew that I acted outrageously, mom," she confessed softly. "But I needed Ben Travis. I knew that I would always have you. Dad is no real father figure to me. And I was looking for a father figure whom I could talk to and give me attention, and make me feel loved. I knew that no matter what I did, you'd be there. And though I knew it was wrong to defy you like I did, I had to get what I needed. Can you understand that, Mom?"

"Yeah Julie, I can understand that." I responded into the darkness.

It was heart-warming for me to hear my Daughter admit to her wrong-doing. But I had to wonder to myself how much of it she would remember when she became sober.

"You don't understand how much I love you, Mom. You fought me with everything you had for three long hard years. You were a friend to me when I couldn't' be a friend to myself. I love you so very much."

"I love you too Julie, very much."

She hugged me and kissed me heavily on the cheek.

"Mom," she continued with her weight bearing upon me. "I've got girlfriends whose Mothers have gone through the same things you have. And their Mothers have become alcoholics and drug addicts. And my friends are embarrassed about their Mothers. But you didn't burden us with being an alcoholic or drug addict. You don't know how much that means to me. I love you, Mom."

It was the first time that I fully realized that one never knows when one's kids are watching how you react to the difficulties in your life. That one can never take for granted that just because they're your kids, you can do anything you want and not risk their judgment. Even when they're doing wrong, they expect you to hold the line and do what is right.

Julie kissed me again and then left to go home. I returned to sleep.

Both Rodrick and I made the Dean's List in our first semester of College. I was elated that my re-entry into the world of learning had begun so auspiciously. But not even the college could provide me a respite from what I had accepted as my "spiritual commitment".

I was standing in line at the college snack shop, when a conversation between two men flowed from behind me. My interest piqued when one of the men stated emphatically his intention to kill his sixteen year old daughter's boyfriend. He could no longer tolerate this guy's insults and abuse. He insisted that his daughter's defiance of his order to break up with the boyfriend was tantamount to a declaration of war.

"Please excuse me for interfering in your discussion," I stated to the two startled middle-aged black men, and ignoring the inner voice that cautioned me to mind my own business, "but you are handling this the wrong way. You will end up losing your daughter and maybe even ruining her life and achieve nothing."

"What do you mean?" the man with the daughter asked testily.

"Well, which would you rather do, get rid of this bum or get rid of your daughter? She will not appreciate you killing the love of her life. She will hate you forever. Is that what you want?"

He stared at me quizzically as I continued. "What you want to do is show your Daughter that what she wants is a Man just like her Father, not a loudmouth bum. So I would be the best 'Gentleman' I could be. When the guy comes by, ask him if he'd like coffee or tea. Serve him cake. Ask him how his day went. Talk about sports or whatever you both might have in common. Whatever you do, don't fight with him. You'll force her to choose sides. She will undoubtedly take his. Sooner or later he's going come out of his super macho bag just to show your Daughter that he's badder than you. She'll see him for what he is and he'll be dead meat. It'll be hard, but you got to figure out what you want."

I bought my hot dog and left the man pondering my advice.

About five months later, I was eating at a restaurant when a man with a small bunch of pansies approached my table and offered met the flowers. I thought this was a strange pass.

"These are for you." He said smilingly. "Do you remember me?"

"I'm sorry, but am I supposed to?" I said uneasily.

"You gave me some advice about my sixteen year old Daughter. Well, last month she dropped the bum. You don't know how you really helped me. When I saw you sitting here through the window I had to drop in and say thank you. You kept me from going to jail and I got my Daughter back. What you told me to do was the hardest thing I ever had to do. But I can't thank you enough for your help."

"That's wonderful. I'm so glad it all worked out for you." I said graciously as I recalled him from school. "Your gratitude is greatly appreciated." I then accepted the flowers even though I suspected that the man had pilfered them from the garden of the restaurant.

Stan Jamison had been right. The College had proved an ideal tonic for my depression. I was especially fascinated with Philosophy and Anthropology and actually nurtured plans to complete my studies at a University. My popularity with teachers and fellow students grew steadily. At first, the students in my philosophy class resented my constant engagement with the instructor on various points of logic and theory. They seemed contented to learn by role or osmosis, while I believed that education consisted of an exchange of ideas and perceptions between student and teacher. One day during a class break, some of my classmates gathered around me and to my surprise, began pummeling me with questions about my beliefs and philosophies. After class one of my fellow students told me that before I had arrived the instructor informed the students that they would not have done as well on their mid-terms were it not for my arguments and observations on the material we had covered.

"Professor Smith really came to your defense today. She made us realize that we were wrong in resenting you constantly challenging her." She said as we walked towards my car. "We learned a lot from you without even knowing it. So that's why we wanted to talk to you at break time. We wanted to know more about your philosophies and your views."

I was gratified to hear that I had made some impact, no matter how minor, in the learning process.

Rodrick and I were enrolled in the same cultural Anthropology course. For me it was a marvelous opportunity to revisit a world from which I was only a generation removed. But for Rodrick and my classmates, that world seemed distant and remote in both time and space. To them, the Eskimos, Masai and other cultures that we viewed through the eyes of film documentaries were little more than unfortunate, exotic and often entertaining species that were logged in at a notch or two beneath them on the evolutionary scale. Since my Father taught me almost nothing about the rituals and beliefs of the Achee culture, I could draw no distinctions between it and the cultures depicted in the documentaries. Had not my Father been banished, he would have taken his rightful place as chief of his Achee village and may well have been an object of study in the area of primitive exotica. Instead, he became a passionate, dedicated and respected participant in the struggle for his nation's freedom and the most intensely fought ideological struggle in the history of the western world. And yet this transformation of what my Father might have been to what he ultimately became was accomplished by not much more that a boat ride from the jungles of Indonesia to the urban sprawl of New York City.

But Rodrick was his Father's son and therefore, doggedly maintained the imperious Eurocentric detachment and condescension reserved for those who did not use forks and wore no shoes. During one of our class sessions, he posed a question to the instructor that struck me as not only trivial, but culturally demeaning. When the instructor did not respond to his satisfaction, he began to press the issue. I intervened to cut off what I could see would become an endless and futile exchange that had no bearing on the subject of instruction.

"Rodrick, why don't you just let it slide." I implored.

"No, Mom. Why should I?" He retorted defiantly. "I have as much right to ask questions as anybody in the class."

Within a cocoon of palpitating silence, Rodrick and I commenced our war of wills. I knew that it had escalated beyond whether or not the question and answer were appropriate. His defiant response made it an issue of authority between Mother and Son rather than an issue of contention between classmates.

"That's not the point, Rodrick. You asked your question and got an answer. I'm asking you to let the rest of it go and we'll discuss it later."

"I want to discuss it now with the teacher. Not you!"

"Now I'm not asking you again." I fumed. "I'm telling you to let it go."

"What the hell do you care? You get A's and B's. What do you care about how my question may affect my grade."

"What are you talking about Rodrick? We both made the Dean's List. Don't talk to me like I'm some idiot on the street." I said threateningly. "Don't make me get up out of this chair. I'm telling you for the last time. Stop and don't answer me back."

Rodrick could barely contain his rage as he slumped down into his chair. The class remained suspended in its uneasy silence as Rodrick, the instructor, and I recomposed our selves. Rodrick said very little in class after that. That evening Rodrick announced that he would never take another class with me again.

The rift that the incident created between us healed slowly. For a long while afterwards, we spoke to each other begrudgingly. One evening I read a paper to my Sociology class, a paper based upon my experiences and conclusions regarding dysfunctional families. To my joyous surprise, the class awarded my effort with a standing ovation. When I left the classroom, there was Rodrick standing outside the door, beaming with pride. At least there was a sign of a thaw in our icy relationship.

Towards the end of the same Anthropology course, I voiced aloud my concern that the documentary films we had been watching were actually records for posterity of doomed cultures. I had deep seated feelings that the encroachment and expansion of "civilization" would eventually overwhelm their fragile environments and passive lifestyles. A look of despair formed on the instructor's face as she nodded knowingly. To Rodrick, the demise of such cultures was simply the unfortunate natural order of things. In his mind, the march of progress, advance of technology, and the need for structured governments transcended into the survival of mere primitives. But after the last class, he conveyed to me a bit of insight that offered me the hope that the time he spent in the class had not been wasted.

"Mom, you realize you don't belong in this society, don't you?" He said solemnly.

"I know, Rodrick. But where am I supposed to go? This society is

totally dedicated to the pursuit of power, exploitation, and self interest. But then who wouldn't be if the opportunity was laid in their lap.
Perhaps in a tribal village people can exercise values like cooperation,
selflessness and sharing. But not in a society like this. Once in a great
while someone like a Dr. King comes along and taps into the societal
conscience. But that only lasts for a little while. Our insatiable lust for
wealth and power makes it impossible to sustain conscience. We have
no qualms about destroying every other culture on the face of the earth
in the name of ideologies and then placate our conscience with only
half hearted remorse. I appreciate your compassion, but there's nothing
you can do for me. I'll muddle through somehow. I'm not concerned
with whether I fit in or not. I've been through a lot and I know where
I'm at."

I watched as the sadness formed on Rodrick's face as he placed a
reassuring hand on my shoulder before heading for his bedroom. Over
the next few days, it was very much in evidence to me that Rodrick was
attempting to reconcile the myriad of issues that had been imposed
upon his life. The institutional mentality had served him well in the
Army. But now he was confronted with a world where self determination and independent reasoning were the currencies of growth and
success. The world that he saw through the eyes of his Father was not
the world that he saw through mine. In some ways they were in conflict.
In others, they were complimentary. But there were always possibilities
for compromises and even mergers. For the sake of spiritual awareness,
there must also be room for forgiveness. My nonconformist views had
thrown Rodrick's illusions of himself and the world into a tailspin. He
felt that he had to somehow find a way to fit them into an acceptable
societal niche. One evening he turned down the sound on the television and sat beside me on the sofa. I could see in his eyes that he was
both troubled and disturbed.

"You know, Mom," he began haltingly. "I learned about overt and
covert violence in the army. I understand why you gave me that beating
when we lived back on Budlong in Watts."

"Then you must know that I didn't want to and I didn't like it either. But you forced confrontation and I couldn't let it slide."

"Yeah, I know," he said forcing a knowing smile.

"Mom, I really can't see what kind of Christianity you practice." Rodrick sprung from seemingly nowhere almost in the form of an accusation. "You don't go to Church. You're Ordained as Reverend, but you don't preach. You're non-denominational. You counsel atheists without pressuring them to convert. And you're an evolutionist instead of a creationist. You seem more inclined towards humanism than religion."

"That's because I'm basically an existentialist and I try not to act like a religious fanatic."

"I don't understand," he said as he got up and ambled to the fireplace across the room.

"We exist as a form of thinking, and reasoning matter." I began slowly and reflectively. "Whether we like it or not, we all need each other or we will not survive. Therefore, we are all equal in our human dignity. I have as much right to do things my way as you have to do it yours. Ideally, we will use our powers of choice and self determination in ways that will best contribute to both our mutual survival and ultimate happiness."

"I understand all that." Rodrick stated impatiently. "But what does that have to do with Christianity?"

"Well we Christians believe that there is an ultimate spiritual force that we refer to as God and that this person who we know of as Jesus Christ is an incarnation of God."

"But in Existentialism, if God is not a form of matter, He doesn't exist. So how can you be an existentialist and believe in God? That seems like a contradiction to me," Rodrick stated with a trace of a triumphant smile.

"But you are presuming that gases, solids and liquids are the only forms of matter in the universe. All things stem from some form of creativity. What form of matter is creativity? What form of matter is a thought of an idea? What form of matter manages the universe? Revelation promised that there will come a time when we will discover these truths. Until then, I accept Christ as the son of God, which is that form of matter that we do not understand, but believe has His own capacity for creativity and self determination. Other religions use other motifs to define the existence of this Divine Spirit. The atheists who come to me believe there is no God, but they acquiesce to my faith. And in that moment of acquiescence they accept the existence and even the presence of God. It really doesn't matter whether we worship the Spirit through religion or not. All that really maters, is that there exists a form of matter whose powers of creation are infinitely greater than ours.

"Oh. So you're an existential Christian?" Rodrick asked.

"I never thought of it that way. But that's as good a description as any. As far as being an evolutionist is concerned, you misunderstand what I believe. All things are a creation. But all things are also works in progress, even we humans. We know that there have been points in time when pivotal and sudden changes in species occur. But these changes are part of an evolutionary process, not creation. You may argue, for example that Adam and Eve were the creation of our species. But then where did Cain's wife come from? Where did the men come from that Cain feared would kill him? Were these other humans who inhabited the earth the product of an evolutionary process that Genesis fails to explain? Or were Adam and Eve simply a symbolic representation of a pivotal change in us as a species?"

"Mom, I can see your point. But that's not what I'm getting at," Rodrick stated. "The existentialists believe that man is the master of his fate. But in Christianity, God is the master of man's fate. So who is really the master of my fate? Me or God? How can it be both?"

It was obvious to me that Rodrick had been doing more in his room than just sleeping. He was never one to be placated with stock answers and then sent skipping off merrily back to his room. I had to figure that his persistent quest for an answer from our Anthropology instructor served as a prelude to our conversation. I paused and tried to formulate an answer that would transport us along a road with which I was at least comfortably acquainted.

"You're looking for an either-or answer. It is nowhere near that simple. Both are masters of your fate. You are the master of your personage. You chose to reason or not to reason. You chose what you will believe in or not believe in. You chose whether you will be controlled by your emotions or will control them. You are master of your destiny only to the extent that you have the capacity to choose a destiny and the route you will stake towards achieving it. But you do not have the final word. This being that we call God also has a self-determination of His own, and you and all of creation are a part of that self-determination. He has precedence to override any choices that you or any of us make. Since we do not know the substance of this Divine Will, all that we can do is live in accordance with Christ's percepts and trust in His knowledge for our salvation. That is why we call it faith, and we pray seeking peace and harmony so that we can be at one with God's Will, whatever it is. Since I believe that, as an incarnation of God, Jesus Christ showed us the best way to accomplish this, I am a Christian. But I also recognize that I am a being composed of matter with the capacity to feel and reason. I am endowed with free will. That makes me an existentialist. Either way, when all is said and done, I will be held accountable for the choices that I make."

Rodrick mulled over my theology in front of the fireplace for a long while. He formed his mouth to speak, but decided not to. He returned to his bedroom without leaving me as much as a "thank you" or "goodnight."

Over the next few days, Rodrick seemed to have retreated into a world of his own, excluding everyone-including me. He attended his classes, but his heart did not seem to be in it. I had no idea as to what was churning around inside his head. I was very much concerned, but said nothing. I wondered if I had made a mistake in placing so much emphasis on the spiritual aspects of life. After all, he was a man in his late twenties. There were temporal matters that he should have been considering and putting into play by now. He had said nothing to me about raising a family or any substantive plans for his future. I could only hope that he understood what I had expressed to him in a spiritual context was intended to run concomitant with a normal life and not instead of it. While part of me found no fault in him carving out some time for earnest introspection, another part of me wondered how he intended to apply it.

One afternoon there was a break in the clouds hovering over Rodrick's hazy world. His face still reflected his concerns and quandaries. The fact that he had come out of his room and was absently adjusting the pokers and screen in front of my never used fireplace while I watched from the sofa indicated that he was prepared to allow me a glimpse of what had been so deeply troubling him. I had firmly resolved in my mind that any conclusions he had drawn would be steered towards urging him to build a life for himself with wife, kiddies, house and a job.

"Mom, I've hit a life inflation." He stated solemnly. "Life has passed me up and I can't catch up to it. So I've looked to the Lord to help me overcome. I've witnessed for the Lord, and brought people in for salvation and I've worked in the Church. Even in the Army, I worked as a chaplain's assistant. But I don't see why God hasn't given me my glory. When does God give me my glory, Mom?"

My contempt for his arrogance soared to the ceiling and then choked my heart as I glared at him in utter disbelief.

"Who in the hell do you thing you are!" I said, fighting to contain my anger. "What gives you the right to presume that you are entitled to glory? We work for the glory of God. Not for ourselves. Our glory is worth nothing. Don't you know that? How dare you tempt God in this way? Where do you get such arrogance? Rodrick get out of my face. You're making me very mad."

Rodrick stared at me in shock. I could not believe that after so much soul searching, that that was the only conclusion he could settle upon. I thought he understood that the quest for one's own glory is inevitably destined to be labor lost. But, of all people, I should have understood that a life so plagued with rejections, disappointments and crises desperately yearned to hitch its faith to some force that he perceived to be flawless, omnipotent, and infallible. Had I not done the same? But I expected salvation and not an earthly glory. He had condensed the entire panorama of existence to a system of earthly reward and punishment. He had suffered, endured and served. He now fully expected his reward.

Rodrick's dilemma was further heightened by the fact that his younger brother, Nathan, was getting along quite well with his life. He had accepted a position as Media Engineer at a major local television station and was living in the San Fernando Valley. As far as Rodrick was concerned, Nathan had been rewarded for his religious service with material advancement and could not understand why his had been so long delayed. He decided that his fortunes may change for the better elsewhere. He took up residence in a house with three roommates in Simi Valley, a town located in the northwest corner of the county. He found work as a clerk in a home supply store while completing his studies at a nearby College.

Now only Victoria and I were left at home. Victoria's fiery temperament and almost pathological obstinacy had relegated her to working at a series of fast food restaurants. When not working, she was gadding about with a shamelessly raucous and undisciplined crowd. She remained respectful of me and my home, but she embarked upon a lifestyle that was well beyond my ability to control.

For all intents and purposes, I was pretty much alone. I had gone as far as I could go at the junior college and lacked the finances to transfer to a university. So I had no choice but to suspend my academic pursuits. Despite Stan Jamison's admonition that I should not work, there was no way that I could afford to sit around the house all day. I was able to find temporary bookkeeping jobs at various Beverly Hills accounting firms to keep from starving. But with the children no longer my primary concern, an ever billowing feeling of loneliness began to creep into the void.

Except for going to work, I rarely ventured beyond the nearby restaurant and bar. There were men that I knew at the "Wichstand" restraunt, but none with whom I felt I could sustain a lasting and intimate relationship. Men had not changed very much since the days that my mother spent a decade casting her net for a suitable replacement for my Father. Most of them who entered and exited my life were mentally stifling, insufferably arrogant, brutishly macho, or simply pathetically uninspiring. Of course I would be remiss in not including the hopelessly alcoholic, blissfully unmotivated, sexually perverted, and the criminally inclined. There were those who were fun and charming to be around as long as there was no chance of them being around me for a lifetime. Vanity forbids me from harboring the thought that my perfect soul mate had crossed my path, but, for whatever reason, was unattainable.

Outside of a few minor tiffs with Victoria and occasional visits from friends and suitors, I settled in for evenings of house cleaning and television watching. One night the picture on the screen began to scramble. Nothing I did brought the picture into focus. The next day I called a repairman. A stock, well build man with a courteous manner responded to my call. He made short work of my television problem and then, to my surprise, invited me out to dinner.

George Barber was pleasant, soft spoken and exuded strength and self confidence. He was essentially a jack of all trades who specialized in repairing appliances. He was one of very few blacks that I encountered who still had his hair chemically processed to make it straight and wavy. He had lived a multi-faceted life that included a stint as a "man of the streets". I gathered that George was transitioning into a life of middle aged stability and respectability. He was attentive, reliable and sensuous. Just when I thought that our friendship was growing in the direction that I had hoped, he announced to me one evening, that he would not be able to see me again.

"Why? What have I done? I asked in a quandary that fell just short of alarm.

"You're starting to tug at my heartstrings and I'm beginning to really care about you," George began solemnly. "You're a good woman. I don't want to hurt you. So it's better if we stop now."

"But why?" I queried as I wracked my brain for an answer that would make sense. I could think of nothing that could not have been overcome with a little time and patience. We both had been around the track enough times to know that perfection was basically the stuff of romance novels, not real life.

"I guess you haven't gotten it. And I guess the men you've dated didn't have the heart to tell you. So I'll tell you, but it's going hurt."

"Then tell me already. I want to know," I insisted irritably.

"No black man in his right mind would get involved in your situation. A black man would have to see himself as head of the family and protector of his home. He could not tolerate living with the threat of a "White Father" hanging over some children that aren't even his and messing over their black Mother. And he certainly couldn't stand the idea of having a "White Court" over his head. Like I said, you're a good woman and I wish you luck. But I just can't handle it."

My mouth fell open as his words reeled inside my head. Amidst the mental turbulence I heard his goodbye and the door close behind him. I hurried into my room, fell across the bed, and cried myself to sleep.

George's words lingered in my mind among the debits and credits that I entered in the books of my firm's client. I did not regard them as an end of doom, but as an epitaph to my life as a woman. I certainly had not lost the capacity to love—and to love deeply. But I had to concede that George's rejection of me was not without merit. I had lived his words since my divorce from Chuck about fourteen years earlier. But hearing them spoken for the first time in this manner was unabashed truth firing booth barrels and striking me right between the eyes. My God! How could this be? I had devoted myself to those whom I loved most, only to find that the happiness I most desired in this life would never be more than the hopeless pursuit of an impossible dream.

# CHAPTER TWENTY-TWO

# Disrespect Your Father,
# Disrespect Me

Just as Stan Jamison and I had established a fruitful working rapport, an auto accident left him laid up for about four months with a shattered ankle. During his recovery, the county consolidated his facility with another in the adjacent city of Compton and transferred him there. I located another facility closer to home. Fortunately, I was assigned a therapist who was as sensitive to my needs as Stan Jamison. But with Paul Manning I was back at square one. Stan tended to be free flowing and experimental and understood that the psychological aberrations of the inner city dwellers were more often the result of stress and circumstances than of flaws in characters. Paul rarely strayed beyond established and traditional procedures and yet was inclined to provide the emotional support I needed.

Rodrick called me one morning and asked to accompany me to my session with Paul. Julie had already called and told me that Rodrick had decided to re-enlist in the Army. He knew how I felt about the military. I suspected he figured that I would be more responsive towards his decision in the presence of my shrink.

"Well, what is it that you want to tell me?" I asked impassively after we went into Paul's office.

"Mom, I'm going back into the Army." Rodrick announced solemnly. "I thought I'd tell you with your therapist present because you might get upset and he could give you some emotional support. I know you're a pacifist and you disapprove of the military. But ever since I was a kid, I loved to play soldier. I guess that's who I am. And I can't make it out here. I need the structure and every so often I get ribbons and promotions."

"Rodrick I try not to think about it." I said as the anger began to swell within me. "but since you want to talk about it, I'm going to tell you what I feel." I paused to gather myself as best I could.

"I carried you in my womb and gave you life," I continued with deliberate control of my seething anger. "My children are my hope for a future of peace and understanding. How could you think that I would expect my son to become a trained killer all because he wants to play soldier? Isn't that what the military does? Train killers. You yourself told me that after the first twenty minutes, you are expendable. Well, you're not expendable to me. Ever. You are my son. What pride can I take in knowing that my son is a trained killer? That my son has no other purpose but to go out to kill some other mother's son because the government deems that he's your enemy. Don't you see that he's a child of God just like you? I am ashamed that human life means nothing more to you than ribbons and promotions. You have betrayed every principle that I honor and live by. You are an abomination to me and everything that I stand for."

I was desperately fighting to control my anger. I didn't know whether or not I could. But I had to say what I felt.

"And you're a hypocrite as well. You talk about God's love and bringing people in for salvation. And yet you have the nerve to tell me that all you are is a trained killer. Is this how you love God? To serve as an instrument of death to your fellow man? Is this how you honor the love that I gave you? I hate you! You sold out your own principles for the security of three hots and a cot! I hate you!" I screamed and then began to sob hysterically.

Rodrick stared sullenly at the floor while Paul stared at me in utter dismay. But neither one said a word.

"Don't you yet understand why I'm a pacifist?" I shouted tearfully. "Because war starts from the violence in each man's soul. Your Dad and I broke up because of the violence in his soul, which triggered the violence in mine. You can't shine that on. Someone has to say stop. Someone has to start talking instead of hating and killing. There has to be another way.

But you're a grown man, Rodrick. You do what you want to do. You don't have to justify it to me. That's between you and God. But if you ask me to talk about it, then all I've got to say is get out of my face!"

Rodrick said nothing more as he got up and left. The intensity of my rage rendered Paul into virtually a state of shock. I assured him that I did not expect the world to stop because of my rage. Nor was I going to do anything rash or foolish because I felt betrayed. Neither was I going to enter into a conspiracy against myself when other people want to con me into accepting their wrongdoing—even when it is my own children.

"You have some strong views," Stan stated incredulously.

"Yes. There was a time when I compromised my beliefs, but not anymore. I've been punished for that already. Now I just try to be tolerant and understanding towards everyone. I don't judge Rodrick. I told him what I believed and felt. The judgment is ultimately between him and God. I'll continue to treat him as my son. But I must also tell him the truth as I see it. Maybe nobody likes it, but I'm not crazy and I'm not going to act like I'm the one who is. Don't you think that it's degrading that he has to tell me in front of my therapist to provide me emotional support? I don't need therapy just because he wants to re-enlist. I need therapy to cope with the disrespect my children perpetrate towards me, like I'm some kind of jackass. How can I love my children when they disrespect me? And yet I have to find it within myself to keep trying. And I'm tired."

Had Stan remained my therapist, he would have most likely applauded me for my position whereas Paul inculcated them into a form of patchwork therapy to enable me to cope with my feelings.

I arrived home that evening to find Rodrick sitting at the dining room table staring despondently into space. I watched him until the anger began to stir within me.

"Rodrick, snap out of it," I said. "You knew that's how I felt or you wouldn't have met me at the shrink. So why are you so depressed? You made your decision and you should be happy about it. So cut this moping shit out."

I began to understand what Rodrick was going through. Try as he might, he could not shed himself of the institution mentality. The structure and security he sought was not here in the streets. Although the military could offer him this, the price was often mindless and pointless violence. In a way, Rodrick expected absolution from me. I could not give him my blessing for something as callous and repulsive as specializing in war. He was the apple of my eye, but my heart was spent. My only consolation was that he had not been drawn to the institution of prison.

A few days after our session, Rodrick revealed something else within him that caught me totally by surprise. My outburst must have pierced his soul. He could no longer deny or suppress his feelings, so they began surfacing a bit at a time. I watched him bewilderedly from the couch as he paced pensively in front of the fireplace to gather his thoughts.

"I have been thinking about things," Rodrick stated. "I've come to the conclusion that dad didn't love me. I don't think he loved any of us."

"How dare you say that about your father," I retorted vehemently.

Rodrick stared at me in shock. I suspected that he assumed that I would agree with him on at least one point before he left for his stint in the military.

"What do you think all this court stuff was about? You guys are the most loved kids in the whole universe. You had your Father and Mother fighting tooth and nail to love you. Maybe your dad had a misunderstanding about how to love, but he fought to have the right to love you the best way he knew how. If that wasn't love, I don't know what to call it. Don't you ever in your life tell me that about your father. Do you hear me?"

Anger formed slowly in Rodrick's face, but he said nothing and scurried back to his bedroom. I knew that I could never make Rodrick understand. I had been robbed of my father through deportation. I was not about to rob my children of their father because of divorce. A few days later, Rodrick left for an Army base in Florida. But the inner torment that plagued him would give him no peace. About a month later, he called me in the middle of the night. He was hysterical and I had to wait for him to collect himself.

"Mom, why do I play 'kick me-kick me'?" He asked referring to a passage from a psychology book called "The Games People Play". His ongoing introspection had brought him to a point where he was willing to face the truth. From the desperation in his voice, I knew that my son was in great pain and I had to be gentle with him.

"Rodrick. A battered child always seeks the love and acceptance of the batterer. If the only ways you can get their love is to be battered, then you will say, in effect, 'kick me, kick me'. But you will take that attitude with you in all of your relationships until you cut it off."

"Is that why I kiss up to dad like I do?" Rodrick asked pressingly.

"Yes, Rodrick. That's why you seek his recognition. But you're a grown man now. You don't have to keep this game up."

"Mom, why do I also play 'pity me, pity me'?" he asked in a whimpering voice.

"Don't you think you deserve great pity after all you've been through? But you have to give yourself the pity and not expect it from other people. They won't give it. They'll try to step on you instead."

"So what do I do?" Rodrick asked, his voice quaking from his inner rage. "How do I get over this?"

"You're starting to do it right now, Rodrick. You're facing the outrage as well as the rage. Each time you face it, you forgive your Father, and then you live your own life. There's no easy way through this. You'll have to go through this time and again."

"Thank you, Mom." Rodrick said gratefully and then hung up.

By the time Rodrick came home on a leave a short while later, he had placated his rage enough to where he could confront Chuck and forgive him. Together, they set new rules to maintain a relationship where he could feel confident that his father loved him.

In a dream of long ago, Chuck and I sat on either side of the judge before a composite personification of my children. In the eyes of God, we had equal standing as parents. Therefore, I could not condone any of my children dishonoring their father without dishonoring me also. I could not permit the inevitable mean-spiritedness that goes with divorce to cloud the truth that I too was a party in my children's suffering. Without realizing it, when Rodrick forgave his father, he forgave me also.

My sister Gracie and I had not spoken to each other in about three years when she called. Our lives had gone in different directions since Mom died and we had lost touch. She told me that she and her husband had spent a three week vacation in Indonesia.

"We went through the jungle to meet Ray's family. He didn't want to take me because of the snakes. But I told him that snakes didn't bother me. So he took me," Gracie said laughingly.

"So you had a good time. I'm glad."

"I've got something to tell you, but don't get upset."

"Okay."

"Your dad died. They wrote a whole page about him in the newspaper because he was considered the nation's most successful herbologist."

"You mean my dad went back to Indonesia to become a voodooman?" I said incredulously.

"I guess so."

As I rang off, I experienced only a fleeting sense of loss at the death of my Father, Rodrick Beden. I had forgiven him long ago and dismissed all hopes of ever seeing him again. Suddenly, I was seized with laughter. I couldn't help myself. It was so ironic. In his letters he was excited about finding a lucrative capitalistic or political niche in his fledgling nation. By me not sending him the seed money that he requested, Dad was forced to return to the spiritual center of his youth. No doubt he applied the western psychology that enabled him to survive in New York to the tribal healing arts he had learned from his Mother before him. Dad may well have thought that he was capitalizing on the superstition of ignorant people. But I preferred to believe that, without realizing it, Dad had helped his people regain faith in themselves, and in doing so, came full circle in affirming the spiritual essence of his own heritage.

It was about the time that I made my final peace with my Father, that Rodrick came home on Thanksgiving leave and made peace with us. Julie offered to prepare a family dinner at her house. At the time, I was dating Ernest Thompson, a single, black man. He was pleasant enough to be around, but a lasting relationship was virtually out of the question. He was too prone to engage in power games and was too much of an alcoholic. Since he had no plans for Thanksgiving, I invited him to escort me to the family dinner. We intended to just eat and run. I had no idea that my bringing a friend to dinner would spark yet another major family crisis.

Julie's boyfriend at the time was, by her description, "a racist redneck from Georgia". When she told him that she was part Puerto Rican and part white, he assumed because of Julie's blonde hair and hazel eyes, that Puerto Ricans were white. As the day of the dinner approached, Julie began strongly hinting that I come to the dinner alone. On Thanksgiving Day, I was doing payroll and invoices at a bakery when Julie called. She asked me to pick up some wine to bring to the dinner, but also made one last pitch at convincing me not to bring Ernest.

"Mom, this is a family dinner. I don't want you to bring your friend."

"Why?" I asked, growing more and more perturbed by her ungraciousness. I knew "why". I just wanted to hear her say the words.

"Because I'm going to have some of my friends here and they might feel very uncomfortable with your black friend being here."

"But he's not your friend. He's my friend. You mean your friends cannot be civil towards a black man? They can't accept that he's not your friend and wait until we leave to let their hair down?"

"Well, that's not the point. He's not my family nor my friend. And I don't want him here," Julie concluded emphatically.

"Julie, let's get down to the nitty gritty," I said irritably. "This has nothing to do with my friend. This has to do with me. What is it Julie?"

"Well, I told my friends that you were Puerto Rican. If you come here with a black man, they'll know that Puerto Ricans are part black. And I'll have a lot of explaining to do."

"Julie, if that's how your friends think, then they ain't shit. And you going along with it makes you less than shit.

You're a disgrace in God's eyes for putting the racism of your friends before your own Mother. Forget I'm your Mother! Don't speak to me anymore. If I pass you on the street, I will not know you. If I get sick don't come to my bedside. I don't even want you to come to my funeral. I don't know you and don't ever want to speak to you again." I slammed down the phone.

One of the bakery owners overheard of the conversation. Being Jewish, he was intimately acquainted with racism.

"I couldn't have said it better myself. You were absolutely right. You are a fine woman and I'm sorry your daughter has done this to you. Keep up the chin."

My well-used tear ducts opened and I spent the workday alternating between balancing the accounts and crying. When I got home, Rodrick and Nathan were waiting to take up Julie's cause. Rodrick pressed Julie's assertion that it was a family dinner and Ernest would be out of place.

"You don't get it Rodrick," I said. "If it was about a family dinner, then there would be no friends of hers there for her to explain that Puerto Ricans are part black. That is racism against me. It is morally wrong to deny your Mother, and I won't give up my principles of racial equality for the sake of some damn free dinner."

"But Mom, the rest of us want you there," Rodrick insisted.

"Rodrick," Nathan interjected. "That is Mom's social ministry. God was using Mom to declare in open court and before everybody that racism is wrong. Mom cannot give in to Julie. Mom has to answer to God for her ministry."

"I gotcha, Nathan," Rodrick said, nodding knowingly at his brother. And then he turned to me.

"Mom, I won't go back there tonight. We'll go to Pann's and have dinner together."

So that Thanksgiving night, Rodrick, Nathan and I ate dinner at a nearby restaurant while Julie, Victoria, Anita, Sarrah and friends enjoyed a home cooked "family dinner".

Despite going to therapy, it seemed that for two weeks all of my feelings had shut down. I was used to venting my emotions. But in trying to relegate this crisis to a state of insignificance, my emotional system went into shutdown mode. I felt no love, no anger, no joy, no sadness, and no rage—nothing. I couldn't even cry. And crying was my middle name. I felt like a zombie. And then terrified. I began to wonder how long this would last and what I would do when I snapped out of it. Would I be violent or withdrawn? I only knew that I would have to ride it out and assume a positive sense of being. Finally, I saw myself as naked with my back against a wall, ready to pounce in defense of myself. I then realized that I was in such pain that I was emotionally poised to attack anything that posed the slightest threat to me and my misery. I wanted someone to hurt me so that I could feel the physical pain my Daughter had inflicted upon me emotionally. When I began to understand what I was going through, I was able to cry again. Ernest and I drifted apart as his alcoholism became unbearable.

The feud between Julie and me continued well into the next year with no sign of a resolution in sight. We were not on speaking terms. Despairing of her inability to make headway in what had become to her, a personal crusade, Victoria came by and insisted that I accompany her to dinner. When I waffled in accepting the invitation, she recommended that we dine at 'Little Bali'. She was as well aware of my weakness for Indonesian food and it was one of her reason for inviting me.

"Why don't you give up this feud with Julie?" Victoria insisted as the colorfully attired waitress serves us the appetizers.

"I'm not trying to make everybody take sides, Victoria. But what Julie said to me was morally wrong. And she knows it. I don't want you to get in the middle of this. Julie has to face her own conscience."

"Well I don't understand. What did she do that was so wrong?" Victoria asked plaintively.

"She's trying to pass for white. So she's willing to deny me because I'm not white."

"She didn't say that. She said it was because you wanted to bring a friend to a family dinner."

"She didn't want my friend there because her friends would think that Puerto Ricans are not white. That's a slap at me, Victoria. And I'm not going to accept that. Furthermore, I don't want to talk about her anymore."

We finished the dinner in silence. But Victoria was not about to let go. Resolving the feud was, for her, nothing less than a personal crusade. A month later, on my birthday, I arrived home to see Julie's Sunbird parked at the curb. In my living room stood a huge rubber tree plant that I had not seen before. I could hear whispering and moving between the bedroom and the bathroom, but I decided to let things play themselves out. After I sat down on the sofa and started to watch television, Victoria came out of the bedroom and sat next to me.

"Mom, why don't you try to see Julie's side?"

I expended a sigh of resignation as I realized that I was no match for Victoria's persistence. "Why don't you just tell Julie to come out? I know she's in there and she's gonna hear what I have to say."

Julie was apprehensive and tentative as she came out of the bedroom and sat on a chair in front of the fireplace across from me. I wanted to be first without being hostile towards her.

"Julie, I'm not going to lecture you. I assume that you came to ask my forgiveness or you wouldn't be here. You have my forgiveness, just as anyone on the street would. But I will not forget. You hurt me more than you know. I will watch you like a hawk. If you ever do this to me again, believe me, I will never speak to you again. It's that simple. So don't try me. The next time you deny me, I will not forgive you. And you can take that to the bank."

A look of remorse grew on Julie's face. She finally understood the pain she had caused me. Victoria expended a sigh of relief that her efforts had been successful. They came to me, kissed me on the cheek and then left.

My own alcoholism had become increasingly unbearable. I began to feel more and more paranoid as I spent more and more time home alone. My shrink diagnosed me with "empty nest syndrome". It made sense, since the children now rarely called or came by to visit. I envisioned something happening to me and no one finding my body for weeks. I started hanging out at the neighborhood bar until it closed. And then I would go home and fall asleep without having to battle through a million nagging thoughts.

One night I sat next to a man that I had not seen at the bar before. He seemed totally absorbed with his own thoughts as he pensively nursed his drink. I did not think much of him except that he might be someone to talk to as I wiled away the time.

"I'm not trying to make a pass at you," I said tepidly into the dark face that regarded me curiously. "But we're both sitting here like two bumps on a log. I wonder would you mind if we talk to each other?"

"No, I don't mind."

"I'm Miki."

"I'm Taft."

"Why don't we talk about philosophy?"

"Okay," he answered with an accommodating smile.

For about an hour, we talked about what we knew and what we thought we knew. We debated and discussed the ideas of Greek, Oriental and European philosophers. After trashing Plato, debating Hume and mutually embracing Pascal, he turned to me and smiled broadly.

"You won that argument."

He then excused himself to go to the restroom. As I watched him return, I had the feeling that I not only won, but he very much enjoyed the intellectual jousting—and so had I.

# CHAPTER TWENTY-THREE

# The Man Who Loved

After our first meeting, Taft returned to the bar almost every night at about eleven. Each time we either picked up where we left off on the previous night or we engaged each other on a different subject. It took him about three weeks to ask me out on a date. We began with a rather spotty relationship, until he moved in with me about a year later.

According to Taft Newman-Williams, man was placed on this earth to accomplish two missions. The first was to seek out the eternal truths of God. The second was to avoid steady employment. In both efforts he was maddeningly persistent. When Taft graduated from Howard, a predominantly black university in the nation's capital, he accepted a commission in the Army. Upon returning from Vietnam and ascending to the rank of captain, he resigned from the military. He reasoned that since America seemed intent on waging such contemptible wars, he saw no reason to expose himself to fighting them. After launching a foray into the world of corporate management, he retreated after four years when it became apparent to him that he lacked what he described as a "corporate soul". He made his way to Los Angeles to try his hand at screenwriting. A teleplay of his was not only produced by the then highly rated comedy television series, "Sanford and Son", but was also submitted for Emmy award consideration. Unable to penetrate the thick racist hide of Hollywood, Taft tumbled into a stint on skidrow where he worked as a day laborer out of the various "slave markets". When he and I met, he was booking horses out of a house in the mid city part of town.

Taft may well have been the ultimate free floater. He believed that the purest form of happiness is achieved when life leads and one follows. One can never comprehend the Eternal Truth that is God until he has committed himself to finding his own spiritual center. When one functions within his own spiritual center, bad choices are, hopefully, forgiven and good choices enables one to evolve to a higher spiritual plane. For Taft, life consisted primarily of following whatever breadcrumbs fate placed before him as best he can and leaving God to assess his worthiness.

Taft was hardly without flaws. He indulged such values as ambition, the work ethic and economic gain only in a trasistory manner. He was inordinately persistent in those things that others would regard as trivial and seemingly impervious to those things that I, and most other humans regarded as vital necessities of living. He struck me as a man who had no concerns about losing a thousand battles, because he had an unshakeable faith in his ability to win the war.

He had a severely malocclusion, but a face that was alive with an astonishing array of expressions. He no longer wrote comedy, but readily displayed a gift for inducing laughter from those around him, seemingly at will. One evening I expressed to him in dismay that a man with such an intelligent and agile mind would find himself on skidrow.

"It was just a place I went through to get somewhere else." Taft began matter-of-factly. "I was staying at one of the fleabag hotels downtown and was just about to launch a major job hunt, when somebody ripped out all the wires from under the console of my car. I got the car started and pulled it around the corner so that I could park it out of a time zone. And then I lived out of it for about five months. I showered at the Greyhound bus station, bought clothes from the Salvation Army, and worked out of the casual labor agencies. One day

I was cleaning and detailing cars at a used car lot that specialized in the sale of Cadillacs. A man driving a large truck came onto the lot and started looking over the cars. As he waited for a salesman, he expressed to me an interest in breaking into the entertainment industry. When I told him about my teleplay being aired, he recalled that he had recently seen it on television. I called the Writer's Guild to check into the possibility of a residual payment. As it turned out, the Guild had me listed as deceased and sent the seven hundred dollar residual check to my widow. Eventually, I did get the money and then went to work hustling metal with John Henry, the guy with the truck. So instead of going to work at the Post Office or selling real estate, I met a brother who introduced me to a few interesting show biz types. We worked our asses off scrounging aluminum, iron, copper and anything else that could turn a buck. Do you understanding what I'm saying?"

"Not really." I responded bewildered.

"Sometimes things just happen. You don't sit in judgment over them. You just deal with them. Maybe God just wanted to see how I would act in a place with nothing in front of me but despair. During the time I was down there, I never took a drop of alcohol, consorted with any women, or used drugs. Every place that I worked, I gave a full day's measure. If I had been one of those 'woe as me' kind of guys, I might have been crushed by the nickel (you know, that's what they call Fifth Street) and blown my own brains out. But I didn't let it get me down and I didn't worry about getting out of it. I knew that a train would come through with my name on it. It did and I rode right out of there."

In a chilling sort of way, I understood what Taft had said, but I was not about to commit my life to waiting for his 'train'. As we grew closer, I began to realize that Taft was an affable man with a good conscience and deep insights, but terrified of commitments beyond himself. More than that triggered in him rebellion and a yearning for escape. I now understand why he never married. Our first date started off badly and almost derailed our relationship before it got out of the station.

Victoria watched me rant and rave while I waited for Taft to show up to take me to dinner. When he finally arrived, her dark eyes lowered as she looked him over and then admonished him with haughty contempt.

"I don't know who you are, but I'm warning you. I'm not going to let anybody mess over my mother. Would you want some strange man messing over your mother? So you better treat my mother right. You got that?"

"Fair enough." Taft answered, forcing an impassive smile.

I was embarrassed and tried to repair the damage as best I could.

"Taft, please excuse my daughter. All of my children are very protective of me. I've been through some bad experiences and they don't like to see me hurt."

"I understand. It's okay." Taft replied. "It speaks well of you that your children feel as they do."

With Victoria placated, I asked him to join me in the bedroom where I could properly vent my own anger.

"We had a date for eight o'clock. It's now ten o'clock and everyplace is closing. Where the fuck have you been?"

Taft sat on the edge of the bed and buried his face in his hands. When he looked up at me with both pain and anger in his eyes.

"I don't appreciate your vulgarity," He began in a voice straining to contain his anger. "I always talk to you with respect and dignity. I wish you would extend me the same courtesy. As far as being late is concerned, two old ladies came by the joint to collect their winnings and needed a ride home. But en route to where they wanted to go, they decided to go somewhere else. So I got stuck with being their chauffeur. I couldn't very well leave those old ladies out on the street. I should have called and let you know what happened. That's my fault and I'm sorry. But I don't curse at people, primarily because I don't tolerate people cursing at me."

"Okay, I'll accept that. So now, are you going to take me to dinner or what?" I stated defiantly.

He smiled and took my hand, and off we went to dinner.

Although Taft had gotten off on the wrong foot with me, he passed two of my tests with flying colors. He handled my confrontation very well. Secondly, he had a conscience. He detested violence; especially violence spawned from vanity and ego. He had no use for evil committed in the name of social policy or good done to mask evil intentions. He was not always honest with me, but he was always trying to do right by me. I realized that he and I could have an ongoing friendship without fear of violence. He seemed contented with maintaining a telephone buddy relationship with occasional dates thrown in from time to time. I wanted more. When I expressed as much to him, he was caught totally by surprise and then he began to put off a decision. I became incensed and ordered him not to call me again.

Four days later, he called me at work. I told him that we had nothing to talk about. When he offered to take me to dinner after work, I informed him that I had an electrical fire in the car and would have to take the bus home. I would be too tired to go out.

"Then I'll pick you up after work." Taft insisted hopefully.

"No, I don't want to see you," I responded firmly and then slammed down the phone.

To my surprise and dismay, Taft was waiting for me outside when I got off from work. He had driven all the way from mid central Los Angeles to Beverly Hills, apparently to say nothing of consequence. He insisted that I join him for a drink at "Dr. Munchies", a bar located on the first floor of the building where I worked. I didn't want a drink, but he ordered one anyway. There was a smug self assurance in his voice as he explained how he preferred that our relationship remain on a friendship basis.

"Oh, so you want a telephone buddy and a sexual toilet," I responded contemptuously. "Not me. I'm not going for that. That's too degrading. You must be crazy, or think I am. If this relationship is going nowhere, then I have the right to decide if nowhere is where I want to go. And it ain't." I concluded loudly enough that other patrons overheard and then they began inserting their own commentaries. Taft was embarrassed. I was mad. We finished our drinks and left.

Taft was very quiet as he drove me home. All of a sudden, he turned into the parking lot of a donut shop, turned off the motor and began pounding on the steering wheel with his fists.

"Oh Goddamn!" He blurted frantically. "Why can't we just keep things as they were? Why do we have to change things?" He concluded angrily.

At first, I was frightened by his sudden outburst and moved my hand to the door handle. But then I felt a surge of overwhelming pity for Taft. I realized that he was having a commitment crisis. He had finally realized that he would not have things his own way. He was in love, and compromise was part of the bargain.

Taft was hardly the sort of man to commit himself to a relationship at the instigation of an emotion. His heart, soul, and mind had been betrothed to something beyond my grasp. But I was willing to settle for what I could get—for the time being. He moved in with me a short time later. He gave up booking horses and went to work driving a taxi at night. He was intrusive and oftentimes aloof. He was not disposed to ordering me around and that endeared him to me all the more. He listened easily and readily. Victoria decided to attend cosmetology school and moved back in with me. She, like all of my children, grew to respect Taft, even though they found him complex and impenetrable.

Taft had both a strange and lingering effect upon both people and animals. Animals were attracted to him because he was a soft touch and they sensed that he had a gentle heart. Before moving in with me, Taft lived in a house located behind the much larger house where he booked horses. It was a pleasant little house with a kitchen, living room and bedroom. It was sparsely furnished with a sofa, rollaway bed and a marvelous electric organ that could replicate the sounds of about twenty other instruments that he never learned to play. One evening he invited me over. The moment we entered the yard between the houses, we were set upon by seven eager, frisky dogs. The largest and most intimidating was Brutus, a mixture of German Shepherd, and about two or three other breeds. He belonged to the owner of the house and was used to guard his various construction jobs. His tail wagged excitedly as he climbed up to Taft's chest and received Taft's heartfelt greetings. He and Taft were best pals. They were such good pals that Brutus helped him manage the six puppies that had been let into the yard by their mother and abandoned. Taft and Brutus parented the puppies until, one by one, they left to seek their place in the world.

At my house, Victoria's Siamese cat, Saphire took to him almost immediately. Not long afterwards, a second cat mysteriously found her way into our household. Victoria named her Baby Cat. No one knew that Baby cat was pregnant when she joined the family. Putting her back on the street was out of the question. The bond between Taft and Baby Cat was every bit as strong as the enmity between Saphire and Baby Cat. After Baby Cat viciously attacked the frail and older Saphire, Taft patiently and gently negotiated a state of tolerable coexistence between them. Whenever he was home, they would lie on either side of him on the sofa while he gently stroked them, taking care to allocate his attentions equally.

Taft watched with childlike wonder as Baby Cat delivered four kittens. We found homes for two from the litter and kept two. We named one Peaches. Because of her black mustache the name that was brought to mind from the actor Groucho Marx, we called the other Groucho. As especially fierce and battle tested tomcat accommodated both of them within days after they went into heat. Our cat population swelled to fourteen, when under Taft's constant vigil, Peaches delivered a litter of four and Groucho a litter of six. Having no children of his own, Taft readily took on the role of the proud poppa. He was totally absorbed with the birth and nursing of the kittens, and would even forego his trips to the racetrack to insure that our brood was well stocked with food and cat litter. Eventually, we found homes for all of the cats except Saphire. She was old and infirm. When we had no choice but to put her to sleep, Taft closed himself into the bedroom. Through the door, I could hear him crying.

People also liked Taft, but could not understand him. He was articulate, intelligent and blended comfortably into virtually any gathering. But everyone was at a loss as to why he had not advanced to a better station in life. At the restaurant that we frequented, there were two divergent groups of men who embraced Taft with an almost proprietary passion. The first group were his "horseracing buddies". Since we lived near Hollywood Park, the morning hours were at the "Wichstand Restaurant" were usually alive with talk about the races of the previous day or analyzing those of the day. The "Dean" of the group was Earl, an elderly white Okie who was in attendance at the opening day of Santa Anita race track almost fifty years before. He had witnessed virtually every great jockey and horse to hit the track since that time. Taft was fascinated with Earl's range of knowledge about horseracing. He became obsessed with the art of handicapping. It became the consensus of the group that no one knew more about picking winners than Taft. But there was also a common agreement that Taft may well have been the worst horseplayer to ever step up to a betting window.

Taft referred to it as a "cosmic affliction". It was a curious anomaly where one spends most of the night poring over the Racing From, calculating an astounding array of figures, while assessing the various machinations and tactics of horse, jockey, trainer, and track conditions to arrive at the "winner" only to reach the window and bet a fleeting fancy or a bolt of illusion. The next morning, he cheerfully accepted the plaudits of his "horseracing buddies" for picking winners even though he had not a penny in his pocket to show for it. Although he would go weeks at a stretch without hitting a single race, Taft persisted in the belief that there was a "spiritual relevance" in his playing the horses. I strenuously disapproved of his gambling and regarded his reasoning as utter nonsense—even blasphemy. As it turned out, I was gloriously wrong.

It was well into his affair with horseracing that it dawned on me that, despite his incredible losing streaks, Taft has a knack for winning whenever we were confronted with a critical need for money. One evening he came home from the track and hurriedly went to the bathroom. After he came out, he approached me, his face contorted in dismay.

"What happened to the water?" He asked.

"They turned it off," I responded impassively. "We didn't have the money to pay the bill."

"Oh." He said matter-of-factly. "Well how much it is?"

He reached into his pocket and pulled out some bills. He handed me two one hundred dollar bills to cover the water bill and then a hundred for me.

"Now. Let's go eat." He said as he extended his hand to help me from the couch.

But the "spiritual relevance" that he referred to occurred much later and concluded yet another seemingly interminable losing streak. There was a form of wagering called the "Pick Six" in which one needed only to select six consecutive winners to win a great deal of money. Undaunted by his legendary losing streaks, he assured me that he would hit the "Pick Six" and then set out in hot pursuit of his Holy Grail of handicapping. One morning he joyously announced that he had the track by the "short hairs". He had received his income tax refund and was going to make a major run at the "Pick Six" He devoted the remainder of the morning to plotting his strategy with his race track buddies and then headed for Arcadia to do battle at Santa Anita.

I was waiting for him at the "Wichstand", growing more worried by the moment. He had taken the bus to the track and was later than usual in returning. By the time he showed up, I was fit to be tied.

"Why are you so late?" I asked angrily.

"I had to wait forever for that damn 42 bus. I think that's the slowest line in the city. So let's eat." He said as he handed me ten one hundred dollar bills.

"You hit!" I said excitedly. "How much did you win?"

"I told you I would, didn't I?" Taft responded with a mischievous grin. "There's just one problem."

"What's the problem?"

"I was in such a hurry to make out my slips this morning that, like an idiot, I filled out one of them twice." He said dejectedly and then paused as a look of apprehension formed on my face. "I should have won four thousand dollars. Instead we got eight thousand." He announced triumphantly.

"We got what!" I blurted out loudly.

We embraced excitedly and then ordered the thickest, juiciest steaks they had—with all the trimmings.

The next day, Taft left me enough money to pay off all of our bills and to buy a washer and dryer. He then took off in his cab and returned with a personal computer. He pored over the seemingly mountain of manuals that accompanied it until he learned how to operate it well enough to resurrect his creative writing aspirations. He also resurrected his losing habits at Hollywood Park. Try as he might, he never hit the 'Pick Six' again. But the computer enabled us to start a bookkeeping business and work out of our home.

The second group that claimed Taft as it's own, was his "talking buddies". It was the larger of the two groups. Some mornings there would be as many as seven men seated in a booth discussing and debating virtually every topic under the sun. They were older than Taft and from all walks of life. There was a doctor, dentist, commodities broker, gardener, and one of the original Tuskegee airmen. They came and left all during the day. Taft loved the give and take and good natured verbal jousting. Sometimes I would sit in with them, and Taft and I would "mop the floor with them" (Taft's words; not mine). There was one morning that Taft was at the top of his game. It was not long after the Humphrey-Hawkins full employment legislation went down to defeat in Congress.

"As far as the race issue is concerned," Taft began assuredly, "America shot itself in the foot. But as far as the survival of its civilization is concerned, I really believe it shot itself in the head."

"What do you mean?" asked Dan, the commodities broker.

"I mean that it's a clear violation of the first law of civilization building. No nation can survive without providing a floor of survival for its people. In its fear of blacks pouring onto the job market and breaking our dependency on whites, Congress pulled the floor out from under its people. There's no law that says that capitalists must provide jobs for the American people. So if America as a nation is unwilling to guarantee employment for everyone willing and able to work, then who's going to look out for the little guy when the economy starts hurtling downhill. And believe me it will.

"I can't see it being that bad," stated George, the gardener.

"I do," insisted Taft. "Don't take my word for it. Ask the French. Think about it. Many a French nobleman would have kept his head had they asked themselves just one question and answered it honestly."

"And what was that?" inquired Dan.

"What would I do if I were forced to eat pig slop?" Taft stated slowly and deliberately, and waited impishly for his listeners to mull over his question.

"I don't get it." Fred, the former Tuskegee pilot irritably admitted. "Man, what are you talking about?"

"Prior to the French Revolution, the noblemen threw lavish feasts and banquets. After the feasts, the noblemen threw the leftovers to pigsties, and then, for their amusement, watched the starving peasants fight with the pigs for the scraps. So had the noblemen asked themselves what they would do if they were in the peasants' place, they would have seen the revolution coming and would have avoided the guillotine by doing the right thing by their suffering people."

"And you think that these white folks are not going to do the right thing?" Asked George the gardener.

"Not without a fight. They haven't done it in two thousand years. I see nothing in the American version of white folks that'll break the chain." Taft concluded solemnly.

Like virtually every black man who came into my life, Taft hated white people. But unlike any black man I ever met, he had analyzed and agonized over his hatred to the point that he concluded that his hatred was every bit as valid a natural force as the Law of Gravity or the Law of Supply and Demand.

I agonized with him through virtually every scene of the television miniseries of "Roots" and the hundreds of daily slights and offenses against his humanity and that of his people. In a lot of ways, he reminded me of my Father. Their convictions and feelings ran deep and, more often than not, they seemed to be intent on making mountains out of mole hills. But as I reflected upon my life as both a woman and a minority, I began to realize that mole hills that are ignored by one generation, become mountains to be climbed by the next. Even when people are powerless against those forces that seek to diminish their humanity, they must never lose sight of them or submit to them as the natural order of things. To do so, not only empowers those forces of evil, but also denies the eternal will of God and inevitably turns them into enemies against themselves.

Taft had experienced racism and the struggle for equality from almost every possible angle. As a boy growing up in the nation's capital, he attended four different elementary schools, while according to him "every human life form in his neighborhood attended Wheatley Elementary School as long as that human life form was not black." He witnessed policemen beating a black man so badly that an eyeball fell out his head and dangled from his face by the tendons. One night two cops threatened to hurl him off a bridge if he could not show proof that he belonged in that commercial and financial hub of the city. Fortunately, he had a wage slip indicating that he worked as a dishwasher at the Shoreham Hotel, a major Washington hotel located a block away.

For him the defining moment in his "education in racism" occurred when he met Malcolm X. It was during the early sixties when Taft was attending Howard University and participating in rallies under the auspices of the Student Nonviolent Coordinating Committee headed by fellow student Stokely Carmichael, that he met the Muslim nationalist leader. It was after what Taft described as an "incredibly exhilarating debate" between the passionate black activist and the eminent black pacifist Bayard Rustin, that Taft and other students approached Malcolm to meet him. What Taft remembered about the meeting was, that no matter what expression appeared on Malcolm's face, the rage in his eyes remained unchanged. In his eyes, Taft saw what he referred to as "a fire in the soul".

"He stared at you," Taft recalled to me during one of our many discussions on race, "as though he were searching for the same fire in your soul that he had in his. That's why he came down so hard on blacks who confronted him. Because he could not understand how every black did not feel as he did."

Taft knew that the look in Malcolm's eyes was too sincere and deeply felt to be contrived for the sake of the movement. He had seen the same look in Stokely Carmichael and others, but nowhere near as intense as that which radiated from Malcolm X. But there was no fire in Taft's soul. Despite all that he had experienced and knew about discrimination, Taft had no concept of "The Movement" beyond the quest for civil rights. He had not had enough contact with whites to lay claim to honest feelings, good or bad. One afternoon, he spoke at a Civil Rights rally across the street from the White House at Lafayette Park. He realized that his speech lacked passion and focus. He began drifting away from "The Movement". When he enrolled in the advanced ROTC program, formally, he detached himself from it entirely.

It was during the six weeks at ROTC summer camp that the eyes of Malcolm X imposed themselves upon his consciousness. There were about three thousand rising college seniors. About ten percent of them were black. Each night he listened to about fifty young white men talk about their futures with all the absolute certainty of a man sitting at a poker table holding four aces. They all expected to graduate from college, enter the army as officers and achieve their visions of the

"American Dream". But Taft could only sit and sulk and hope that Congress would pass a law or the Supreme Court would render a decision that would permit him to dream the dreams that the others regarded as virtually in the bank. Almost all of them spoke as though they were in total control of their destinies. They had already selected the corporations they would go to work for, where they would live, even where they planned to take their vacations. He detested the reality that his skin color had relegated him to a life of having to fight,... to get to the fight,... in order to fight, and to stay in the fight in a dog eat dog society. Then he began to hate the whites around him with their airs of divine superiority and surly contempt for those not anointed with their pallid hue. By the end of summer camp, Taft had become well aware of the source of Malcolm X's passion. He did not yet have the fire in his soul, but he could feel the heat form a flickering flame.

In 1967, blacks and their allies marched, suffered, and died while taking their righteous yearnings into the jaws of the "Great White Beast". To him, the most courageous Americans were in the streets of Mississippi, Georgia and Alabama, not the jungles and rice paddies of Southeast Asia. Taft concluded that he had devoted a year of his life helping the beast appease an appetite for power and domination that would not be satiated until it devoured the world. He agonized over the choices that he had been confronted with. He felt like a traitor to his people by serving his country in Vietnam. For a moment he had flirted with the notion of becoming a traitor to his country when the opportunity was offered him to serve his people by participating in a Freedom Ride that passed through North Carolina. But he had committed himself to serve in the military and could not bring himself to betray it.

By the time he returned from his tour in Vietnam, the fire had taken hold in his soul and his mind was riddled with anger and confusion over the direction in which to steer his life.

On the day that Dr. Martin Luther King was assassinated, Taft had been back from Vietnam four months and had been promoted to the rank of Captain the month before. From the officer's club, he watched on television as Stokely Carmichael exhorted the people of Washington to get their guns and take to the streets. The next day, Taft was ordered to the Tactical Operations Center. As postal officer for Fort Bragg, he was charged with the task of insuring that troops got their mail in the event they were dispatched to quell the riot that had erupted in the nation's capital. The ironies of the situation mounted within Taft as he listened to the briefing Colonel refer to the rioters as "the enemy".

The last that Taft had seen and spoken to Stokely Carmichael was about four and a half years earlier on the day President Kennedy was assassinated. Taft had heard the news over a radio in the student union building while he was typing a term paper on Rommel's North African Campaign for an ROTC class. He recalled offering words of consolation to the grief stricken Civil Rights Activists as they joined the other students in an almost zombie-like walk towards the School of Religion.

One of the staging areas for the troops was only a few miles from the house that Taft grew up in and where his Mother and Father then resided. It was the site of RFK Stadium which had not many years before been the fairgrounds. Taft dreaded the prospect of having to possibly confront people he had known all his life who were engaged in an action in which he was wholeheartedly sympathetic.

The troops were not dispatched from Fort Bragg to quell the riot. But Taft was drained of all emotional attachment to white America. He droned through the eight months of military service he had remaining and then drifted aimlessly in North Carolina, supporting himself selling encyclopedias. He had been accepted to three law schools, including Howard University but could not summon the motivation to attend any of them.

It was during the early years of affirmative action, and most corporations were trying to comply with the equal employment directives from the government. Somehow word got out that there was a "black College Graduate", who had attained the rank of Captain and served in Vietnam traipsing about Fayetteville, North Carolina, unspoken for and unclaimed. Within fifteen minutes after showing up at a career seminar, Taft was scheduled for no less than ten interviews. By the end of the day, he had eight job offers. He accepted a position in industrial relations at McGraw Edison, a transformer production company, in Canonsburg, PA. He was responsible for hiring and promoting plant workers. There were about twenty five hundred workers in the plant, mostly of Italian and Eastern European descent. Only about fifty of the workers were black. Within months after arriving at the position, Taft found himself caught up in the midst of determined and contentious forces. The various Civil Rights organizations in the area demanded that Taft step up the pace in hiring more blacks. The labor union, which had no aversion towards violence, insisted that Taft slow down his determined effort to hire blacks. The company, whose letterhead appeared on his paycheck, maintained a constant vigil to insure that he in no way betrayed their often conflicting interests.

About three years into the job, Taft was chosen as a delegate to represent Pennsylvania at the NAACP convention that was held in Minneapolis. During an especially contentious meeting, the delegates of the northern states walked out of the auditorium in protest of an obviously irregular method of arriving at a site for a future convention. After Taft saw himself on television that night walking out with his delegation for him, "The Movement" was over. The billowing hatred within him was beyond the reach of temporal issues and programs. It became totally an issue between him and God.

"We're not white folks." He said one evening when I chastised him for an angry outburst about whites. "White folks contrive and manipulate hate as a means to accomplish their vile and insidious ends. They hate the Russians because they challenge them for world domination. They hate the Vietnamese because they would not lie down and play dead when they sent a million men to kill them. They hate Castro because he would not permit his country to be their social and economic toilet like Batista did. And they hate us because our presence in this land reminds them that their words espousing freedom and justice belies their actions.

I see whites as a great, venomous serpent in the middle of a road. My objective is not to harm, abuse, or destroy the serpent. It is to get past the serpent and continue on my way. Eventually, someone will come along who will be endowed with the resources to dispose of the serpent, and will. For me hate is the emotional propellant that enables me to transcend this evil force."

One evening, Taft and Victoria stormed into the house, snorting from rage. I couldn't imagine what had gotten them so upset. Anxiously, I asked what had happened. Taft explained that he had picked up Victoria from the dentist and they were stopped on Wilshire Boulevard by the police because of a broken tail light. While one of the policemen ordered Taft out of the car to interrogate him on the street, the other ordered Victoria around a corner to query her about being in the car with a black man.

The encounter with the police was a searing reminder to Taft that white power would remain a constant and persistent malevolence in his life. Taft was not furious because the police did not accept Victoria's claim of him being her stepfather. He was furious because Victoria had not given him cause to ask anymore than her name and no reason whatsoever to ask her to exit the car. The sole consolation that Taft derived from the incident was that in their single minded intent on nailing him for some violation against Victoria, the police neglected, and completely forgot to give him a ticket for the broken tail light.

Having been a bookie, Taft was no stranger to contact with police. But then he knew that he was breaking the law and affixed no blame upon them for doing their jobs in enforcing it. Because the horseplayers who frequented the establishment were mostly working or retired people who mainly came by to also socialize, eat, and watch the soap operas on television, the relationship between Taft (as a Bookie) and the police was mostly cordial. More often than not, they would call him on the phone to let him know that it was his turn to be arrested so he could arrange for a replacement. The police never arrived until he had taken his bets for the fifth race. The misdemeanor bookies would usually be the first miscreants hailed before the arraignment judge.

According to Taft, "We all wanted to plead guilty, pay our fines and be back at our telephones in time to take bets for the first race. As long as there was no violence and no drugs used or sold on the premises, the police didn't see us as criminals."

The incident with the police triggered the hate in Taft to the point that it bordered on rage. It was the closest I had come to seeing him lose control. But, as with losing at the racetrack, he calmed down quickly. He understood how vital it was to regain control of his feelings as soon as possible and then put matters in their proper prospective. I had little tolerance for hate and anybody who did. Taft and I needed to talk about hate and seek to understand each others sentiments on the subject. I did not want hate to drive a wedge between us where we would end up as enemies instead of friends. We were alone after Victoria left to see a friend.

"Taft, I think I understand how you feel about white people. I grew up under racism and I was married to a white man." I began deliberately, as I joined him on the sofa. "But I still believe that hate is wrong. Nothing good can come out of hate."

Taft smiled at me knowingly as he took my hand in his. There was no emotion in his voice as he stated his case.

"Just as truth comes out of honest love, so it does from honest hate. When one honestly examines an emotion, one comes to understand the source of it. And truth is ultimately revealed. What I feel has nothing to do with a single white person on the planet. I have never met a white man that I hated. I don't even hate those two cops. They just function under a mandate from a synergy that is evil. Their mandate isn't to just protect and serve. They are charged with the responsibility of keeping us contained and under control. The white power structure creates an environment of dependency and despair for blacks. And then they employ the police to insure that the environment is maintained.

I don't hate whites just because they are white. That would be morally wrong. I hate them because slavery, racism, genocides, and the development of weapons of total mass destruction are manifestations of the nature of their collective souls. They are the personification of absolute evil. That is how their existence on this planet will ultimately be resolved. They will be consumed by their own evil. But in the meantime, the rest of us are compelled to endure abject suffering and humiliation until that time comes."

"But Taft, how can you have time to devote yourself to love and service God and yet be so full of hate?" I asked plaintively.

"God is truth. That is all He is. Nothing more, nothing less. What validates or invalidates what we believe is its relationship to the eternal will of God. White folks contrive beliefs in their minds and then configure them in order to impose them upon humanity as truth. Hatred is merely a valid emotional reaction to those who mask their lust for wealth, power, and violence as the eternal Will of God. And the main thing to remember is that I am still accountable to God for the choices I make irregardless of whether I am filled with love, fear, or hate. In the eyes of God, it is just as much a sin to embrace evil out of love as it is to transcend the will of God out of hate."

"But Taft. God is not only the truth. God is the way and the life also. And hate only leads to violence no matter how you figure it. Is that what you want?" I insisted. "I spent many years going to therapy to cope with my hate so that is wouldn't turn to violence or I'd be consumed. I can rationalize feelings of hate, but I have to acknowledge that hate is wrong. God has also given us the capacity to transcend all of our emotions through forgiveness. I now can transcend other people's hatred through my own peace. They cannot affect me even though my physical life can be taken. I can stand before God and know that I have followed in the way, and lived the life. You're right in feeling the hate, but you're wrong to hang onto it. Somewhere in your soul you must find the capacity to forgive and restore your peace. If you cannot do this, then you cannot consider yourself a Christian."

"What I want is irrelevant. What you, me or anyone else believe means nothing when cast in the light of God's Truth," Taft said, his face contorted to reflect the intensity of his feelings. "God's Truth is eternal and universal. If God revealed His aversion to slavery to Moses in ancient Egypt, how could the white man expect God to condone slavery in Alabama? If those civilizations that choose to live by the sword, died by the sword, how can America even begin to hope that it will fare any better holding humanity hostage with the nuclear bomb! Whites perceive themselves as the proprietors of the earth. The rest of humanity perceives itself as stewards of the earth, which is in keeping with the revealed Will of God. The planet cannot possibly be the property of a people who have no compunctions about depleting it clean of its life sustaining resources or blowing it to smithereens if it does not suit their ends. In the eyes of God and the rest of humanity, the ends do not justify the means. In the mind of Whites, their ends are the only ends worthy of pursuing; therefore, their means are the only valid means. Racism is just one of many avenues that the white man has constructed that leads unerringly towards the most horrendous and catastrophic binge of violence that the world has ever known. The only way they will even remotely understand the misery and suffering that they have visited upon this world, will be for them to experience it themselves.

Let me put it this way. The whites use Christianity in the same way that Butch Cassidy used the Hole in the Wall. No act is too egregious for them when it accommodates their lusts for wealth and power or their passion for violence. And then they dart behind the Bible to pray for forgiveness even as they thank God for their ill gotten gains. It is the Eternal Will of God to forgive those transgressions when the sinners "know not what they do". But after two thousand years you can't possibly say that they "know not what they do". There can never be forgiveness for those vile iniquities perpetrated from a malicious and evil synergy whose only intent is to get away with it and avoid atonement and penitence."

"But Taft," I began pressingly, "If all of the energy that is directed towards hate, was directed towards love, all of this ignorance and mistreatment would cease. I understand the reasoning behind hate, and I have suffered because of hate. But God asks all of us to love thy neighbor and that's what I'm going to do. My emotional reaction of hate towards the injustices that I see is insignificant to the love that is the Will of God. And the Will of God is that we forgive each other and love each other and resist the temptation to do evil. In fact, just as we have the holiday of Christmas, we should have a holiday dedicated to forgiveness to remind ourselves of what we must do and must not do. I realize that I am accountable for my actions and I will not be a party to hate no matter how justified it may appear to be. You can call me a sellout to the cause, but I'm not going the route of hate. I will speak up when I see injustice done and, if need be, suffer the consequences. But I will not pursue hating."

"You know sweetheart, I've got to stop saying that you don't understand. You do understand." Taft said as he gently patted my hand. "We are both victims of circumstances over which we have no control. I guess that the best that either of us can ever do is not to make ourselves victims of each other's emotions." He concluded by kissing me tenderly on the lips.

Most of our discussions revolved around subjects that were generally remote and innocuous. We never expected to resolve anything. We both regarded them as calisthenics for the mind. This time I found Taft's logic to be both disturbing and daunting, primarily because he presented it as though he were presenting a thesis on Einstein's Theory of Relativity.

I now understood the basis of our relationship. It mattered not to Taft whether I was a traditional or a liberated woman. Taft has a value for critical thinking which he had not found in the women he had met. He referred to me, on more than one occasion, as his "worthy opponent". It was no concern to him if I ranted or raved as long as I expressed my ideas and substantiated them with a palatable logic. He harbored no grand designs in this temporal life. His purpose for being resided was in the very capable hands of God. He had only subsistent regard for time, space and money, believing to the depths of his soul that he would have the time, space and money to accomplish whatever God expected of him. He readily overlooked and even accommodated my flaws and faults for no other reason than he had no more right to judge me than I had to judge him.

Despite the inherent dangers of driving a taxi in Los Angeles at night, he continued to do so even when it was not necessary. He was robbed, threatened, harassed and had passengers bolt from his cab and run into the night without paying the fare. But he was hopelessly fascinated by the people of the night. We were content to keep our computerized bookkeeping business small. We worked out of the house, serving about a half dozen clients.

He said nothing to change my mind, not I his. In my mind, Taft and I seemed destined for happiness if for no other reason than we were two neurotics who had learned not to step on each other's neurosis.

# CHAPTER TWENTY-FOUR

# The Miracle Of My Family

I n the eyes of the law, five of my children were adults and were free to go their own way. But the status of my youngest, Anita and Sarrah, stilled remained very much the subject of possible contention between me and Chuck.

Everything was going well for me, Taft, and Victoria when Anita and Sarrah came down from Camarillo for a visit. The night before they were to return home, Anita revealed what had been on her mind during the weekend she had spent with me.

"Mom, I'll be eighteen in a few months and I want to leave Dad. But I can't leave Sarrah behind," she said.

I was flattered by Anita's desire to want to move in with me. But there were legal ramifications to be considered. And I was emotionally ill prepared for another round of courtroom confrontations. On the other hand, I could not deny Anita her request.

"I'll try to talk to your father. But I may have to go to court. So you guys better be sure about this." I warned. After the girls returned to their father, I called Nathan with the hope that he could discern how Chuck felt about the move. To my surprise, Nathan not only managed to convince his Dad that the girls had a right to know and live with their Mother, but he extended himself to provide Chuck the emotional support he needed.

"I told Dad about how angry you got when I moved in with room-mates." Nathan said when he called to tell me how it went between him and his Father. "He was shocked that you got upset. I reminded him that all parents get like that when their children leave home and that it was perfectly normal for him to feel that way about the girls. So I suggested that, instead of getting mad, he do what's best for the girls and let them go. I told him that all this court stuff was very hard on everybody and accomplishes nothing over the long run."

Despite the fact that I wanted Anita and Sarrah with me, I was more than a bit apprehensive about having two more girls with me who were approaching adulthood. Julie had been obstinate and Victoria self willed. I had not spent nearly enough time with Anita and Sarrah to know what to expect from them. That summer, they moved in. Before I could settle in with the girls, I first had to contend with Taft.

Although fond of my children, he began to sulk and grumble about the girls' arrival. One evening I was writing checks at the dining room table, when he approached me and stated his concerns.

"Sweetheart, how come you didn't ask my consent for the girls to come?" Taft asked sullenly.

I didn't think that his question required an answer. There were times in life when events occurred that were beyond one's control. Surely he understood that.

"Sweetheart, I'm asking you something." He insisted.

"Taft, what if I had asked you?" I responded irritably. "Would you have said no?"

"Of course I wouldn't have said no."

"Then I assumed that you had no objection to their coming. So what's the sense in me asking you? If you had said 'no', we would have had to separate. I hope you didn't expect me to put you before my own children."

"My answer is not the issue." Taft stated sternly. "It's that you should have extended me the courtesy of asking me how I felt about it.

There are two of us in this relationship and we should come to a consensus about these things. I don't like feeling that you are conducting an 'I' relationship and I'm just along for the ride. I don't claim the right to make decisions for you, but I expect to be consulted."

"Please forgive me, Taft. I didn't mean to hurt your feelings or berate your opinion. But this is a situation that just happens. There's nothing that even I can do about it. I'm their Mother. That's what God made me to be. When they want or need me, how can I refuse? Taft, you have a little understanding and you'll see that there's nothing to discuss and that I'm not running an 'I' relationship.

With Taft assured that he was not in an 'I' relationship, I returned my attentions to Anita and Sarrah. Whereas Anita was effervescent and extroverted, Sarrah was more distant and introspective. Both girls had become very close to both of her half-sister Beverly and her stepsister, Melissa, and my daughters felt very guilty about leaving them behind. Sarrah was only just beginning to adjust to life without them. But Melissa would not let go so easily. It was on a pleasant September day when I picked up the phone and was confronted with yet another crisis.

"This is Melissa. I'm at the downtown Greyhound. Can Sarrah come and pick me up? I've run away from home."

"Yes, Melissa." I said wearily. "We're on the way."

I knew that a potentially major problem loomed before me. It would be a small matter for Chuck and his wife to accuse me of being an accomplice in her running away from home and hold me accountable for anything that happened to her. I had to make Sarrah understand that their relationship could not continue as before.

"Sarrah, I'll try to be gentle," I began as we drove towards downtown Los Angeles. "But she can't stay with us. I would have to be her guardian and her Mom would never consent to that. I'll have to inform her Mother that she's here and safe. Maybe she'll let Melissa stay a few days. But I can't keep her. Sarrah, you're not her Mother. She has to learn to cope with her own Mother. You have a right to your Mother just like she has to hers. You can't be the buffer for her problems. She'll never grow up. I'll tell her so she won't feel that I'm welcoming her and then betraying her."

Although Melissa was a year younger than Sarrah, she was much larger. She had long, straight reddish-blonde hair, despondent blue eyes, and was tentative and ungainly in her movements. According to Sarrah, she had little standing in the household other than the family klutz and the object of derision. She wore faded blue jeans that accentuated her bulk and an ill fitting polo shirt that gave her the appearance of being a formless sack of cotton. I liked Melissa and would have no problem with her staying with me. She had a good and sensitive heart despite being consigned by fate to a household that seemingly prided itself on being heartless. There was nothing I could do for her except to treat her as my own. But if I thought it was morally wrong for her Mom to interfere in my relationship with my children, then it was wrong for me to interfere in her prerogatives of Motherhood.

After we pulled into the driveway of my house, I explained as delicately as I could to Melissa why she could not stay with me and why it was wrong of her to run away from home. Then I went into the house to call her parents. Chuck answered the phone. He was very much relieved that Melissa was safe and offered to come and get her, but at a loss as to why she ran to me, of all people. I was in no mood to banter about blame and recriminations. He offered to come and get her right away. I did not think it was a good idea and offered an alternative.

"Chuck, before you do that, will you listen to me, please? Melissa is feeling abandoned by Sarrah and Anita. She is missing her sisters and is upset and confused. Her world has been turned upside down. She came for her sisters, not for me. Why not let her stay here until she's ready to go home. I've already told her that she can't stay, but I think it would be better if she came back on her own. She might feel like she's being coerced if you come and get her right now. It'll give you and your wife a little more time to talk about this between yourselves. And Melissa will have a little time to settle down and think things through.

Assure your wife that I'll send Melissa back as soon as she calms down. Try to have some understanding, Chuck. Don't push her right now. She's not used to being without her sisters. Try to get your wife to let up a little."

"Well that makes sense. Okay. I won't come to get her."

"In fact, maybe for next Easter break, all of the girls can come down and spend the week together. Why don't you think about it?"

"That sounds like a good idea. I'll talk to my wife about it and plan for it."

I turned the phone over to Melissa to talk to her Mother who immediately launched into an angry tirade. To the amazement of us all, Melissa matched her Mother word for word in both volume and rage. Before our eyes she had crossed the line from a passive retiring girl into the realm of self awareness. The next day after she had calmed down and we were alone, I counseled her about what had happened and how best to proceed from there.

"You have to remember Melissa," I began as I sat next to her on the living room couch. "She is your Mother and she is what she is. It's not your place to change her or to judge her. She will always be your Mother, and despite her faults, she will always love you. In two years, you will be eighteen and free to make your own life. So the most important concern in your life right now should be to figure out what kind of life you want to build for yourself and start preparing for that and not tear down the bridge between you and your Mother. There will be many times when you may need her. I can promise you that."

Melissa smiled at me knowingly. During the three days that she spent with us, she withdrew into herself. When she returned home, she and her Mother co-existed in, as best I could comprehend, a state of reserved tolerance.

Anita was very much concerned about the well being of her sister, Sarrah. There was that Christmas of long ago that still haunted me, when she cried incessantly as a small infant. No one could tell me why. When the state changed foster homes, I heard no more about the condition and pursued it no further. Although Anita apparently suffered no physical abuse, the images of what Sarrah had endured remained with her. In her mind, Anita believed that Sarrah was very much affected by the abuse, even though she was a baby at the time and could not recall it. From my own experience, I knew that the effects of abuse could remain with victims for a lifetime with them having no cognitive awareness of having been abused. One day Anita approached me quietly while I was gardening in the front yard. She sat on the steps next to me and watched pensively as I turned over the soil.

"Mom, can I talk to you?" She asked.

"Yes, of course you can."

"I tried to talk to Sarrah about suing the County of Los Angeles for the abuse she suffered in the foster homes. Mom she's got burn marks, perfectly round cigarette burns everywhere. But she doesn't know how she got them," Anita began to cry, "The cigarette scars are on the top of her scalp and the insides of her thighs. Mom, the first time I met her we were just little and I remember looking at this little girl who looked just like me. Mom, they striped her down naked, and then they used the word, "malnutrition". I looked at her, the little girl who looked like me… she was so frightened and her protruding stomach stuck way out. That was our first meeting.I didn't know ….I didn't even know; she was my sister" Anita continued to weep profusely yet quietly because her sister, Sarrah was inside the house. "She could win easily. But she doesn't want to come forward. Maybe you can get her to do it."

My first inclination was to rush to Sarrah and see the burn marks for myself. But then I would not know where my anger would take me. Inside, I was seething at the thought of what my Daughter suffered— and at my own helplessness. Outwardly, I offered a calm assurance to Anita as I gripped the trowel handle as tightly as I could. I realized that I had to make Anita understand that there was more to it than suing the County of Los Angeles.

"I understand how you must feel, Anita." I began solemnly as I sat next to her on the step. "But you're a fighter and can probably take the grilling that they would put you through. Sarrah isn't strong the way you are. To dredge up the experience might cause problems that no amount of money could solve. She might even wind up in a mental hospital. She knows something happened to her. But she was a baby and doesn't know what, why or who did it. They'll make a laughingstock out of her in court. And that'll only add to her trauma. I think Sarrah understands that she cannot fight for her future while re-tripping the past. As much as I'd like to cream the "State" for what they did to all of you, we all have to close that door behind us and push forward. I'm glad that you love your sister enough to care so much about her. But we have to leave the decision totally up to her. In the meantime, what she needs is for you to respect her wishes and be the best sister you can be."

Tears began to well up in Anita's eyes. I put my arms around her and fought back my own tears. Sixteen years later and the 'State" was still affecting our lives in ways too painful to ever forget.

Somehow, we managed to pull together a functioning household. Victoria was doing well in cosmetology school. Anita and Sarrah used Julie's address in order to attend high school in the South Bay, Manhattan Beach area. Taft continued to drive a taxi at night, thereby avoiding the early morning bathroom rush. He and the girls got along extremely well. He remained un obtrusive but always accessible. He was both understanding and protective towards them. He had no problems with coming from work at four or five in the morning and gingerly stepping over the sleeping bodies of my daughter's and often their friends. Even though virtually all of my daughters' friends were white, Taft was always cordial and respectful towards them. On one occasion, he spent almost the entire night consoling and counseling Anita's boyfriend after he and she engaged in a particularly nasty argument. They reconciled the next morning. And then there was that one evening when Taft outdid even himself.

Anita brought home a young man who was a buddy of Anita's boyfriend and asked if he could stay a few days because he had been kicked out of his home. He was extremely handsome and well mannered with solid, muscular build of the dedicated surfer that he was. He began setting up housekeeping in a shed in our backyard. From the chatter that went on among the teenagers, Taft detected something that stirred his suspicions. With the skill of a trained surgeon, he sought to uncover the truth of the young man's plight.

Through a gentle, but persistent, inquisition, Taft learned from the young man that he had been cast out of his parent's house and had been crashing with friends. From that Taft deduced that he drank a lot of liquor and used a lot of drugs. Since the young man had no job to support his party lifestyle, Taft pressed his quarry, until he admitted that he had burglarized a house and was attempting to evade capture by the police.

"I won't have this house and family placed in jeopardy." Taft stated sternly. "You have to go, right now."

The young man was taken aback and disconcerted. But he gathered his things and left the house. I never saw nor heard from him again.

About twenty years ago, my first analyst, Dr. Knox used the analogy of the pioneers and Indians to warn me that the odds of me enjoying a life of happiness and fulfillment were very much against me. Although I wasn't prepared to proclaim that Dr. Knox had grossly erred, I felt entitled to treat myself to a few congratulatory pats on the back. I have come to believe that all life is a miracle unto itself. Therefore, I could append no noble significance to what I may have accomplished. Every life serves as a potentially vital link in the unbroken chain of humanity that began millions of years ago and will continue until either God's Will, or our arrogance and ignorance terminate the existence of our species. The severity of the crisis in my life was to me not unlike sitting in a den of lions like Nathan or suffering the trials of Job. Fortunately, God permitted me to foresee the manner in which my life would be transformed, through visions and his ever imposing wisdom. That gave me comfort and reassurance. If, with the concurrence of God, I could do no more than to lay claim to my life as a social ministry against racism and perpetuate that ministry through my children, I will not bemoan those successes and accomplishments that might have eluded me.

I was a happy, exuberant baby with large expressive eyes, black hair topped with a great white bow. Someone had dressed me in a lacy white dress, white socks and shiny black patent leather shoes and seated me in a wooden high chair. At the dining table in front of me, eight people who were strangers to me indulged themselves in joyous feasting. I climbed over the high chair top and onto the table. Happily, I crawled along the table scooping food from each plate as I passed. No one took notice of me or tried to stop me. After I had eaten my fill, I used the high chair to climb down to the floor and then scuttled off to the living room. It was most curious to me that, although my face and clothes were smeared with food, I was perfectly clean when I climbed down the floor even though no one had touched me.

I awakened from this dream amidst a gentle flow of rapture that sustained me through the rest of the day. It had been the best of all possible dreams to have at the outset of the Christmas season. I felt that I had been restored to my original childlike innocence in order to begin life anew. The dream served to heighten the joy of not only feeding my loved ones in the flesh, but also of hopefully feeding them through their souls.

Perhaps it was because of the ever swelling feeling of euphoria that I wanted this Christmas to be special. I decided to invite all of my children to join me in a home cooked Christmas feast. Victoria, Sarrah and Anita were excited by the idea. Julie and Nathan assured me that they would come. Only Rodrick, who was stationed in Florida, remained a question mark. I could only hope and pray that he would be able to come home from the military for the holiday. I threw myself into the project, with Taft and others standing ready at my beck and call. Everything was going joyously when Rodrick called me from Florida. He was in much distress over an incident that disheartened us both.

"Mom, they sent me to human relations school. At the first session, the instructor asked all the whites to sit on one side of the room and all the minorities on the other. I took my chair and sat between the two groups."

"Rodrick, you're a trip and a half." I stated laughingly.

"Well the instructor made me pick a side. I sat with the non-whites."

"I'll bet that raised a lot of eyebrows."

"It was much worse than that, mom." Rodrick said as his voice began to reflect his pain. "After class, about five black guys jacked me up against the lockers. They started screaming at me that since I could pass for white, why didn't I sit with the white guys. Mom, they actually wanted to beat me up."

"What did you do, Rodrick?" I asked in a mounting panic.

"I told them that they better get their hands off of me or I'd kick their ass."

"I'm so sorry, Rodrick."

"They let go of me, but one guy couldn't let go of his rage. He just couldn't understand why I didn't try to pass for white. Mom, why were they so mad at me? Why did they want to hurt me?"

"Rodrick, in their mind, they would have done anything for a chance to pass for white. When you didn't, you made them have to face their feelings of inferiority that society had imposed upon them. You had a choice. They had no choice. You chose to be inferior. No person chooses to be labeled inferior. They could not see that you chose to be seen beyond color. Had everyone pulled their chairs into the middle with you, there would have been no need for this kind of class. Your actions made them face up to the fact that they were morally wrong to want to be something they weren't. You served as a mirror and they didn't like what they saw in themselves. You had the courage to accept who you are and they didn't. You did great, Rodrick. I'm so proud of you."

"I was so scared." Rodrick admitted. "I couldn't fight five guys. When they let me go, I was trembling. I still haven't gotten over it."

"I know Rodrick. On the streets you would be their enemy just by your looks. But now, they have to question their own stereotypes about white people and their perceptions of themselves. Now they have to deal with non-whites who refuse to deny their racial heritage no matter how white they may appear to be. But you got first hand experience about the great subliminal damage that racism does to the human psyche and how irrational racism is. I'm just glad that you're alright. Now can you let it go and move on?"

"Yeah, Mom." He concluded with a sigh and then a pause. "Oh, Mom, by the way, I'll be on leave for Christmas. I'll be home in a few days."

The knowledge that Rodrick would be attending our feast heightened my efforts to make this the best Christmas ever. There were extra strands of lights strung around the hedges outside to proclaim to the world that this was a house that had much to be thankful for.

Through the large bay window of my dining room, I beheld in the twilight a scene that was at first surreal and then hilarious. A large Christmas tree hovered above the lawn and was pointed towards the house like a missile. And then under the tree, emerged two legs churning over the slope of the lawn. The huge tree wavered precariously from side to side as it moved towards me, only to move backwards, steady itself and start forward again. It then lunged forward, only to collapse into the bushes in front of the window. I wanted to rush and get my camera, but I was laughing so hard that I could only manage to open the front door. The tree re-gathered itself and squeezed past the doorway into the house. Through the green pine needles, I followed the sounds of huffing and puffing and found Taft, smiling triumphantly. It was a glorious tree-high, thick and fresh. The aroma of pine soon filled the house and drew us all into the spirited determination to adorn the tree as beautifully as possible. We joked and clowned and reminisced as we worked. From time to time hysterical laughter would fill the room as we shared our visions of Taft's valiant struggle to deliver to us our wonderful Christmas tree.

On Christmas Day, I fussed over every detail in the preparation of dinner and meticulously set the table. From out of the South Bay Julie, radiant and sensuous arrived with Rob, her roommate. Rodrick had flown in from Florida a few days before and drove in from his Father's house in Camarillo, stopping along the way to pick up Nathan. Everyone gathered around the table and Taft offered the prayer. My dream of a few weeks before flowed into my mind as I watched everyone fill their plates and eat with gusto the giant chef's salad, roast Cornish hens stuffed with cornbread dressing, Caribbean style shrimp fried rice with plantains, baked yams, peas, cranberry sauce,all of this was topped off with chocolate cream, custard, pumpkin pies, and an assortment of drinks and spirits. Now I realized that the strangers eating at the table in the dream had not been strangers at all. They were the loves of my life, my family. My taking of food from their plates had been a communion of our spirits. We now were partaking of a communion of the flesh. For all intents and purposes, I had stayed the course, and in my heart I believed that God was well pleased.

The dinner surpassed any that I had eaten before. The banter and gaiety about the table passed through my ears as hymns sung by angels. With my eyes, heart and mind, I visited each of my children, one at a time.

Rodrick, my eldest, had finally confronted all of those issues that could drive him to wanton violence and hopeless desperation. He had believed that life had passed him by and that God had abandoned him. God had not abandoned him. Rodrick was much too innocent and sincere for God to turn a dead ear. He had been ordained to become a seeker of wisdom and not of wealth. In time, he will accept it.

Nathan, self centered and self assured, had never been as open and expressive towards me as I wished. However, there have been moments where he revealed insights that I found uncanny and heartwarming. I had all the faith in the world that when confronted with moments of truth and crisis, Nathan will draw from resources that have nothing to do with acquisition and temporal stability.

Julie, My beautiful Julie. She was my pride and joy. She had gone through hell and returned stronger and wiser. Her exotic dancing supported her while she pursued her interest in etching glass. She had been my prodigal child. And my heart was feasting upon her return. She still has a little way to go, but I have every confidence that she'll get there.

Tempestuous and willful, Victoria still struggles to come to terms with a world that has caused her mostly grief and torment. She asks so little of it, and yet even that manages to elude her. Her cosmetology studies now consume her interest. But nothing means more to her than her family. Victoria constantly reminds us that, come what may, we must always stick together as a family.

Anita has grown into our happy-go-lucky, eternal optimist. She approaches life with the same uncompromising, indomitable spirit that she does as a member of her high school softball team. She refuses to remain embittered by her experiences with life. She was more than willing, and had an ability to confront life on whatever terms it lay before her.

And last but hardly least, there is Sarrah. She and I have loved in silence. Only time will tell whether the chasm between us will be narrowed. From now on, we are both imprisoned by the haunting presence of the abuse that was inflicted upon her in the cradle. She was my beautiful, loving baby. I could not give up on her in a million years. I had to trust that time and my perseverance will somehow reassure her that in my heart, she was never abandoned and is much loved.

Rob was Julie's roommate. He graced my table with his friendship and Julie's life as an influence of order and stability. He tolerated Sarrah and Anita often imposing themselves upon his lifestyle during much of the school year and made no complaint.

Taft came into my life searching for a buddy, but found his own capacity to love instead. He gave more of himself than he thought possible and asked little in return. He quelled whatever exasperations that I expressed about the children by reminding me of the goodness he saw in them and the ways their values were similar to mine. He was an endless fountain of patience and tolerance. Where I thought that I had given up on men, I thank God every day for his presence in my life.

My mind drifted back to my painting of the sparrow that I gave my father when he was deported. Hidden beneath my intentions that the painting was to be a token of remembrance of me to my father, there may well have been the budding knowledge that I too must take flight and commend my fate to whatever resources that came to hand. Through the turbulences and storms that tossed and buffeted me against seemingly perpetual angry unyielding and unforgiving skies, I finally settled upon the currents of faith, humility and compassion. On this holiest of nights, they have delivered me, joyful and ever so grateful to this occasion of utter fulfillment. The perplexed, bewildered stares of my children returned me to the present. Everything was evolving as Baby Jesus had promised in the dream so many years ago. And I was beginning to enjoy it. What more could I want out of life? I had my children home, in my love and care. I dispatched a gracious smile.

"Now, who's going to make the coffee?" I prodded gently. "Who's going to serve the pie?"

CPSIA information can be obtained at www.ICGtesting.com
Printed in the USA
LVOW090718100812

293631LV00004B/23/P